Biblical Christian Ethics

Biblical Christian Ethics

David Clyde Jones

 Baker Books

A Division of Baker Book House Co
Grand Rapids, Michigan 49516

Published by Baker Books
a division of Baker Book House Company
P.O. Box 6287, Grand Rapids, MI 49516-6287

Printed in the United States of America

Library of Congress Cataloging-in-Publication Data

Jones, David Clyde.
    Biblical Christian ethics / David Clyde Jones.
    p. cm.
    Includes bibliographical references and indexes.
    ISBN 0-8010-5228-9
    1. Christian ethics—Reformed authors. I. Title.
    BJ1251.J615 1994
    241'.0404—dc20   94-1888

Contents

Preface

My father, who grew up on a small red-clay farm in the South Carolina Piedmont before he turned to dry-goods for a living, used to love to tell the story about the county farm bureau agent who took a bunch of brochures on contour plowing, crop rotation, and the like to a farmer in his district, handed them to him, and said, "Here, read these; they'll improve your farming." The farmer took them, looked them over, handed them back, and said, "Shucks, I ain't farming now as good as I know how."

A book on Christian ethics is supposed to help us improve our living, but if the truth were confessed, we're not living now as well as we know how. Our crucial lack is not information. Unless the Holy Spirit breathes life into our bones, we will remain on the valley floor, disjointed and very dry. Still, the Spirit works by and with the Word, and a fuller vision of what God is calling us to be and to do may be instrumental in motivating us to seek improvement in the Christian life. In that hope I offer my brochures, such as they are.

The title *Biblical Christian Ethics* is intended to underscore the unity of theology and ethics. Given the evangelical assumption that the holy Scriptures of the Old and New Testaments are the only infallible rule of faith and practice, the Bible is the source and norm of Christian ethics as well as Christian doctrine. On this view ethics and dogmatics are not properly separate disciplines but integral parts of the whole study of God's revelation of himself and his will for humankind.[1] Christian ethics is properly a subdivision of systematic theology; it could be called the doctrine of the Christian life.

When I first started teaching theological ethics some twenty years ago, the organizer of a conference on Christianity and politics asked me in casual conversation who had been the most formative influence on my ethics. Taken off guard I facetiously replied, "Moses." The truth is I was embarrassed to admit I hadn't read that widely in the field and furthermore couldn't tell how I had been influenced by what I had read. Now I would say that I follow the Reformed tradition in ethics, especially Augustine on the goal of the Christian life, Calvin on its norms, and Jonathan Edwards on its motive. In addition, I

---

1. Ethics and dogmatics have been treated as separate disciplines only since the late sixteenth century. In the Reformed tradition Lambertus Danaeus published his *Christian Ethics* in 1577. The better-known Lutheran theologian Georgius Calixtus followed suit with *Epitomes Theologiae Moralis* in 1634. The same development may be observed in Roman Catholic moral theology around 1600.

have sought to listen carefully to evangelical Lutherans on the proper distinction between law and gospel, and I admit to an admiration for the structural analysis of Thomas Aquinas, though I make no claim to being more than a "peeping Thomist," as the saying goes.

Confessionally I am committed to that remarkable committee report published in 1647 as *The Humble Advice of the Assembly of Divines, Now by Authority of Parliament Sitting at Westminster, Concerning a Confession of Faith*, known since as the Westminster Confession of Faith. According to its own principles it is "not to be made the rule of faith, or practice; but to be used as a help in both" (31.4).[2] Citations from the Confession and its companion catechisms are made in that light.

Special thanks to the board of trustees of Covenant Theological Seminary for their generous sabbatical policy, which enabled me to write this book. Also to John W. Sanderson, Jr., my teacher, colleague, and friend (who got me into ethics in the first place when he was chairman of the systematics department at Covenant) for reading the first seven chapters on foundations and making numerous valuable suggestions. And to Sue Ellen Bilderback Jones, my intimate life companion and committed partner in ministry, who shares my hopes, calms my fears, encourages my writing, and—as an English teacher and more—generally improves my style. But though she tells me I can't use a double modal, I still say I might could.

---

2. The Westminster divines echo Augustine almost to the letter: "As regards our writings, *which are not a rule of faith or practice, but only a help to edification*, we may suppose that they contain some things falling short of the truth . . . [for] there is a distinct boundary line separating all productions subsequent to apostolic times from the authoritative canonical books of the Old and New Testaments." Augustine, *Reply to Faustus the Manichaean*, trans. Richard Stothert, in *A Select Library of the Nicene and Post-Nicene Fathers of the Christian Church*, ed. Philip Schaff, 1st series (New York: Scribners, 1901), 11.5 (emphasis added).

Abbreviations

ASV American Standard Version
GNB Good News Bible
JB   Jerusalem Bible
KJV King James Version
LXX Septuagint
NAB New American Bible
NASB New American Standard Bible
NEB New English Bible
NIV New International Version
NRSV New Revised Standard Version
RSV Revised Standard Version
TEV Today's English Version

1

The Questions of Ethics

What goals ought we to pursue in life? What sort of persons ought we to be? What practices ought we to follow? These are the great questions the discipline of ethics seeks to answer.

The questions imply that human conduct is subject to a threefold evaluation from a moral point of view. First, the end the agent seeks to realize must be good, intrinsically worthy of human pursuit. Second, the motive of the agent must also be good, so that the end is sought because it is worthwhile, the mark of a good character. Third, the means to the end must be good, conforming to the standard of what is right, since neither a good end nor a good motive is compatible with a bad means. For conduct to be morally praiseworthy it must be good in all three respects, not least because end, motive, and means are not finally separable.

Moral evaluation, of course, implies standards of judgment. Ends are judged good or evil by criteria of intrinsic value; agents are judged good or bad by criteria of moral virtue; actions (including mental acts or attitudes) are judged right or wrong by criteria of moral obligation. What are these criteria, and how do we know them? This is the most pressing question of ethics; no particular instance of ethical choice can be resolved without presupposing an answer to it. The answer is necessarily dependent upon some broader philosophical perspective, some view of human beings and their place in the universe.

From a biblical point of view, the question of criteria for goals, persons, and practices comes down to this: *What is God calling us to be and to do?* Since God's salvific call is not a bare invitation but a manifestation of his sovereignty and power, the question is more fully: What is God summoning and enabling us, his redeemed people, to be and to do?[1]

---

1. Formally this agrees with the practical moral question put by James M. Gustafson: "What is God enabling and requiring us to be and to do?" *Ethics from a Theocentric Perspective* (Chicago: University of Chicago Press, 1981), 327. Cf. John Murray: "[B]iblical ethics is concerned with the manner of life and behaviour which the Bible requires and which the faith of the Bible produces." *Principles of Conduct: Aspects of Biblical Ethics* (Grand Rapids: Eerdmans, 1957), 12.

Effectual calling has been helpfully defined by Anthony Hoekema as "that sovereign action of God through his Holy Spirit whereby he enables the hearer of the gospel call to respond to his summons with repentance, faith, and obedience."[2] By including obedience within the definition, Hoekema draws our attention to the goal-directed aspect of effectual calling that often emerges in the New Testament. We are called to salvation by the sanctifying work of the Holy Spirit and belief of the truth so that we may share in the glory of our Lord Jesus Christ (2 Thess. 2:13–14). The ultimate goal of our calling is eternal life (1 Tim. 6:12), the heavenly prize (Phil. 3:14), God's kingdom and glory (1 Thess. 2:12). We are called to belong to Christ (Rom. 1:6), and since our calling brings us into fellowship with him (1 Cor. 1:9), we are called to live a holy life (1 Thess. 4:7) and to follow his example of suffering for righteousness' sake (1 Pet. 2:21).

In effectual calling we are united to Christ and consequently called to a distinctive way of life in him, a way of life made possible by divine grace. The classic text is Romans 12:1–2, which in the unsurpassed cadence of the King James Version reads:

> I beseech you therefore, brethren,[3] by the mercies of God, that ye present your bodies a living sacrifice, holy, acceptable unto God, which is your reasonable service. And be not conformed to this world: but be ye transformed by the renewing of your mind, that ye may prove what is that good, and acceptable, and perfect, will of God.

The chief interest of this text for ethics lies in its climactic description of the will of God as the standard of the Christian life. But the truths about human nature presupposed in the terms of Paul's appeal ought not to be overlooked.

"By the mercies of God" (the plural represents the Hebrew *rahamim*, translated "tender mercies" in the Psalms) alerts us to the affectional aspect of human nature. Motivation in ethics must reach the dispositional complex of desire and feeling that Scripture calls "the heart." The full extent of God's mercy is revealed in the cross, as Paul earlier has said: "God demonstrates his own love for us in this: While we were still sinners, Christ died for us" (Rom. 5:8). This is the profound truth by which we are moved to respond to God's call. "We love because he first loved us" (1 John 4:19).

"To present your bodies" brings into sharp focus the volitional aspect of human nature. Paul's powerful appeal is addressed to free agents whose choices are morally significant. It assumes that human conduct involves acts of conscious determination toward good or evil. As Christ voluntarily laid down his life for sinners, so Christians, having been made alive by the Spirit

---

2. Anthony A. Hoekema, *Saved by Grace* (Grand Rapids: Eerdmans, 1989), 86.
3. As in the original, "brethren" refers to the whole Christian community. Read: "brothers and sisters."

of God, are called willingly and actively to offer themselves to God as perpetual oblations of thankfulness and praise. The best commentary on "living sacrifices" is Hebrews 13:15–16: "Through Jesus, therefore, let us continually offer to God a sacrifice of praise—the fruit of lips that confess his name. And do not forget to do good and to share with others, for with such sacrifices God is pleased."

"Which is your reasonable service" highlights the ethical significance of human nature as rational. Both the New International Version and the New Revised Standard Version have "spiritual worship" instead of "reasonable service," but the latter appears to be closer to the sense of the original. The word translated "worship" or "service" is *latreia*, which in the Septuagint and the New Testament always means "divine service," predominantly with reference to the offices of the tabernacle and the temple. Under the new covenant believers are themselves said to be the temple where God dwells by his Spirit. Since in the context it is the whole of life that is to be consecrated to God, "service" would seem to be the more suitable translation than "worship," especially in view of the broad use of the related verb *latreuō* (to serve) in both Testaments (e.g., Deut. 10:12; Luke 1:74–75; Acts 27:23; Heb. 9:14).

More importantly, the modifier translated "spiritual" or "reasonable" (NRSV has "spiritual" in the text and "reasonable" in the margin) is *logikos*. Although the word is rare in biblical Greek, the only other instance being 1 Peter 2:2, it was commonly used in contemporary philosophical discourse with reference to human nature as "possessed of reason, intellectual." There is no cause to suppose that Paul's use is fundamentally different; his usual term for "spiritual" is *pneumatikos*, yet here he says *logikos*, "rational." This nuance suits the context well. Christian service is not a matter of unthinking activity or rote performance; it engages the mind as well as the heart and the will.

Human nature is affectional, volitional, and rational; it is also fallen. Thus Paul issues the twofold exhortation, "Be not conformed . . . be transformed," so that, renewed by God's grace, we may be able to "approve" the will of God, making God's moral judgments our own and putting them into practice. "The will of God" is in apposition to "the good, and acceptable, and perfect"; each term bears a particular ethical significance.

"The good." The prophet Amos long ago called for adherence to what in philosophical discussion is referred to as the first principle of practical reason: "Seek good, not evil . . . hate evil, love good" (Amos 5:14–15; cf. Rom. 12:9, which is practically identical, and Rom. 16:19, "I want you to be wise about what is good, and innocent about what is evil"). "Good" is the most comprehensive term for what human beings ought to be and to do. The biblical ethic is distinctive in that it identifies the good with the revealed will of God. In the great summary declaration of the prophet Micah: "He has showed you, O man, what is good. And what does the LORD require of you? To act justly and to love mercy and to walk humbly with your God" (Mic. 6:8). To this verse, with its threefold specification of what the Lord requires of his people, we will in due course return. For now we simply note its assertion of God's revelation of the good that human beings ought to seek.

"The acceptable." The will of God is further described as *euarestos*, "acceptable" or "well-pleasing" to God. This word-group (*euaresteō, areskō*, and derivatives) figures prominently in the New Testament vocabulary for moral conduct. The benediction of Hebrews 13:20–21 is typical: "May the God of peace . . . equip you with everything good for doing his will, and may he work in us what is pleasing to him, through Jesus Christ, to whom be glory for ever and ever." It is God's approval that ultimately counts in ethics, doing "what is right in his eyes," as the Old Testament puts it (e.g., Exod. 15:26; Deut. 12:28; 1 Kings 11:38). The standard to which we are called to conform is not impersonal law, but rather the personal will of our Creator and Redeemer.

"The perfect." The will of God is finally described as "perfect" or "complete." The true fulfillment of human nature consists in being conformed to the will of God, which is essentially God's own moral perfection transcribed for creaturely imitation. As Jesus says in the Sermon on the Mount, "Be perfect, therefore, as your heavenly Father is perfect" (Matt. 5:48). Self-denial in the Christian life is aimed not at eradication of the human personality but rather at eradication of sin. The goal of sanctification is the perfection of human nature created in the image of God.

To sum up, Christians ethics may be defined as the study of the way of life that conforms to the will of God—the way of life that is good, that pleases God and fulfills human nature.[4] This leads to practical questions: How do we know the will of God? How do we know what God is calling us to be and to do?

"The will of God" can refer either to God's decree or to God's purpose and direction. Where human response is called for, the latter sense is intended. God does not reveal what he has decreed as a guide for human decision-making; what he has revealed is his direction, his law (in Hebrew *torah*, divine instruction in the way of life) by which his purpose and desire for his people may be realized. The question is more precisely: How do we know the revealed will of God? The short answer is: By knowing the holy Scriptures, which are able to make us wise for salvation through faith in Christ Jesus (2 Tim. 3:15). The Scriptures are both clear and sufficient for this purpose, so that we may be thoroughly equipped for every good work (v. 16).

---

4. The New Testament word for "way of life" is *anastrophē*. See 1 Tim. 4:12; Heb. 13:7; James 3:13; 1 Pet. 1:15, 18; 2:12; 3:1–2, 16; 2 Pet. 3:11. The English word *ethics* represents *ta ēthika* in Greek, the technical term for the study of principles of conduct. *Ta ēthika* was derived from *ēthos* (alternately, *ethos*), meaning "way of doing things, mode of behavior, customary pattern of conduct." As used in the New Testament, *ethos* refers to "custom" and does not imply moral judgment, except for the one instance of the ionic spelling (*ēthos*) in the Greek saying cited in 1 Cor. 15:33, "Bad company corrupts good *morals*" (NASB).

Even so, the answer is not as simple as it might seem. The will of God must be discerned through a whole-souled engagement of heart and mind and will. This is the perspective of Philippians 1:9–11, which may be rendered in English as follows:

> And this [is what] I am praying: that your love may abound more and more in knowledge and all insight for [the purpose of your being able] to approve the values that excel, that you may be pure and blameless unto the day of Christ, filled with the fruit of righteousness which is through Jesus Christ to the glory and praise of God.

This comprehensive prayer begins with the impelling motive of the Christian life (love) and ends with its controlling purpose (the glory of God). Paul prays for love's increase in both knowledge (*epignōsis*), which denotes an intelligent understanding of the directing principles of the Christian life, and insight (*aisthēsis*), which is the existential grasp of their application in concrete circumstances.[5] Christians whose love abounds in this twofold way will be able to make true moral judgments and approve the values that excel (*ta diapheronta*), which is equivalent to knowing the will of God (cf. Rom. 2:18, "if you know his will and approve of what is superior [*ta diapheronta*] because you are instructed by the law").[6]

The biblical view of values is that they are objective and normative. It says, "These things are valuable and therefore ought to be desired and sought." This stands in opposition to the subjective or descriptive view, which says, "These things are desired and sought; therefore they are valuable, at least to those who seek them." As one author puts it, "Human beings are value and whatever they value is value."[7] But some human beings value revenge, others cruelty, still others forms of sexual activity aptly labeled "bondage." Such practices obviously do not represent intrinsic human goods; so far from being values, they are instead disvalues, destroying rather than fulfilling human nature.

Paul's classic list of the values that excel, values that are objectively true and intrinsically worthy of human pursuit, is found in Philippians 4:8–9.

---

5. The noun *aisthēsis* is used only here in the Greek New Testament. Arndt and Gingrich give as its meaning "insight, experience beside *epignōsis*, which means intellectual perception." The verb *aisthanomai* also occurs only once, at Luke 9:45, where the disciples did not "grasp" what Jesus was saying. *Aisthēterion* is a third single-instance term in this word group; Heb. 5:14 speaks of "faculties" trained through exercise to distinguish between good and evil.

6. Phil. 1:10 and Rom. 2:18 are the only instances of *ta diapheronta* in the New Testament. The verb *diapherō* can mean either "to differ from" or "to be superior to," so that *ta diapheronta* could refer to "the things that differ" (i.e., right and wrong) or "the things that are superior." Most of the English versions adopt the latter at Phil. 1:10, and translate "the things that are excellent" (KJV, ASV, RSV, NASB) or "what is best" (NIV, NRSV). The NAB has "so that you may learn to value the things that really matter."

7. Joseph Fletcher, "Humanistic Ethics: The Groundwork," in *Humanist Ethics: Dialogue on Basics*, ed. Morris B. Storer (Buffalo, N.Y.: Prometheus, 1980), 258.

Whatever is true, whatever is noble, whatever is right, whatever is pure, whatever is lovely, whatever is admirable—if anything is excellent or praise worthy—think about such things. Whatever you have learned or received or heard
from me, or seen in me—put it into practice.

The double imperative ("these things think . . . these things practice")
brings out the unity of contemplation and action in the pursuit of moral
excellence. Without going into a detailed analysis of each item in Paul's list,
we may note that there is an objective world of value grounded in the God of
truth to which we are invited to attend with all our mind. We are not called
to create our own values but rather to contemplate the values God has
ordained. Contemplation through the renewal of the Holy Spirit leads to the
desire to embody these values in our lives, so that the things communicated
by apostolic teaching and example may be put into practice.

The apostolic witness points us to Christ, the definitive embodiment of
moral excellence. And as the writer of Hebrews reminds us, "Jesus Christ is
the same yesterday and today and forever" (Heb. 13:8). Though we live in a
changing world, God does not change, nor does his ideal purpose for human
beings made in his image. Consequently the world of values does not change,
however complex our world may become through advances in technology.
We have in Christ and the holy Scriptures the permanent deposit of the
directing principles of the Christian life, to be learned and applied in our own
day through the illuminating and enabling work of the Holy Spirit.

Thus, by way of summary, Christian ethics is the study of the way of life
that conforms to the will of God as revealed in Christ and the holy Scriptures
and illuminated by the Holy Spirit. It seeks to answer the practical question,
What is God calling us, his redeemed people, to be and to do? Expressed in
term of goals, persons, and practices, a threefold answer may be proposed:
The controlling purpose of the Christian life is the glory of God; the impelling motive of the Christian life is love for God; and the directing principle of
the Christian life is the will of God as revealed in Christ and the holy Scriptures.[8] These basic propositions will be the subject of the next three chapters.

8. This phraseology derives from lectures on theological anthropology delivered by John Murray at
Westminster Theological Seminary in the academic year 1960–61.

2

The Goal of the Christian Life

Wh at is the chief end of man?" Generations of children brought up on the Westminster Shorter Catechism have been taught to answer, "Man's chief end is to glorify God and to enjoy him forever." It's a good answer. So good, perhaps, that few pause to ask why the Catechism begins with this particular question. Only the child who hasn't yet memorized the answer is likely to stall by asking, "What do you mean 'chief end,' and why do you want to know?" It's a good question.

The Catechism presupposes that there is some supreme purpose for human beings, some ultimate goal or *telos* that fulfills human nature, some highest good of intrinsic value that is to be most sought after in life. It thus identifies with the goal-oriented or teleological tradition in Christian ethics encapsulated in the famous saying of Augustine: "[T]hou hast made us for thyself, and restless is our heart until it comes to rest in thee."[1] The Catechism begins the way it does because it understands that we are purposeful beings, that "whatever else man may be—emotional, rationalizing, mortal, brutish, reasonable, whatever—he is very much a teleological animal."[2] It wants to know what we should aim at in life as a whole, for this will determine all our notions of virtue and duty and sustain our commitment to them. There is, of course, a history behind its remarkably comprehensive and concise answer.[3]

By the time Augustine was converted to Christianity the question of the highest good or *summum bonum* had long been the subject of philosophical discussion. Aristotle, for example, taught that the end or goal (*telos*) of human existence is *eudaimonia*, traditionally translated "happiness" but now commonly rendered "flourishing" in an attempt to express in one word Aristotle's complex notion of being good and faring well. Not to be confused with *hēdonē* (pleasure), *eudaimonia* involves rational and virtuous activity, for these are dis-

---

1. Augustine, *Confessions*, in *Augustine: Confessions and Enchridion*, ed. and trans. Albert C. Outler (Philadelphia: Westminster, 1955), 1.1.

2. Paul Ramsey, *The Truth of Value: A Defense of Moral and Literary Judgment* (Atlantic Highlands, N.J.: Humanities, 1985), 91. This is Paul Ramsey the poet, not Paul Ramsey the ethicist.

3. See Benjamin B. Warfield, "The First Question of the Westminster Shorter Catechism," in *The Westminster Assembly and Its Work* (New York: Oxford University Press, 1931), 379–99.

tinctively human characteristics and therefore necessary to human fulfillment. Ask Aristotle, "What is the chief end of man?" and he would reply, "To flourish through moral and intellectual excellence—plus a little bit o' luck."[4] (The element of luck was necessary because Aristotle could not guarantee even the minimum physical conditions of life—food, health, shelter—let alone the income required for a contemplative lifestyle. "Happiness" is being good and faring well, but Aristotle had to admit that the twain do not always meet.)

In certain formal respects Augustine agrees with the classic teleological analysis of human conduct.[5] He acknowledges that the desire for happiness, understood as fulfillment-cum-satisfaction, is a human given. He further concedes that human activity is driven by the pursuit of happiness, even going so far as to say in one of his sermons, "If I were to ask you why you have believed in Christ, why you have become Christians, every man will answer truly, 'For the sake of happiness.'"[6] The highest good, however, is not happiness but "that which will leave us nothing further to seek in order to be happy, if only we make all our actions refer to it, and seek it not for the sake of something else, but for its own sake."[7]

For Augustine, God is the "highest good." The desire for happiness has been implanted by him and is intended to lead us to him so as to find in him our all in all. God is the absolute value, infinite, eternal, and unchangeable, and the good life consists in knowing and loving God. The pagan philosophers erred, not in seeking happiness (for God made us with this itch), but in trying to find happiness in themselves and in this life only. From Augustine's point of view the virtues that made for pagan happiness (Aristotle's intellectual and moral excellence, for instance) were vitiated by the pride of self-fulfillment—not the fulfillment of a self, which is the work of divine grace, but fulfillment by oneself, a strictly human achievement. No matter how resplendent the natural virtues may be, they fall short of the glory of God.

Christian happiness, on the other hand, transcends both the human self and the present life. As Augustine says in his climactic description of the celestial city, God is the happiness of the redeemed.

> God himself, who is the Author of virtue, shall there be its reward; for, as there is nothing greater or better, he has promised himself. What else was meant by his word through the prophet, "I will be your God, and ye shall be my people," than, I shall be their satisfaction, I shall be all that men honourably desire—life,

4. See Aristotle, *Nicomachean Ethics*, trans. Martin Ostwald (Indianapolis: Bobbs-Merrill, 1962), 1.7.10.

5. The ambiguity of the term *teleological* is the source of some confusion in ethics. Its classic use for the perfection of human nature in conformity with right precepts should be distinguished from the modern use for the view that the rightness or wrongness of an action is determined solely by its consequences. Cf. Thomas W. Ogletree, *The Use of the Bible in Christian Ethics: A Constructive Essay* (Philadelphia: Fortress, 1983), 42 n. 9.

6. Cited in John Burnaby, *Amor Dei: A Study of the Religion of St. Augustine* (London: Hodder, 1938), 46.

7. Augustine, *The City of God*, trans. Marcus Dods (New York: Modern Library, 1950), 8.8.

and health, and nourishment, and plenty, and glory, and honour, and peace, and all good things? This, too, is the right interpretation of the apostle, "That God may be all in all." He shall be the end of our desires who shall be seen without end, loved without cloy, praised without weariness.[8]

Thomas Aquinas embraced Augustine's perspective on ethics and applied his architectonic genius to the development of a comprehensive teleological system.[9] In doing so he made full use of the threefold formal structure of Aristotle: "human-nature-as-it-happens-to-be, human-nature-as-it-could-be-if-it-realized-its-*telos*, and the precepts of rational ethics as the means for the transition from one to the other."[10] This is regularly regarded by evangelical Protestants as having compromised Augustine, but Aquinas' Christian frame of reference entails such fundamental changes that it is rather Aristotle who is "compromised."[11] As Alasdair MacIntyre points out, the introduction of theism means that "the precepts of ethics now have to be understood not only as teleological injunctions, but also as expressions of a divinely ordained law."[12] Again, the human problem of living rightly is not simply a matter of error, as Aristotle taught, but of sin; the solution, for Aquinas no less than Augustine, is God's grace.

Calvin in his ethics retained the Augustinian orientation but made no use of the Thomistic system.[13] Like Augustine, Calvin took the question of happiness as the starting point for discussion of the knowledge of God, only with this difference: whereas Augustine had begun with the universal desire for happiness, Calvin emphasized the need to be existentially aware of *un*happiness. The self-knowledge that leads to the knowledge of God is not so much the "mighty gifts" with which human nature is endowed as it is the "miserable ruin" that results from the Adamic revolt. The first lesson in the pursuit of happiness is humility, a virtue tellingly absent in Aristotle and the classical tradition.[14] Calvin's point is best made in his own words:

8. Ibid., 12.30.
9. For a concise, authoritative introduction to Aquinas's ethics see Vernon J. Bourke, "Aquinas," in *Ethics in the History of Western Philosophy*, ed. Robert J. Cavalier et al. (New York: St. Martin's, 1989), 98–124.
10. Alasdair MacIntyre, *After Virtue: A Study in Moral Theory*, 2d ed. (Notre Dame, Ind.: University of Notre Dame Press, 1984), 53.
11. Cf. Arvin Vos: "Aquinas approached Aristotle . . . with the intent of appropriating such truth as he could from the philosopher and incorporating it into considerations of the issues that were important in his own day. He does not simply recapitulate Aristotle; rather, he silently corrects and enriches his position. He employs Aristotelian principles in contexts and ways Aristotle never used them." *Aquinas, Calvin, and Contemporary Protestant Thought: A Critique of Protestant Views on the Thought of Thomas Aquinas* (Grand Rapids: Christian University Press, 1985), 166.
12. MacIntyre, *After Virtue*, 53.
13. Vos concludes that the *Institutes* do not reveal a firsthand knowledge of Aquinas's writings. *Aquinas, Calvin, and Protestant Thought*, 38.
14. MacIntyre observes that humility, along with thrift and conscientiousness, "could appear in *no* Greek list of the virtues." *After Virtue*, 136.

Each of us must, then, be so stung by the consciousness of his own unhappiness as to attain at least some knowledge of God. Thus, from the feeling of our own ignorance, vanity, poverty, infirmity, and—what is more—depravity and corruption, we recognize that the true light of wisdom, sound virtue, full abundance of every good, and purity of righteousness rest in the Lord alone. To this extent we are prompted by our own ills to contemplate the good things of God; *and we cannot seriously aspire to him before we begin to become displeased with ourselves.*[15]

In his brief chapter on eschatology in the *Institutes*, Calvin echoes Augustine's (and for that matter Aquinas's) description of God as the highest good and happiness of the redeemed:

If God contains the fullness of all good things in himself like an inexhaustible fountain, nothing beyond him is to be sought by those who strive after the highest good and all the elements of happiness. . . . If the Lord will share his glory, power, and righteousness with the elect—nay, will give himself to be enjoyed by them and, what is more excellent, will somehow make them to become one with himself, let us remember that every sort of happiness is included under this benefit.[16]

Calvin observes that we are taught in many biblical passages to seek God as the highest good (e.g., Gen. 15:1; Pss. 16:5–6; 17:15; 1 Pet. 1:4; 2 Thess. 1:10). Even so, teleology is not a prominent structural feature of his ethics. His "Meditation on the Future Life" affirms enjoyment of the presence of God as the summit of happiness, but the chapter as a whole is not written from the point of view of attaining the goal of our creation and redemption.[17] With his profound understanding of fallen human nature and its proud self-assertion in opposition to divine authority, Calvin appears more concerned with the immediate issue of obedience to God's commandments.

The Reformed tradition has largely followed Calvin in this regard and concentrated on ethics as decision-making in relation to the biblical standard of right and wrong. This is certainly an important part of ethics, but it needs to be seen in the larger teleological context of the Christian calling. Because of the modern confusion of teleological ethics with consequentialism (the view that the rightness or wrongness of an action is determined solely by its consequences for good or evil), evangelicals tend to reject the label *teleological* and

15. John Calvin, *Institutes of the Christian Religion*, ed. John T. McNeill, trans. Ford Lewis Battles (Philadelphia: Westminster, 1960), 1.1.1 (emphasis added).

16. Ibid., 3.25.10. Cf. Aquinas: "Clearly, then, nothing can satisfy man's will except such goodness, which is found, not in anything created, but in God alone. Everything created is a derivative good. He alone, *who fills with all good things thy desire* [Ps. 102:5], can satisfy our will, and therefore in him alone our happiness lies." St. Thomas Aquinas, *Summa theologiae*, trans. Thomas Gilby (New York: McGraw, 1969), 1a2ae; 2.8.

17. Calvin, *Institutes*, 3.9.

opt for "deontological" instead.[18] But this is a false choice; a goal-oriented ethic does not automatically exclude absolute principles of moral obligation.

The structural orientation of the Westminster Shorter Catechism thus remains viable for Christian ethics. God's will is in the first place his purpose for us in Christ, and then his direction of us in achieving that purpose. As we consider the goal to which God is calling his redeemed people, we find in Scripture a rich variety of overlapping themes, especially the glory of God, the image of Christ, the kingdom of God, and eternal life.

The Glory of God

The heavens declare the glory of God, and so, of course, do the holy Scriptures. As the whole earth is full of his glory, so is the whole Bible. God is the God of glory (Acts 7:2); the Father, the Father of glory (Eph. 1:17); the Son, the Lord of glory (1 Cor. 2:8); the Spirit, the Spirit of glory (1 Pet. 2:8). God's name is glorious (Neh. 9:5), which is to say, God is glorious in his entire being, wisdom, power, holiness, justice, goodness, and truth.

God's glory is revealed in all his works, but especially in the salvation of his people. The King of glory exercises his sovereignty in redeeming a people to himself, thereby manifesting his glory in, by, unto, and upon them. God's plan from all eternity is to have a people, chosen in Christ, redeemed by Christ, called through Christ, to the praise of his glory (Eph. 1:3–14). It is this truth that evokes Paul's sweeping doxology: "For from him and through him and to him are all things. To him be the glory forever! Amen" (Rom. 11:36).

This much may be read off the face of the biblical text. That is not to say it is less important for being conspicuous; still, it is necessary to probe more deeply into how God is glorified in his works.

The most profound treatise on the glory of God is Jonathan Edwards's dissertation *Concerning the End for Which God Created the World*.[19] According to Edwards, God's ultimate and supreme end in creating the world was "that there might be a glorious and abundant emanation of his infinite fullness of good *ad extra* [outside himself]." God was "moved" to this end by a perfection of his own nature, namely, "the disposition to communicate himself or diffuse his own fullness."[20] The ema-

---

18. *Deontological:* from the Greek *deon*, meaning "duty" or "obligation"; *teleological:* from the Greek *telos,* meaning "end" or "goal." For an example of their polarization, see Norman L. Geisler, *Christian Ethics* (Grand Rapids: Baker, 1989), 24.

19. Jonathan Edwards, *Ethical Writings*, vol. 8 of *The Works of Jonathan Edwards*, ed. Paul Ramsey (New Haven: Yale University Press, 1989), 403–536. This volume contains *Charity and Its Fruits* (Edwards's sermons on 1 Corinthians 13 preached at Northampton in 1738) and *Two Dissertations, I. Concerning the End for Which God Created the World. II. The Nature of True Virtue*, published posthumously in 1765. Edwards's *Treatise Concerning Religious Affections*, which may also be numbered among his ethical writings, is volume 2 in this series.

20. Edwards, *Concerning the End*, 433.

nation of God's fullness of good is essentially threefold: it consists in the communication of God's knowledge, holiness, and happiness to the creature.[21] God is glorified as we come to know God, to love him, and to rejoice in him. Since reflection
of the divine fullness constitutes human fulfillment, God's glory and our good, so
far from being opposed, are not properly and entirely distinct.[22]

A generation that remembers Edwards only for his sermon "Sinners in the
Hands of an Angry God" may be surprised to learn that he believed God created the world for the communication of his goodness and especially his happiness. True, Edwards did hold that God's justice is glorified in the damnation of the wicked, but not without making a crucial distinction:

> According to the Scripture, communicating good to the creatures is what is in
> itself pleasing to God . . . what God is inclined to on its own account, and what
> he delights in simply and ultimately. For though God is sometimes in Scripture
> spoken of as taking pleasure in punishing men's sins . . . yet God is often spo-
> ken of as exercising goodness and shewing mercy, with delight, in a manner
> quite different, and opposite to that of his executing wrath. For the latter is spo-
> ken of as what God proceeds to with backwardness and reluctance; the misery
> of the creature being not agreeable to him on its own account.[23]

Edwards thus resisted the temptation to make election and reprobation
"equally ultimate" in God's creative purpose, and the two doctrines remain
asymmetrical in his thought. The glory of God's justice in the damnation of
the wicked is radically subordinate to God's supreme and ultimate end in creating the world, the glory of God's goodness in the salvation of the elect.[24]

The latter theme figures prominently in the epistles of Peter. The great
confessing apostle writes to God's elect in the name of "the God of all grace,
who called you to his eternal glory in Christ" (1 Pet. 5:10). There is a strong
eschatological note: faith results in praise, glory, and honor when Christ is
revealed (1 Pet. 1:7). But there is also present glory in following the example
of Christ: "If you are insulted because of the name of Christ, you are

21. Ibid., 441–42, 528–29.
22. Cf. Richard Baxter: "The glorifying himself and the saving of his people are not two decrees with
God, but one decree, to glorify his mercy in their salvation, though we may say that one is the end of the
other: so I think they should be with us together intended. We should aim at the glory of God, not alone
considered, without our salvation, but in our salvation. . . . Christ himself is offered to faith in terms for
the most part respecting the welfare of the sinner, more than his own abstracted glory. He would be
received as a Saviour, Mediator, Redeemer, Reconciler, Intercessor. And all the precepts of Scripture, being
backed with so many promises and threatenings, every one intended of God as a motive to us, do imply as
much." *The Saints' Everlasting Rest*, abr. John T. Wilkinson (1650; reprint, London: Epworth, 1962), 31.
Baxter's classic was reprinted often throughout the next two centuries.
23. Edwards, *Concerning the End*, 503.
24. One can only hope that literary critics will someday recognize that Edwards's "Heaven Is a World
of Love," the climactic sermon of *Charity and Its Fruits*, belongs in the canon of American literature alongside the often anthologized "Sinners in the Hands of an Angry God."

blessed, for the Spirit of glory and of God rests on you" (1 Pet. 4:14). The climax is 2 Peter 1:3–4.

> His divine power has given us everything we need for life and godliness, through our knowledge of him who called us by [or to] his own glory and goodness. Through these he has given us his very great and precious promises, so that through them you many participate in the divine nature and escape the corruption in the world caused by evil desires.

The arresting feature of Peter's doctrine of glorification is the thought of sharing (*koinōnos*) in the divine nature. Not that believers are somehow absorbed into God's being, but that they are called to nothing less than to reflect God's own glory and moral goodness (*aretē*).[25] Though the great and precious promises reach into eternity, they include everything necessary for life and godliness now, particularly enablement to answer the summons to holy practice: "Just as he who called you is holy, so be holy in all you do" (1 Pet. 1:15). God's purpose is to have a people who mirror his holiness, who display his excellencies (1 Pet. 2:9), who share in Christ's sufferings (1 Pet. 4:13), and whose transformed lives proclaim: "To him be glory both now and forever!" (2 Pet. 3:18).

Since believers are called to respond consciously to the revelation of the goal of their redemption, the glory of God may be said to be the controlling purpose of the Christian life. This is the force of Paul's great comprehensive imperative: "Whether therefore ye eat, or drink, or whatsoever ye do, do all to the glory of God" (1 Cor. 10:31 KJV). Earlier in the epistle Paul had reminded the believers at Corinth that they were not their own, that they had been bought with a price; therefore they should glorify God in their body (1 Cor. 6:19–20). In that context the chief application was to shun sexual immorality as something radically incompatible with the calling to belong to Jesus. Believers are the temple of the Holy Spirit, and life in the body, including the sex lives of the saints, is to be lived for the glory of God.

The context of the great imperative (1 Cor. 10:31) is more broadly the life and witness of the church. Paul follows up the comprehensive principle of seeking the glory of God in everything that we do with an application to his immediate concern: "Do not cause anyone to stumble, whether Jews, Greeks or the church of God" (1 Cor. 10:32). God is not glorified by actions, however innocent in themselves, that hinder the progress of the gospel. Paul appeals to his own example of self-subordination for the sake of others: "For I am not seeking my own good but the good of many, so that they may be saved" (1 Cor. 10:33). Then comes the clincher: "Follow my example, as I

---

25. *Aretē* (excellence, especially moral excellence or virtue) is used four times in the New Testament, three times by Peter (1 Pet. 2:9; 2 Pet. 1:3, 5) and once by Paul (Phil. 4:8).

follow the example of Christ" (1 Cor. 11:1). God is glorified in the imitation of Christ in all things great and small, for the image of Christ is the supreme expression of the glory of God.

The Image of Christ

Bernard Ramm, in a rare separate treatment of the doctrine of glorification, points out "that God intends to share his glory with his children in the form of their glorification, and that our present salvation, already begun, is a process which shall terminate in end-time, eschatological glory."[26] The classic Pauline passage on glorification is Romans 8:28–30. The familiar and measured rendering of the King James Version reads:

> And we know that all things work together for good to those who love God, to them who are the called according to his purpose. For whom he did foreknow, he also did predestinate to be conformed to the image of his Son, that he might be the firstborn among many brethren. Moreover whom he did predestinate, them he also called: and whom he called, them he also justified: and whom he justified, them he also glorified.

The goal of redemption in God's eternal purpose is conformity to the image of his Son. Glorification consists in being made like Christ, the perfect image of God in human nature. The goal is finally attained in the age to come; the resurrection of Christ carries with it the assurance that "just as we have borne the image of the man of dust, we will also bear the image of the man of heaven" (1 Cor. 15:49 NRSV). God's open secret (*mystērion*) is "Christ in you, the hope of glory" (Col. 1:27). Even now those whom God calls "are being transformed into [the Lord's] likeness with ever-increasing glory" (2 Cor. 3:18). The Christian life has a definite shape as Christ is formed in us (Gal. 4:19); renewal in the image of God (Eph. 4:24, Col. 3:10) has a tangible meaning in the person and example of Christ.

The latter references in Ephesians and Colossians hark back to the original creation narrative:

> Then God said, "Let us make humankind in our image, according to our likeness; and let them have dominion. . . ." So God created humankind in his image, / in the image of God he created them; / male and female he created them. God blessed them and God said to them, "Be fruitful and multiply, and fill the earth and subdue it." [Gen. 1:26–28 NRSV]

Human beings were created to be the visible representation of the invisible God. The content of the image is not precisely defined but some inferences may be drawn from human distinctives in the context, especially the mandate to sub-

---

26. Bernard Ramm, *Them He Glorified: A Systematic Study of the Doctrine of Glorification* (Grand Rapids: Eerdmans, 1963), 62.

due the earth (1:28), the vocation to work and take care of the garden (2:15), the commandment not to eat of the tree of the knowledge of good and evil (2:16–17), the naming of the animals (2:20), and the use of language as a medium of expression (2:23). The implication is that human beings are self-conscious, rational, moral agents, that after the pattern of what God is uniquely and transcendently, humans are personal beings with a divine calling to fulfill. (Personality, we should note, requires relationship for expression, a point underscored by the creation of male and female in the image of the tripersonal God.)

The Bible continues to speak of human beings as the image of God even after the fall (Gen. 9:6; James 3:9), though obviously a thorough renewal is necessary if we are to reflect the glory of God as originally intended (Eph. 4:24; Col. 3:10). To accommodate both poles of the biblical teaching theologians frequently distinguish between the image in a broader and a narrower sense. The former refers to "the entire endowment of gifts and capacities that enable man to function as he should in his various relationships and callings," whereas the latter means "man's proper functioning in harmony with God's will for him."[27] Renewal of the image refers to the restoration of its proper functioning.

To be renewed in the image of God is to be made like Christ, who not only is God but who also as a human being functioned in perfect harmony with the will of God and so fulfilled all that human nature was intended to be. From his example we learn that human fulfillment is to be found in the path of reverent submission (*eulabeia*) to God's will (Heb. 5:7). In Christ we see the glory of God truly and perfectly reflected in human nature, and he calls, "Follow me."

If we think of glory in terms of outward splendor we will surely distort or miss altogether the doctrine of present and progressive glorification as taught in such passages as 2 Corinthians 3:18. The Gospel of John, which could well be called "the gospel of glory" in view of its frequent use of the verb *doxazō* (twenty-three instances as compared to Luke's nine), broadens our understanding by directing us to the glory of Christ in his humiliation. Leon Morris comments on the well-known statement "we beheld his glory" (John 1:14):

> John is speaking of that glory that was seen in the literal, physical Jesus of Nazareth. As He came in lowliness we have an example of the paradox that John uses so forcefully later in the Gospel, that the true glory is to be seen, not in outward splendor, but in the lowliness with which the Son of God lived for men and suffered for them. John thinks, it is true, that the miracles showed the glory of Christ (2:11, 11:4, 40). But in a deeper sense it is the cross of shame that manifests the true glory (12:23f; 13:31).[28]

The new human being is created to function as God's image "in true righteousness (*dikaiosunē*) and holiness (*hosiotēs*)" (Eph. 4:24). This combination

27. Anthony A. Hoekema, *Created in God's Image* (Grand Rapids: Eerdmans, 1986), 70–71, 72. Hoekema's treatment—exegetical, historical, and theological—is excellent throughout.

28. Leon Morris, *The Gospel According to John* (Grand Rapids: Eerdmans, 1971), 105.

of terms appears in one other place in the New Testament, in Zechariah's song of thanksgiving (Benedictus) at the birth of his son, John the Baptist: "[The Lord has come] to rescue us from the hand of our enemies, and to enable us to serve him without fear in holiness (*hosiotēs*) and righteousness (*dikaiosunē*) before him all our days" (Luke 1:75). In redemption the image is restored to proper functioning in relationship to both God (*hosiotēs*) and other human beings (*dikaiosunē*) after the pattern of Christ, the preeminent and exemplary Servant of the Lord, through whom the original mandate to rule over the earth for the glory of God is fulfilled.

The Kingdom of God

The first Beatitude bestows the kingdom of heaven upon the poor in spirit; the fourth guarantees that those who hunger and thirst for righteousness will be filled; the seventh assures those who are persecuted in the pursuit of righteousness that the kingdom of heaven is theirs (Matt. 5:3, 6, 10). The Beatitudes thus prepare Jesus' disciples for his striking assertion of the highest good: "But seek ye first the kingdom of God and his righteousness, and all these things [food, drink, clothing] shall be added unto you" (Matt. 6:33 KJV). In a work that deserves to be better known, Martin Franzmann comments:

> [Jesus] thereby makes the blessing bestowed in the first Beatitude the imperative force in their lives. The Kingdom is given to the poor in spirit, to men [and women] who stand before God unhindered and undeceived by the security of things, in the need of their bare humanity. The gift of the Beatitude has become the dynamic of their existence: they seek first the first gift. Likewise the blessing of the fourth Beatitude has become the imperative that shapes their lives. God gives His righteousness to men [and women] who hunger and thirst for it, who see in their need for righteousness the supreme need, the need which must be met if they are to live, a need before which the need for things recedes . . . so that it becomes a footnote on the page whereon is written: "The LORD is our righteousness."[29]

In keeping with the focus of the Beatitudes, New Testament narrative characteristically sums up a given unit of its history by reference to the kingdom of God. Matthew, for example, gives this synopsis of Jesus' Galilean ministry: "Jesus went throughout Galilee teaching in their synagogues, preaching the good news of the kingdom, and healing every disease and sickness among the people" (Matt. 4:23; cf. 9:35). Luke, for his part, sums up Jesus' ministry between his resurrection and ascension with the notice: "He appeared to them over a period of forty days and spoke about the kingdom of

29. Martin H. Franzmann, *Follow Me: Discipleship According to Saint Matthew* (St. Louis: Concordia, 1961), 58.

God" (Acts 1:3). Significantly, the Book of Acts ends with this encapsulation of Paul's Roman ministry: "Boldly and without hindrance he preached the kingdom of God and taught about the Lord Jesus Christ" (Acts 28:30; cf. 19:8). Jesus himself gave this advance summary of the activity of the whole period between his first and second coming: "And this gospel of the kingdom will be preached in the whole world as a testimony to all nations, and then the end will come" (Matt. 24:14). It is evident that the hub of New Testament theology is the proclamation of the kingdom of God. What does it mean?

As in English, the Hebrew and Greek words for kingdom can mean either "reign" or "realm." When the Bible speaks of God's kingdom, the predominant reference is to his reign, the sovereign exercise of his authority and power:

> All you have made will praise you, O LORD;
>   your saints will extol you.
> They will tell of the glory of your kingdom
>   and speak of your might,
> so that all men may know of your mighty acts
>   and the glorious splendor of your kingdom.
> Your kingdom is an everlasting kingdom,
>   and your dominion endures through all generations.
>
> [Ps. 145:10–13]

The idea of a realm, the sphere in which God's rule is exercised and experienced, follows in close succession. Thus Psalm 103:19, "The LORD has established his throne in heaven, and his kingdom rules over all."

As these passages indicate, God's reign is both universal and perpetual. How then can it come? The answer is, God's kingdom comes as he manifests his sovereignty in a world of apostasy and revolt and restores the vicegerency of humankind (expressed in the creation narrative as cultivative and protective dominion over the earth) in Christ. The theme of the coming kingdom is heralded immediately after the fall had rendered God's purpose for humankind unachievable without divine intervention. The Creator-King rules by putting enmity between the serpent and the woman and between their respective seeds—a divine decree that carries with it the promise of ultimate victory over the evil one (Gen. 3:15).[30] The seed of the woman will triumph, though not without suffering; the serpent will bruise the Redeemer's heel before being finally crushed beneath his feet.

---

30. Cf. Derek Kidner: "Remarkably, it [the first glimmer of the gospel] makes its début as a sentence passed on the enemy (cf. Col. 2:15), not a direct promise to man, for redemption is about God's rule as much as about man's need (cf. Ezk. 36:22, 'not . . . for your sake . . .')." *Genesis: An Introduction and Commentary* (Chicago: InterVarsity, 1967), 70.

The royal conflict theme is amplified in Jesus' explanation of the parable of the weeds among the wheat (Matt. 13:37–43):

> The one who sowed the good seed is the Son of Man. The field is the world, and the good seed stands for the sons of the kingdom. The weeds are the sons of the evil one, and the enemy who sows them is the devil. The harvest is the end of the age and the harvesters are angels. As the weeds are pulled up and burned in the fire, so it will be at the end of the age. The Son of Man will send out his angels, and they will weed out of his kingdom everything that causes sin and all who do evil. They will throw them into the fiery furnace, where there will be weeping and gnashing of teeth. Then the righteous will shine like the sun in the kingdom of their Father. He who has ears, let him hear.

The kingdom comes as God exercises his sovereignty in a fallen world in salvation and judgment. Thus, "The LORD sat as King at the flood" (Ps. 29:10 NASB),[31] bringing judgment upon impenitent apostate humanity but saving a remnant preserved by his grace. Again, God ruled at the exodus, saving his chosen people and bringing judgment upon the powers—human and demonic—that arrayed themselves in opposition to him. "Thus the LORD became king in Jeshurun" (Deut. 33:5 RSV). While God is king of all the earth and reigns over the nations (Ps. 47:7–8), he is in a special sense the king of the Jews, Israel's creator and redeemer (Isa. 43:15; 44:6). "For the LORD is our judge, the LORD is our lawgiver, the LORD is our king; it is he who will save us" (Isa. 33:22). God's reign in the Old Testament dispensation established "a community of people who constituted his own kingdom and received his gifts and his laws" (cf. Matt. 8:11–12; 21:43).[32]

While the kingdom was manifest in the redemption and subsequent history of Israel, the Old Testament looks forward to a coming kingship that would usher in the full realization of God's rule, not only over Israel but redemptively over all nations (e.g., Pss. 96:10–13; 98:8–9). The prophets speak of a final visitation of God in which he will bring his redemptive purpose to its ultimate consummation (e.g., Zech. 2:11; Dan. 7:13–14). The coming kingdom where the Lord exercises his rule in the full redemptive sense is linked with the Messiah. As Herman Ridderbos points out, the Messiah is the coming ruler of the world (Isa. 11:9–10), and his kingship bears a supernatural character (Mic. 5:2–5). "In short, all that which holds for the coming divine manifestation is to say that it is the Lord, who will again assert his rule over Israel and maintain his kingship over the whole world in and through the coming Messiah-King."[33]

---

31. Ps. 29:10 contains the only instance of *mabbûl* (flood) outside of Genesis 6–9.

32. Ned B. Stonehouse, *The Witness of Matthew and Mark to Christ* (Grand Rapids: Eerdmans, 1944), 229.

33. Herman Ridderbos, *The Coming of the Kingdom*, ed. Raymond O. Zorn, trans. H. de Jongste (Philadelphia: Presbyterian and Reformed, 1962), 7.

The messianic kingdom comes in stages correlative to the work of Christ. Ned B. Stonehouse captures the point well:

> Various aspects of the manifestation of the kingdom must be distinguished. The kingdom is one, and it may be recognized as being basically "eschatological" in view of its consummation through divine interposition. But no contradiction is involved in recognizing that, prior to the consummation at the end of the age, there have been significant preliminary manifestations of the kingdom which are also the consequence of decisive divine action in history. The divine action in view is in and through Christ, and thus the stages of the coming of the kingdom correspond with the stages of the ministry and activity of Christ. The action of the returning Son of Man ushers in the kingdom in its final glory and power. His exaltation to God's right hand also constitutes a most signal triumph of God in the accomplishment of his purposes of redemption, and hence a specific historical turning point in the work of making actual the divine rule. But even prior to this development the very present of the Son of Man upon earth, and his victory over the works of Satan, signalizes that the kingdom has actually come.[34]

The practical importance of recognizing the stages of the coming of the kingdom is twofold. We may not lag behind the King in an unwarranted pessimism about history and culture as though his first coming and present exaltation make no difference, nor may we forge ahead of the King with an unwarranted triumphalism in the expectation of establishing a utopian theocracy prior to his second coming. Because the perspective of kingdom stages has a significant bearing on Christian social practice, a brief overview of the main lines of the biblical basis is in order.[35]

The Earthly Ministry of Christ

The New Testament opens with the birth of the King; the annunciation to Mary (Luke 1:30–33), the annunciation to the shepherds (Luke 2:10–12), and the visit of the magi (Matt. 2:1–6) are all regal in substance. Mary's song (Magnificat, Luke 1:46–55) and Zechariah's song (Benedictus, Luke 1:68–79) exalt the inbreaking reign of the Messiah in fulfillment of the Abrahamic and Davidic covenants. Jesus himself begins his public ministry with a royal proclamation announcing the arrival of the messianic era of salvation: "Today this scripture [Isa. 61:1–2] is fulfilled in your hearing" (Luke 4:21). The presence of the King upon earth marks the first phase of the coming of the promised kingdom. Confirmation is provided by consideration of Jesus' total teaching and work and by such explicit texts as Matthew 11:12, "From the days of John the Baptist until now, the kingdom of heaven has been forcefully

---

34. Ned B. Stonehouse, *The Witness of Luke to Christ* (Grand Rapids: Eerdmans, 1951), 152–53.
35. Cf. Anthony A. Hoekema, *The Bible and the Future* (Grand Rapids: Eerdmans, 1979), 41–54.

advancing, and forceful men lay hold of it," and Matthew 12:28, "But if I drive out demons by the Spirit of God, then the kingdom of God has come upon you."

The climactic act of Jesus' public ministry was his laying down of his life on the cross. So far from being a defeat, the cross was the means by which he won the decisive victory over all his enemies and ours. "He forgave us all our sins, having canceled the written code, with its regulations, that was against us and that stood opposed to us; he took it away, nailing it to the cross. And having disarmed the powers and authorities, he made a public spectacle of them, triumphing over them by the cross" (Col. 2:13–15; cf. 2 Tim. 1:10; Heb. 2:14–15). As Anthony Hoekema remarks, "The greatest eschatological event in history is not in the future but in the past. Since Christ has won a decisive victory over Satan, sin, and death in the past, future eschatological events must be seen as the completion of a redemptive process which has already begun."[36]

The Heavenly Exaltation of Christ

In answer to the question of how is Christ exalted in his session at God's right hand, the Westminster Larger Catechism asserts, "Christ is exalted in his sitting at the right hand of God, in that as God-man he is advanced to the highest favor with God the Father, with all fulness of joy, glory, and power over all things in heaven and earth; and doth gather and defend his church, and subdue their enemies; furnisheth his ministers and people with gifts and graces, and maketh intercession for them" (q. 54). The resurrected and ascended Christ enters the full exercise of his mediatorial authority seated at the right hand of God.

Jesus' retrospective on the Old Testament revelation of the Messiah illuminates the two stages of his redemptive accomplishment: "Did not the Christ have to suffer these things and then enter his glory?" (Luke 24:26). As a consequence of Messiah's death and resurrection, repentance and forgiveness of sins are proclaimed in his name to all nations, beginning at Jerusalem (Luke 24:47). The crucified Christ sits enthroned as Lord (Acts 2:36), exalted to God's right hand as Prince and Savior that he might grant repentance and forgiveness of sins to Israel (Acts 5:31) and indeed all nations (Acts 11:18).

The great program of the present stage of the kingdom is the mission to the world in which God shows his concern by taking from the nations a people for himself (Acts 15:14). This perspective is reflected in Paul's prayer for the Colossians' growth in the Christian life, which concludes with "giving thanks to the Father, who has qualified you to share in the inheritance of the saints in

---

36. Hoekema, *The Bible and the Future*, 77.

the kingdom of light. For he has rescued us from the dominion of darkness and brought us into the kingdom of the Son he loves, in whom we have redemption, the forgiveness of sins" (Col. 1:12–14). The kingdom is both a matter of present Christian experience and of future hope. The church is called to follow the messianic pattern of suffering and glory (cf. Rom. 8:18–21).

The Second Coming of Christ

The full manifestation of Christ's power in making actual the divine rule awaits his coming in glory. Although Christ has all power in heaven and on earth, we do not yet see all things subject to him (Heb. 2:8). As the apostle Paul tells us, "He must reign until he has put all his enemies under his feet" (1 Cor. 15:25). The last enemy—death—will be routed at the second coming. "Then the end (*to telos*) will come, when he hands over the kingdom to God the Father, after he has destroyed all dominion, authority and power" (1 Cor. 15:24). In the words of Jesus' own end-time prophecy, "When the Son of Man comes in his glory, and all the angels with him, he will sit on his throne in heavenly glory. . . . Then the King will say to those on his right, 'Come, you who are blessed by my Father; take your inheritance, the kingdom prepared for you since the creation of the world'" (Matt. 25:31, 34).

The kingdom is a present reality in the church as the fellowship of those who receive the divine rule; it is also the future inheritance of the people of God, whose lives attest their faith and love (cf. James 2:5; Matt. 25:34–46; 1 Cor. 6:9–11; Gal. 5:21). Paul brings out the connection between adoption and hope: "Now if we are children, then we are heirs—heirs of God and co-heirs with Christ, if indeed we share in his sufferings in order that we may also share in his glory" (Rom. 8:17). The groaning of the whole creation right up to the present time (Rom. 8:22) should be read as the contractions of "a better world a-coming," to be delivered at the second coming of Christ.[37]

"Therefore, since we are receiving a kingdom that cannot be shaken, let us be thankful, and so worship [or, 'serve,' *latreuō*] God acceptably with reverence and awe" (Heb. 12:28).

Eternal Life

> What comfort do you derive from the article of *the life everlasting?*
>
> That, since I now feel in my heart the beginning of eternal joy, after this life I shall possess perfect bliss, such as eye has not seen nor ear heard, neither has entered into the heart of man—therein to praise God forever.
>
> —Heidelberg Catechism, q. and a. 58

37. Ibid., 163.

"Life eternal is the supreme good, death eternal the supreme evil."[38] So wrote Augustine in one of his versions of the *summum bonum*, reflecting a fundamental biblical perspective that goes all the way back to the Garden of Eden. The tree of life in the middle of the garden symbolized more than continued physical existence; it held the promise of unending fellowship with the living God. Adam and Eve were free to choose life and warned against making the opposite choice by eating of the tree of the knowledge of good in evil. By refraining they would have known good experientially; by partaking they came to know evil.

The story does not end there, however. God graciously intervenes and makes provision that the choice may be reversed. Moses' covenant renewal sermon concludes with the eloquent appeal: "This day I call heaven and earth as witnesses against you that I have set before you life and death, blessings and curses. Now choose life, so that you and your children may live and that you may love the LORD your God, listen to his voice, and hold fast to him. For the LORD is your life, and he will give you many years in the land he swore to give to your fathers, Abraham, Isaac and Jacob" (Deut. 30:19–20). The blessing is represented concretely in terms of the Promised Land, but its most crucial aspect is expressed in the striking assertion, "For the LORD is your life." God himself is the good to be sought, the life to be chosen; the covenant blessing consists essentially of union with him.

The hope of *eternal* life in the presence of God, predicated on the messianic prophecy of resurrection, is the arresting conclusion of King David's "inheritance" psalm: "You have made known to me the path of life; you will fill me with joy in your presence, with eternal pleasures at your right hand" (Ps. 16:11). It remained for David's Christ to bring eternal life fully to light through the gospel (2 Tim. 1:10). When we compare the four Gospels, we find that "receiving the kingdom" is characteristic of Matthew, Mark, and Luke, while "having eternal life" is the dominant feature of the Gospel of John. There is, as one would expect, some linkage; the quest for eternal life is an issue in the Synoptics (Matt. 19:16; Mark 10:17; Luke 18:18), and those who enter the kingdom receive eternal life as their inheritance in the age to come (Matt. 19:29, 25:46; Luke 18:30). But although some of Jesus' best-known kingdom sayings are recorded only by John (John 3:3, 5; 18:18), the unifying theme of his narrative is not the coming of the kingdom but the gift of eternal life.

Of particular interest is the definition of eternal life that appears in the prayer Jesus prayed the night of his betrayal: "Now this is eternal life: that they may know you, the only true God, and Jesus Christ, whom you have sent" (John 17:3).[39] The viewpoint of Moses and David—that life consists of fel-

---

38. Augustine, *The City of God*, 19.4.
39. See George Eldon Ladd, "Eternal Life," *A Theology of the New Testament* (Grand Rapids: Eerdmans, 1974), 254–69.

lowship with God—is now reaffirmed with a distinctively christological focus. As John says in his famous prologue, "the Word became flesh, and dwelt among us, and we beheld His glory, glory as of the only begotten from the Father, full of grace and truth" (John 1:14 NASB). To know Christ is to know God; to have the Son is to have life—now and forevermore.

The offer of eternal life in Christ frankly appeals to our self-interest, but this does not make Christian ethics egoistic as that term is commonly understood. The framework—eternal life *in Christ*—makes all the difference. The Lord satisfies the desires of those who delight themselves in him (Ps. 37:4), and in those things in which he delights—kindness, justice, and righteousness on earth (Jer. 9:24). The self that is fulfilled in eternal happiness is not just any self, but the self that hungers and thirsts after righteousness (Matt. 5:6), the self that above all desires God.

The Westminster divines rightly made the enjoyment of God coordinate with the glory of God in answer to the question of our chief end (N.B. not "end*s*"). From time to time theologians have attempted to eliminate self-interest from Christian ethics. Duns Scotus, for example, taught that "self-interest must be *wholly* excluded, and this can only be if in the last resort the self can cease to will even its own being."[40] But as John Burnaby points out, this renders the doctrine of creation unintelligible. "Why should God have brought out of nothing a world which can glorify Him only by a voluntary return to nothingness?"[41] Closer to home, Samuel Hopkins, Jonathan Edwards's chronological successor (but not his theological heir), argued in his "Dialogue between a Calvinist and a Semi-Calvinist" that true love for God is so disinterested that a Christian should be willing to be damned for the glory of God if he so wills.[42] Here is love gone wrong—with a vengeance. It has nothing to do with biblical religion, which is premised on the truth of John 3:16, "For God so loved the world that he gave his one and only Son, that whoever believes in him shall not perish but have eternal life." To think, after all God has done to secure the eternal life for those who believe, that he would be loved with "disinterested benevolence," is to treat God's indescribable gift with contempt. So far from loving the true God, Hopkins's "Calvinist" bows down to the false deity of philosophical abstraction.

Perhaps C. S. Lewis put it best when he said, "It would be a bold and silly creature that came before its Creator with the boast 'I'm no beggar. I love you disinterestedly.'"[43] Jesus came to call the weary and burdened—not the self-sufficient and disinterested—to find rest for their souls in him (Matt. 11:28).

---

40. Burnaby, *Amor Dei*, 274.
41. Ibid., 289.
42. Cf. Edwards, *Ethical Writings*, 648 n. 6.
43. C. S. Lewis, *The Four Loves* (London: Bles, 1960), 12.

To glorify God and to enjoy him are not entirely separate and distinct ends; the saints enjoy God when they glorify him, and God is glorified when they enjoy him. This has led one thoughtful evangelical theologian to suggest that the biblical *telos* is more accurately stated thus: "The chief end of man is to glorify God *by* enjoying him forever."[44] This is certainly an important aspect of the truth—Piper's presentation is rich in biblical exposition of the Christian pursuit of joy—and very much in need of emphasis. Nevertheless, the saints' glorification of God cannot be reduced to their taking pleasure in him. God is glorified by the holiness as well as the happiness of the redeemed.[45] The coordinating particle (to glorify God *and* to enjoy him forever) is necessary to represent the inseparable objective and subjective aspects of the biblical *telos*.

Practical Implications

> The trick is to start at the ending when you write a play. Get a good strong ending and then write backwards.
>
> Woody Allen, *God (A Play)*

One of the most perceptive analyses of the American character in the 1980s was the best-seller *Habits of the Heart*, by Robert Bellah and four associates.[46] The authors, backed up by their extensive sociological research, observe that "Americans tend to think of the ultimate goals of a good life as matters of personal choice."[47] Americans accordingly rank freedom as the highest cultural value. This means that freedom has practically become definitive of the good in the American mind. But as Americans typically describe it, freedom is a *summum bonum* without positive content.

> [F]reedom turns out to mean being left alone by others, not having other people's values, ideas, or styles of life forced upon one, being free of arbitrary authority in work, family, and political life. What it is that one might do with that freedom is much more difficult for Americans to define.[48]

Freedom in the biblical tradition means freedom to do the will of God; in the republican tradition, to participate in working for the common good of

---

44. John Piper, *Desiring God: Meditations of a Christian Hedonist* (Portland: Multnomah, 1986). For a philosophical evaluation of Piper's "Christian Hedonism" see Richard J. Mouw, *The God Who Commands* (Notre Dame, Ind.: University of Notre Dame Press, 1990), 30–42.

45. Although Piper cites Edwards on our being created to reflect God's happiness, he neglects Edwards's other "remanations" of God's glory, namely, knowledge and holiness.

46. Robert N. Bellah et al., *Habits of the Heart: Individualism and Commitment in American Life* (1985; New York: Harper, 1986).

47. Ibid., 22.

48. Ibid., 23.

society. But in modern American individualism, freedom means "freedom of choice" without reference to objective moral criteria. "What does the Bill of Rights mean to you?" a reporter asked a schoolchild viewing the original manuscript on display. "Being free to do whatever you want," was the not unexpected reply. This is how the posterity of the founders of the American republic typically construe the "blessings of liberty" it was the purpose of the Constitution to secure for them. "Choice is what this country's all about" is a proposition of bumper-sticker depth, yet it appears as the trump card in all sorts of public-policy issues. Furriers use it to cut off debate with animal-rights activists; pro-abortionists use it to by-pass discussion of the humanity of the unborn. Freedom of choice functions in American culture as a self-justifying moral absolute. To parody a popular song, "Freedom's just another word for 'no one else to choose'; / My choices may be kooky, but they're me."

When Americans do speak positively about the goal of life, they are more comfortable (itself an illuminating term) talking about "values" than dealing with the question of duties.[49] The reason is plain. It has become the accepted thing to talk about what one values without getting into the question of what human beings ought to value—that might provoke disagreement and even moral criticism, which is interpreted as intolerance. To talk about what is good in itself, or good for human beings as such, implies a universal standard, and it is taken for granted that no such standard exists. Thus Americans no longer probe the good; they only clarify their values. Because of the ambiguity of the term *value* (which can be either objective or subjective), "values-speak" retains the aura of moral decision about the good, but in fact it only refers to the pragmatic choice of what is "good for me" as I see it. The voice is the voice of moral discourse, but the hands are the hands of personal preference.

As the authors of *Habits of the Heart* point out, "if selves are defined by their preferences, but those preferences are arbitrary, then each self constitutes its own moral universe."[50] Right and wrong are determined not by reference to an objective standard of good and evil but by reference to what the individual finds useful for achieving the self's own felt needs and desires. "What kind of world," our authors ask, "is inhabited by this self, perpetually in progress, yet without any fixed moral end? There each individual is entitled to his or her own 'bit of space' and is utterly free within its boundaries."[51] In the popular culture, Madonna is the symbol of this "improvisational self," free to be anything one wants to be—and to change one's self at will. No choice is right or wrong in itself; what counts are results that satisfy the preferences of a self unencumbered by a moral universe not of its own making.

---

49. One hears often enough, "This election is about values!" which is conveniently ambiguous. On the other hand, who could be elected on the slogan, "This election is about *duties*"?

50. Bellah et al., 76.

51. Ibid.

This is far from satisfactory, however, and so difficult to live with consistently that the question of whether we may live in a moral universe not of our making after all intrudes upon our privacy. Is there a fixed moral end at which human beings should aim? Is human life meaningful just making it up as we go along? The question runs through much of Woody Allen's art, including the fine example of theatre of the absurd from which the epigraph at the head of this section is taken. The point seems to be that without a fixed ending to the human drama, the search for significant meaning in life is hopeless.[52]

The question of the goal of human life is not the property of any one culture. Although the *summum bonum* has been the subject of a long philosophical discussion in the West, it is a human question. When anthropologist Jacob A. Loewen asked Indians of the Paraguayan Chaco, "What is the most important desire that you carry in your 'innermost'?" he received the reply: "One wants to become a person. . . . Yes, one wants to become a human being."[53] That answer reflects a profound awareness that there is some norm for human nature that defines its true fulfillment. The gospel makes contact at this point, for it is good news indeed for those who want to become what human beings were made to be.

Beginning with the question of our chief end not only provides an intelligible point of contact for the gospel; it also maintains the distinctly personal orientation of the Christian ethic. The fundamental principle of the Christian life is not adherence to impersonal law but allegiance to God the personal lawgiver out of a desire to please him and to be conformed to him. Self-interest is incorporated, for God has made our interest his own, even giving his only begotten Son that we might hear at last his "Well done, good and faithful servant. . . . Enter thou into the joy of thy Lord" (Matt. 25:21, 23 KJV).

> What, ye ask me, is my prize?
> What the secret to be wise?
> What the wealth I value most?
> What the Name wherein I boast?
> Jesus, Jesus Christ, the Crucified.

---

52. *God (A Play)* is included in *Without Feathers* (New York: Warner, 1976), a collection of Woody Allen's writings that bears as its own epigraph Emily Dickinson's line, "Hope is the thing with feathers. . . ."

53. Jacob A. Loewen, *Culture and Human Values: Christian Intervention in Anthropological Perspective* (South Pasadena, Calif.: William Carey Library, 1975), 91.

3

The Motive of the Christian Life

The short answer to the question of the goal of human life is God: his glory, his image, his kingdom, to enjoy him forever. The problem is, nobody naturally seeks this end; all seek happiness, but no one seeks God. The biblical *telos* is particularly anathama to the humanist mind. Paul Kurtz, for example, writes:

> "Man's chief end," admonishes the Scottish shorter catechism, "is to glorify God and enjoy him for ever and ever." What kind of life can be said to be significant if we are totally dependent upon this God for our existence and sustenance? Is not the life of an independent free man to be preferred to one of eternal bondage? As Bertrand Russell has said, to sing hymns in praise of Him and hold hands throughout all eternity would be sheer boredom. For the free man, Hell could not be worse.[1]

Cosmic hand-holding aside, we may take it that heaven is an acquired taste. Asked by God, "Why should I let you into my heaven?" Kurtz would reply, "Why should I want in? Sounds like hell to me." Left to ourselves our reply would be no different. It is the experience of God's amazing grace that creates the desire to sing his praise for eternity. As Jonathan Edwards observed in his *Treatise Concerning Religious Affections,* a man must first love God, or have his heart united to him, before he will esteem God's good his own, and before he will desire the glorifying and enjoying of God, as his happiness.[2] The real problem of ethics is not in finding the rule to direct us how to glorify and enjoy God but in having the will to make this our aim in the first place. Leopards are not in the habit of changing their spots. Something drastic has to happen for human beings to make God their goal, a change of heart so profound it is like being born all over again, this time from above.

---

1. Paul Kurtz, *The Fullness of Life* (New York: Horizon, 1974), 86. Wittingly or unwittingly Kurtz echoes Milton's Satan: "Better to reign in hell, than serve in heav'n" (*Paradise Lost,* 1.263).
2. Jonathan Edwards, *Religious Affections*, vol. 2 of *The Works of Jonathan Edwards,* ed. John E. Smith (New Haven: Yale University Press, 1959), 241.

The Human Heart

In the Book of Proverbs the wise parent counsels, "Keep thy heart with all diligence; for out of it are the issues of life" (Prov. 4:23 KJV). Put another way, "[B]ehind all overt action is the dispositional character or complex which is the psychological determinant of action."[3] Human conduct—every thought, word, and deed—flows from this spring and shows the kind of person one is. According to Jesus, it is not a pretty sight: "For from within, out of men's hearts, come evil thoughts, sexual immorality, theft, murder, adultery, greed, malice, deceit, lewdness, envy, slander, arrogance, and folly" (Mark 7:21–22). A rotten tree produces rotten fruit; a polluted spring streams polluted water.

Human beings are in a bad fix so far as moral goodness is concerned. The Bible views the human condition as a state of being dead in sin (Eph. 2:1). The natural mind is hostile to God and will not submit to his law; those under its control cannot possibly please God (Rom. 8:7–8). This radical disinclination to godliness must be overcome for moral goodness to ensue. The good news is that God's grace in salvation uproots the hostility of the heart toward God and implants a new disposition of affection for him. The gospel thus transforms moral conduct from within; moral goodness is produced, not by external amendment of life, but by union with Christ through faith. God's law is first written on the heart that it may be practiced in the life (Jer. 31:33; Heb. 10:16). As the Lord promises in Ezekiel's great prophecy of restoration and renewal: "I will give you a new heart and put a new spirit in you; I will remove from you your heart of stone and give you a heart of flesh. And I will put my Spirit in you and move you to follow my decrees and be careful to keep my laws" (Ezek. 36:26–27).

What are the essential characteristics of the transformed heart? What constitutes a virtuous disposition as defined by the Scriptures? Often in the New Testament faith, hope, and love are mentioned together as the basic components of the dispositional change brought about by the gospel.[4] The pervasiveness of this coordination warrants the conclusion that faith, hope, and love form the great trio of gospel virtues (or better, *graces*) bestowed by the Holy Spirit in the application of redemption. There is a radical change in the disposition, affections, and behavior of the person to whom they are given. From the regenerate heart there flows a work produced by faith, a labor prompted by love, and an endurance inspired by hope (1 Thess. 1:3).

Faith, hope, and love always work together, but there is a certain order in their relationship, as Luther was existentially to discover. Unable to love a just and angry God, Luther despaired of the goal of life until he came to under-

---

3. John Murray, *Principles of Conduct: Aspects of Biblical Ethics* (Grand Rapids: Eerdmans, 1957), 13.
4. See 1 Cor. 13:13; Gal. 5:5–6; Rom. 5:1–5; 1 Thess. 1:3; Heb. 6:10–12; 1 Pet. 1:21–22. Col. 1:5 is somewhat different; there faith and love are said to spring from hope in the objective sense, "the hope that is stored up for you in heaven."

stand that the righteousness of God in salvation is a gift received by faith alone. Thereupon, he testifies, "I felt that I was altogether born again and had entered paradise itself through open gates."[5] Justifying faith engenders hope and expresses itself through love (Gal. 5:5–6); faith is thus the pivotal virtue, the gateway to a sure hope and a liberated love.

Christian Freedom

The Reformation produced two classics on motivation in the Christian life, Luther's *The Freedom of a Christian* (1520) and Calvin's chapter on "Christian Freedom" in the first edition of the *Institutes* (1536). Luther published his treatise with an open letter to Pope Leo X in the hope even yet of a reconciliation with Rome. Of this work, which Luther said contained the whole of the Christian life in brief form, John Dillenberger remarks, "If one were to single out one short document representing the content and spirit of Luther's faith, *The Freedom of a Christian* would undoubtedly be at the top."[6]

Luther's aim was to defend the doctrine of justification by faith alone and to show its implications for the Christian life. "Our faith in Christ," he wrote, "does not free us from works but from false opinions concerning works, that is, from the foolish presumption that justification is acquired by works."[7] The motive of proving oneself worthy of salvation Luther discerned to be self-serving and inhibiting. The gospel of justification by faith renders works unnecessary for acceptance by God. "Therefore [the Christian] should be guided in all his works by this thought and contemplate this one thing alone, that he may serve and benefit others in all that he does, considering nothing except the need and the advantage of his neighbor."[8]

For Calvin also Christian freedom was a matter of intense pastoral concern. "Its whole force consists in quieting frightened consciences before God—that are perhaps disturbed and troubled over forgiveness of sins, or anxious whether unfinished works, corrupted by the faults of our flesh, are pleasing to God, or tormented about the use of things indifferent."[9] The doctrine of justification is the answer to the first problem, the doctrine of adoption the answer to the second, and the doctrine of creation the answer to the third. Calvin's main points are briefly as follows.

First, in seeking assurance of their justification before God, the consciences of believers are above and beyond the reach of the law, though the law con-

---

5. Martin Luther, *Martin Luther: Selections from His Writings*, ed. John Dillenberger (Garden City, N.Y.: Doubleday, 1961), 11.
6. Ibid., 42.
7. Ibid., 81.
8. Ibid., 73.
9. John Calvin, *Institutes of the Christian Religion*, ed. John T. McNeill, trans. Ford Lewis Battles (Philadelphia: Westminster, 1960), 3.19.9.

tinues to be instructive in what is good to those who have already been accepted by God. Second, in the process of sanctification the consciences of believers are not constrained by the necessity of the law; rather, "freed from the law's yoke they willingly obey God's will. For since they dwell in perpetual dread so long as they remain under the sway of the law, they will never be disposed with eager readiness to obey God unless they have already been given this sort of freedom."[10] Here Calvin draws out the implications of adoption: "Such children ought we to be, firmly trusting that our services will be approved by our most merciful Father, however small, rude, and imperfect these may be."[11] Third, regarding outward things that are in themselves neither commanded nor forbidden (the so-called *adiaphora*) consciences are free to use God's created gifts as he intended.[12]

Christian liberty and liberty of conscience are also the subject of chapter 20 of the Westminster Confession of Faith, the first paragraph of which is a particularly helpful summary of the doctrine articulated by Luther and Calvin in the preceding century.

> The liberty which Christ hath purchased for believers under the gospel consists in their freedom from the guilt of sin, the condemning wrath of God, the curse of the moral law; and, in their being delivered from this present evil world, bondage to Satan, and dominion of sin; from the evil of afflictions, the sting of death, the victory of the grave, and everlasting damnation; as also, in their free access to God, and their yielding obedience unto him, not out of slavish fear, but a child-like love and willing mind.[13]

"Slavish fear" refers to conformity to the moral law motivated by the threat of punishment. But this is not what the Bible means by obedience. As Augustine observed, "if the commandment be done through fear of penalty and not through love of righteousness, it is done in the temper of servitude not freedom—*and therefore it is not done at all.*"[14] "A child-like love," on the other hand, is motivated by the thought of pleasing one's heavenly Father and so yields the true obedience of a willing mind. The glory of the gospel is that it creates such motivation, though not without internal struggle, as the apostle Paul himself attests (Rom. 7:21–25).[15]

10. Ibid., 3.19.4.

11. Ibid.

12. Ibid., 3.19.7.

13. Westminster Confession of Faith 20.1. Cf. Samuel Bolton, *The True Bounds of Christian Freedom* (1645; reprint, Edinburgh: Banner of Truth, 1964). This is a treatise on Christian liberty and the right use of the law by the last member "superadded" to the Westminster Assembly of Divines.

14. Augustine, *The Spirit and the Letter*, in *Augustine: Later Works*, trans. John Burnaby (Philadelphia: Westminster, 1955), 215 (emphasis added).

15. For a brief exposition of this controverted text, see J. I. Packer, "The 'Wretched Man' in Romans 7," *Keep in Step with the Spirit* (Old Tappan, N.J.: Revell, 1984), 263–70.

The key biblical texts that contrast filial affection and slavish trepidation are Romans 8:14–15 and 1 John 4:18.

> Those who are led by the Spirit of God are sons of God. For you did not receive a spirit that makes you a slave again to fear, but you received the Spirit who makes you sons.

> There is no fear in love. But perfect love drives out fear, because fear has to do with punishment. The man who fears is not made perfect in love.

The word translated "punishment" is *kolasis,* used only here and at Matthew 25:46. It refers to God's retributive justice or penal satisfaction (cf. the verb *kolazō* in 2 Pet. 2:9).[16] The objects of *kolasis* are the unrighteous; "punishment . . . is quite alien to God's forgiven children who love him."[17] Consequently, to be motivated by the threats of the law is sub-Christian. In the words of Toplady's great hymn: "The terrors of law and of God / With me can have nothing to do; / My Saviour's obedience and blood / Hide all my transgressions from view."[18]

We should note that the Scriptures use the word *fear* in two distinct senses. There is the fear of terror and dread, and there is the fear of veneration and honor.[19] The fear of terror makes us want to run away and hide; the fear of honor leads us to stand in awe and worship. The gospel removes the fear of terror as a source of motivation in the Christian life. Punishment has no power to rehabilitate. As John Murray notes, "Even the infliction of wrath will not create the hatred of sin; it will incite to greater love of sin and enmity against God."[20] Fear of punishment must be expelled so that love may reign supreme as the animating principle of the Christian life. Since it is love to God that is in view, it is necessarily a *reverent* love. God is majestic in his holiness, and his acts of redemptive love are awe-inspiring. The only proper response to the crucifixion of the Lord of glory is, "Sometimes it causes me to tremble, tremble, tremble." Believers tremble at the righteous judgment of God against sin. They are no longer afraid of punishment, but they are sobered by the awesome transaction: Christ died for our sins; God made him to be sin for us who knew no sin; he bore our sins in his own body on the tree.

When the Scriptures tell us to "work out [our] salvation with fear and trembling" (Phil. 2:12) they do not mean that we are to live lives of nervous

---

16. The only other instance of *kolazō* is Acts 4:21, where it refers to human threats of retribution.

17. John R. W. Stott, *The Epistles of John: An Introduction and Commentary* (London: Tyndale, 1964), 169. Cf. Gordon H. Clark, *First John: A Commentary* (Jefferson, Md.: Trinity Foundation, 1980), 145–46.

18. This is the hymn that begins, "A debtor to mercy alone, / Of covenant mercy I sing." It expresses the same evangelical theology as Toplady's more familiar "Rock of Ages."

19. Cf. Murray, "The Fear of God," in *Principles of Conduct,* 229–42.

20. Ibid., 236.

apprehension because the completion of our salvation is up to us. The reading of the New American Bible, "work with anxious concern to achieve your salvation" is as misleading as it is common. The full text of Philippians 2:12–13 is as follows:

> Therefore, my dear friends, as you have always obeyed—not only in my presence, but now much more in my absence—continue to work out (*katergazesthe*) your salvation with fear and trembling, for it is God who works in you to will and to act according to his good purpose.

The verb translated "work out" is the only New Testament instance of *katergazomai* in the imperative mood. Although it can mean "to effect or achieve" (cf. Rom. 5:3, "tribulation works patience"; 2 Cor. 7:10, "godly sorrow works repentance") or "to finish [off] or conquer" (cf. Eph. 6:13, "after you have done everything"), it can also mean "to practice or work at."[21] The question is, which is the most likely meaning in this context?

We should mark first Paul's opening note of confidence, "that he who began a good work in you will carry it on to completion until the day of Christ Jesus" (1:6). Salvation is the Lord's doing and the outcome is not in doubt. Paul now grounds his imperative (*katergazesthe*) in this primary truth, "for it is God who works in you to will and to act according to his good purpose" (2:13). "Your salvation" is not a goal to be achieved by human effort but a gift bestowed by divine grace. Significantly, the imperative is in the present tense: "Go on putting your salvation into practice, go on actualizing your salvation." This fits with Paul's reference to the Philippians' established pattern of response: "as you have always obeyed."

We should also recall Paul's earlier prayer (Phil. 1:9) for motivation in the Christian life, "that your love [not fear] may abound more and more in knowledge and depth of insight." "Fear and trembling" is a stereotyped expression (it rhymes in Greek—*phobou kai tromou*) for proper respect (cf. 2 Cor. 7:15; Eph. 6:5). Here it refers to the awed reverence that comes from the realization that *God* (the word order in Greek puts the emphasis here) is the one who is working in us both to will and to act according to his saving purpose. J. B. Phillips's translation is correct: "Work out the salvation that God has given you with a proper sense of awe and responsibility. For it is God who is at work within you, giving you the will and the power to achieve his purpose."

As there is a fundamental difference between the fear of terror and the fear of honor, so is there a fundamental difference between punishment and discipline.[22] The goal of the Christian life is to be like Christ, the image of God. In the transformation process, "God disciplines us for our good, that we may

---

21. Liddell and Scott verify this usage and give in addition the meaning *to cultivate [land]*.
22. Cf. Calvin, *Institutes*, 3.4.31–35.

share in his holiness" (Heb. 12:10). Whereas punishment is the execution of God's retributive justice, discipline is the expression of his corrective love (Heb. 12:6; cf. Rev. 3:19, "Those whom I love I rebuke and discipline").[23] Though the experience of discipline is never pleasant, it is endurable in the knowledge that in the long run it "produces a harvest of righteousness and peace for those who have been trained by it" (Heb. 12:11).

Affliction thus has an entirely different face depending upon whether it appears as punishment or discipline. It is not too much to say that punishment and discipline are as far apart as God's wrath and God's love. Sinners rightly take refuge in Christ to escape the penal consequences of sin, but this is not the continuing motivation of the Christian life other than as a standing warning against apostasy. The message of Hebrews 12:4–11 is not, "If you sin, you will be punished," but "If you are a son or daughter, you will be disciplined." Though painful, discipline is welcome as the sign of God's love. Through it we are led to progressive obedience, not out of fear of the consequences, but out of love for him who first loved us.

Love of God

Asked by a scribe for his opinion on which is the greatest commandment in the law, Jesus replied: "'Love the Lord your God with all you heart, with all your soul, and with all your mind.' This is the first and greatest commandment. And the second is like it: 'Love your neighbor as yourself.' All the Law and the Prophets hang on these two commandments" (Matt. 22:37–40; cf. Mark 12:31, "There is no greater commandment than these"). Systematicians are served notice that there is not just one great commandment but two. The first commandment is inseparable from its close second; the whole biblical revelation ("all the Law and the Prophets") swings as a gate on these two hinges.

It happens that the second great commandment (Lev. 19:18) is cited more often in the New Testament than the first (Deut. 6:5).[24] In the Old Testament the great first commandment immediately follows the *Shema* ("Hear, O Israel: The Lord our God, the Lord is one") and is repeated in Deuteronomy

---

23. The New Testament is remarkably consistent in using *kolazō* and *kolasis* (punishment) with reference to the wicked and *paideuō* and *paideia* (discipline) with reference to believers. The RSV rendering of Heb. 12:6 ("For the Lord disciplines him whom he loves, and *chastises* every son whom he receives") is thus preferable to the NIV ("because the Lord disciplines those he loves, and he *punishes* everyone he accepts as a son"). The verb in question is *mastigoō* (literally, "to scourge") used just this once in the New Testament (citing the LXX of Prov. 3:12) with reference to spiritual discipline. Since everything depends on motive and purpose, "chastises" is preferable to "punishes" in the context of God's paternal correction. This is supported by the New Testament use of *mastix* (literally, "scourge") more broadly for suffering or affliction that serves God's purpose (e.g., Mark 5:29, 34).

24. Deut. 6:5 is cited only in the Gospels (Matt. 22:37; Mark 12:30; Luke 10:27). The citations of Lev. 19:18 are more dispersed as well as more frequent (Matt. 5:43; 19:9; 22:39; Mark 12:31; Luke 10:27; Rom. 13:9; Gal. 5:14; James 2:8).

eight times (Deut. 11:1, 13, 22; 13:3; 19:9; 30:6, 16, 20). The New Testament builds on this imperative foundation; presupposing that God gives what he commands, it addresses believers in the indicative as those who love God (Rom. 8:28; 1 Cor. 2:9; 8:3; Eph. 6:24; James 1:12; 2:5, 1 Pet. 1:8).

Clearly this love is a responsive love: "We love because he first loved us" (1 John 4:19). God loves his people from eternity (Eph. 1:4–5) and demonstrates his love for them on the cross (Rom. 5:8). Through the self-sacrifice of Christ for sinners, believers come to understand what it means to be loved by God: "This is how we know what love is: Jesus Christ laid down his life for us" (1 John 3:16). In response to God's gracious initiative, God's people begin to love. Redeemed by his grace and enabled by his Spirit, they become loving persons, joined to Christ and to one another in a community of faith, hope, and love (1 Cor. 13:13).

What does it mean to love God? The question has received scant attention in recent Christian ethics. This would surely surprise Jonathan Edwards, who wrote, "Unless we will be Atheists, we must allow that true virtue does primarily and most essentially consists in a supreme love to God; and that where this is wanting, there can be no true virtue."[25] Maybe our generation skirts closer to atheism than it would like to think. When asked, "What is love?" few are likely to respond in Augustinian fashion like Thomas Watson: "It is a holy fire kindled in the affections, whereby a Christian is carried out strongly after God as the supreme good."[26]

Love for God is a dispositional complex of affection and volition, traditionally referred to as *complacentia* (satisfaction) and *benevolentia* (good will). William Ames, the continental Puritan divine whose *Marrow of Theology* was the preferred systematics textbook in seventeenth-century New England, puts it nicely: "The love which is satisfaction is that affection by which we approve of all that is in God and rest in his supreme goodness. The love which is good will is the affection which bids us yield ourselves wholly to God."[27] A fuller description is given by Ames's contemporary, St. Francis de Sales, a leader of the Counter-Reformation and bishop of Geneva from 1602 until his death in 1622.

> We express our love for God chiefly in two ways—spontaneously (affectively), and deliberately (effectively). . . . In the first of these ways we grow fond of God, of what he likes; in the second we serve God, do what he enjoins. The first way unites us with God's goodness, the second urges us to carry out his will. The first way gives us our fill of gratification, of benevolence, of spiritual yearnings,

25. Jonathan Edwards, *The Nature of True Virtue* (Ann Arbor: University of Michigan Press, 1960), 18.

26. Thomas Watson, *The Ten Commandments* (1692; reprint, Edinburgh: Banner of Truth, 1965), 6.

27. William Ames, *The Marrow of Theology*, ed. and trans. John D. Eusden (Boston: Pilgrim, 1968), 251.

desires, aspirations, fervour, leading us to commune heart to heart with God; the second way brings to birth in us the firm resolve, steadfast courage, and absolute obedience necessary for carrying out whatever God's will ordains, also for suffering, accepting, approving, welcoming all that he permits.[28]

In our own time, love for God is presented as a dispositional complex in the ethics of John Murray. According to Murray, love is "impulsive affection." By this he means, "Love is both emotive and motive; love is feeling and it impels to action. . . . [It is] intensely preoccupied with him who is its supreme object, and therefore intensely active in the doing of his will."[29] Murray's treatment is brief and unburdened by traditional terminology, but it is one with de Sales's affective-effective distinction. Whatever terminology is used, the idea of love for God as a complex of affection and volition represents a key biblical truth.

Love for God involves a holy delight or satisfaction in the being of God and the desire to do his will—to follow him, to walk in his ways, to be conformed to his image. "Love me, and keep my commandments," is a principle enunciated at Sinai and echoed in the upper room (Exod. 20:6; John 14:15). Loving God and keeping his commandments are not simply equivalent, as though the Lord had said, "Love me, *that is,* keep my commandments." But the relationship between delight in the Lord and the desire to please him is so close that the apostle John can say, "This is love for God: to obey his commands" (1 John 5:3). Devotion to the person of Christ ("If you love me") is exhibited in doing his will ("you will obey what I command"). The one cannot be without the other.

The affectional side of love is directly expressed often in the Psalms—indeed it is the motive of the whole Psalter as the book of God's praise:

"I love you, O LORD, my strength" (Ps. 18:1).

"As the deer pants for streams of water, so my soul pants for you, O God" (Ps. 42:1).

"Because your love is better than life, my lips will glorify you" (Ps. 63:3)

"Whom have I in heaven but you? And earth has nothing I desire besides you" (Ps. 73:25).

"I love the LORD, for he heard my voice; he heard my cry for mercy" (Ps. 116:1).

The affectional is immediately joined by the volitional, for those who love God also love his law: "Oh, how I love your law! I meditate on it all day long"

---

28. St. Francis de Sales, *Treatise on the Love of God,* trans. Vincent Kern (Westminster, Md.: Newman, 1962), 217.

29. Murray, *Principles of Conduct,* 22–23.

(Ps. 119:97); those who delight in God delight also in his commands: "I delight in your commands because I love them" (Ps. 119:47); those who desire God desire also to do his will: "I desire to do your will, O my God; your law is within my heart" (Ps. 40:8). The reason is evident: To love God is to love him who is faithful in all he does, who himself loves righteousness and justice, who has filled the earth with his lovingkindness (Ps. 33:4–5). To love God is therefore necessarily to love righteousness and to want to be just and merciful and faithful, just as he is and as he directs in his law.

Development of the affectional side of love for God through recourse to the means of grace (the Word, sacraments, and prayer) should be a matter of high priority in the Christian life. Its neglect in recent Christian ethics may be due in part to the radical thesis of Anders Nygren, whose *Agape and Eros* is widely regarded as a classic.[30] According to Nygren, Agape must exclude all motives of satisfaction in the object of its desire; otherwise it would be only self-seeking Eros, not self-giving Agape. Agape is "spontaneous, unmotivated love"; it seeks only the good of the other and takes "no side-long glances at anything else."[31] At first sight this seems right since it appears to give an account of the distinctiveness of Christian love. On closer inspection it turns out that some serious cracks have been papered over. John Burnaby summaries the implications of Nygren's thesis:

> The logical conclusion, accepted by Nygren, is that since man may not love God in the sense of *eros*, and cannot love him in the sense of *agape*—the creature cannot "seek the good" of the Creator—the love enjoined in the first great commandment is really indistinguishable from the faith which is man's only proper attitude to God; while the Christian love of neighbour is nothing less than God's own *agape* flowing through human hearts.[32]

Nygren claims in support of his position Paul's "remarkable reticence" to speak about man's love for God. "Man's loving surrender of himself without reserve to God is still, of course, the central thing in the Christian life, but Paul shrinks from applying the term Agape to it. To do so would suggest that man possessed an independence and spontaneity over against God, which in reality he does not."[33] Paul would surely agree that man does not possess such an independence, but how reticent is he to speak about love for God? He characteristically refers to God's people as "those who love God" (Rom. 8:28; 1 Cor. 2:9; 8:3). Believers receive from his pen the benediction, "Grace to all who love our Lord Jesus Christ with an undying love" (Eph. 6:24). That it is

---

30. Anders Nygren, *Agape and Eros*, trans. Philip S. Watson (London: SPCK, 1953).

31. Ibid., 1:213, 215.

32. John Burnaby, "Love," *Dictionary of Christian Ethics*, ed. John Macquarrie (Philadelphia: Westminster, 1967), 199.

33. Nygren, *Agape and Eros*, 213.

technically the verb *agapaō* rather than the noun *agapē* that is used in these instances makes no difference. Besides Paul does use the noun in the famous trio of faith, hope, and love, from which a Godward reference for *agapē* can be excluded only with difficulty. This is especially true of 1 Thessalonians 1:3 with its the parallel expressions, "work of faith [in God], labor of love [for God], endurance of hope [in God]." Paul is less reticent than Nygren suggests, and Agape more complex than his theory will allow. Even so, the Nygrenian contrast of Agape and Eros continues to have its advocates.[34]

To take a recent example, a respected evangelical scholar writes, "*Eros* has two principal characteristics: it is a love of the worthy and it is a love that desires to possess. *Agapē* is in contrast at both points: it is not a love of the worthy, and it is not a love that desires to possess."[35] In other words, Eros is the desire to possess a worthy object, and Agape is the desire to benefit an unworthy object. The author finds it necessary, however, to qualify the contrast at both points. Citing John's Gospel on the love of the Father for the Son and the love of the Son for the Father (John 15:10; 17:26; 14:31), he comments, "These passages show that *agapē* can be directed toward a worthy object." To save the theory he goes on to say, "But because this love is spontaneous it is exercised irrespective of the object's worthiness, and may be directed toward the worthiest of objects as well as those that are unworthy." Love on this theory is not so much spontaneous as it is irrational. As for the absence of Agape's desire for its object, this also has to be qualified because, "there is, of course, a sense in which God desires us; the entire Bible expresses this truth."

Since the contrast runs into major difficulties at both of its critical points, perhaps it was not rightly drawn in the first place. The quite proper insistence on God's love for sinners as love for the undeserving is a far cry from saying that God's love, and hence all love worthy of the name, is "spontaneous and unmotivated." God loves sinners because he created them for himself, and though they are undeserving of his grace they are not worthless in his sight. Calvin, not one easily open to the charge of being anthropocentric or soft on depravity, puts it this way:

> God, who is the highest righteousness, cannot love the unrighteousness that he sees in us all. All of us, therefore, have in ourselves something deserving of God's hatred. With regard to our corrupt nature and the wicked life that follows it, all of us surely displease God, are guilty in his sight, and are born to

---

34. Protestant challenges are rare. Joseph Haroutunian cuts against the grain with this forthright assessment: "[T]he definition of love in negatives as 'unconditional, uncaused, unmotivated, groundless, uncalculating'; as self-giving, self-denying, self-crucifying, simply outgoing; as unprudential, unevaluating, unteleological, etc., leave us with a 'love' that is not only impossible for human beings, regenerate or unregenerate, but also of doubtful Biblical and theological validity." *God with Us* (Philadelphia: Westminster, 1965), 207.

35. Leon Morris, *Testaments of Love* (Grand Rapids: Eerdmans, 1981), 128.

the damnation of hell. But because the Lord wills not to lose what is his in us, out of his own kindness he still finds something to love. However much we may be sinners by our own fault, we nevertheless remain his creatures. However much we have brought death upon ourselves, yet he has created us unto life. Thus he is moved by pure and freely given love of us to receive us into grace.[36]

Though fallen, sinners are still God's creatures and capable of being redeemed—but at an awful cost. It is the willingness to bear the cost that shows the incredible depths of the love of God. "For God so loved the world that he gave his one and only Son, that whoever believes in him shall not perish but have eternal life" (John 3:16). So far from being "spontaneous and unmotivated," God's love according to the Scriptures is volitional and teleological: "In love he predestined us to be adopted as his sons through Jesus Christ, in accordance with his pleasure and will—to the praise of his glorious grace, which he has freely given us in the One he loves" (Eph. 1:4–6).

Love of Neighbor

The first and great commandment summons us to love God with all our heart and mind and soul and strength. Lest we misconstrue this and think that the Christian life has nothing to do with other people, Jesus immediately adds, "And the second is like it: 'Love your neighbor as yourself.'" The likeness is far from superficial—Jesus asserts that the biblical revelation of the will of God hangs on these two commandments. The second is like the first in the importance that God attaches and in the comprehensiveness of its reach. According to the apostle Paul, love for our neighbor is (objectively) the summary and (subjectively) the fulfillment of the law. The classic text is Romans 13:8–10, which may be interpretively translated as follows:

> Owe nobody anything, except [remember] the [debt] to love one another. For the one who loves the other [person] has fulfilled (*peplēroken*) the law. For the [commandments] Do not commit adultery, Do not murder, Do not steal, Do not covet, and if [there is] any other commandment, it is summed up (*anakephalaioutai*) in this word: You shall love your neighbor as yourself. Love does not work evil to its neighbor; thus, the fulfillment (*plērōma*) of the law is love.[37]

The commandment to love our neighbor is found first in Leviticus 19:18. The wider context (chaps. 17–26) is sometimes called the "holiness code"

---

36. Calvin, *Institutes*, 2.16. In the next paragraph Calvin cites Augustine for support.

37. Cf. Gal. 5:14, "For all the law is fulfilled in one word, in the [one that says], You shall love your neighbor as yourself."

because of the key thought, "Be holy because I, the Lord your God, am holy" (Lev. 19:2). The constantly repeated ground of conduct is, "I am the Lord your God," or more concisely, "I am the Lord." The command to love occurs twice (Lev. 19:18, 34); in each case it is helpful to read together with the immediately preceding verse.

> Do not hate your brother in your heart. Rebuke your neighbor frankly so you will not share in his guilt. Do not seek revenge or bear a grudge against one of your people, but *love your neighbor as yourself.* I am the Lord.

> When an alien lives with you in your land, do not mistreat him. The alien living with you must be treated as one of your native-born. *Love him as yourself,* for you were aliens in Egypt. I am the Lord your God.

The Old Testament revelation of the will of God is no mere external morality. Hatred of the heart is forbidden; the attitude of bearing a grudge and the action of taking vengeance are alike condemned. When love is positively enjoined it is also a characteristic that issues in appropriate attitudes and actions—including love's rebuke. As Peter Geach remarks, love is not "a fatuous amiability towards every vagary of misconduct and misbelief."[38] Neither may love be restricted on a narrow interpretation of "brother" or "neighbor" so as to justify discrimination on the basis of birth or race. Israel was commanded to love the alien as well as the native-born. Motivation is provided by appeal to Israel's experience in Egypt. The Lord's loving deliverance of his people is an example for them to follow: "He defends the cause of the fatherless and widow, and loves the alien, giving him food and clothing. And you are to love those who are aliens, for you yourselves were aliens in Egypt" (Deut. 10:18–19; cf. Eph. 5:1–2).

Love for our neighbor, like love for God, is rightly understood as a dispositional complex of affection and volition. To think, "I must love my neighbor but I don't have to like him," is to make an unwarranted separation between attitude and action. Love is an affection that wills the other person's good; its relation to love for God is brought out by Jonathan Edwards:

> Love to God is the foundation of gracious love to men. Men are loved either because they are in some respect like God, either they have the nature or spiritual image of God; or because of their relation to God as his children, as his creatures, as those who are beloved of God, or those to whom divine mercy is offered, or in some other way from regard to God.[39]

---

38. Peter Geach, *God and the Soul* (New York: Schocken, 1960), 116.
39. Jonathan Edwards, *Ethical Writings,* vol. 8 of *The Works of Jonathan Edwards,* ed. Paul Ramsey (New Haven: Yale University Press, 1989), 133–34.

Affection for God flows out in affection for other persons as they are in relation to him, willing and doing what love requires appropriate to each relationship. Persecutors, for example, are to be loved and prayed for, not hated and cursed, for they are God's image and the gospel is offered to them (Matt. 5:44; James 3:9; 2 Pet. 3:9). Hungry enemies are to be loved and fed, not despised and starved, for they are God's creatures and he is merciful and kind to them (Luke 6:35; Rom. 13:20; Prov. 25:21). Paul's great text on the use of Christian freedom joins affection and volition as he calls upon members of the body of Christ to "serve one another through love" (Gal. 5:13).[40] Actions laudable in themselves, such as giving one's possessions to the poor, do not count as Christian obedience if they are void of affection (1 Cor. 13:3). On the other hand—and far more common—professed affection that does not lead to action is certainly not love. "If anyone has material possessions and sees his brother in need but has no pity on him, how can the love of God be in him? Dear children, let us not love with words or tongue but with actions and in truth" (1 John 3:17–18).

Granted that love of one's neighbor is affectional and volitional, how are we to understand the stipulation "as yourself"?[41] Should we think in terms of quantity: "Love your neighbor *as much as* you love yourself"? Or of quality: "Love your neighbor *as a person* like yourself"? Taken in a quantitative sense, "as yourself" would strictly mean "no less and no more than yourself." But the Bible does not require across-the-board equalization of benefits (implied in "no less"), and it commends self-sacrifice even to the point of preferring the lives of others to one's own (excluded by "no more"). On the other hand, recognition that my neighbor is a person like myself elicits an empathy responsive to human wants and needs. Reading the second great commandment in a qualitative sense also fits with Jesus' other comprehensive principle of love: "So in everything, do to others what you would have them do to you, for this sums up the Law and the Prophets" (Matt. 7:12; cf. Luke 6:31).[42]

Love for our neighbor is *beneficent affection* for persons like ourselves. Love acts for the good of other persons out of affection for them, which influences the perception of what truly serves their interest and how it may be carried out in the diverse circumstances of life. Persons exist in various relationships to us, and love rightly takes these into account. Christian love extends to those

40. *Dia* with the genitive may denote manner or medium; the emphasis falls on the attitude in which service is performed.

41. Cf. Garth L. Hallett, *Christian Neighbor-Love: An Assessment of Six Rival Versions* (Washington, D.C.: Georgetown University Press, 1989). The six versions are: Self-Preference, Parity, Other-Preference, Self-Subordination, Self-Forgetfulness, and Self-Denial. As Hallett points out, none of these positions will suit all turns; life is more complicated than any one version suggests, and so is love.

42. Leo Baeck suggests this reading of the command in Hebrew: "Love thy neighbor; [he is] as thou." *God and Man in Judaism* (New York: Union of American Hebrew Congregations, 1958), cited by Shubert Spero, *Morality, Halakha, and the Jewish Tradition* (New York: KTAV, 1983), 125.

from whom no response is expected, but if this were its only valid expression, only enemies could be loved, never friends. The sharp distinction between sacrificial and mutual love renders John 15:13 (and much else in the biblical ethic) unintelligible: "Greater love (*agapē*) has no one than this, that he lay down his life for his friends." The application of love for one's neighbor is universal, but it is appropriately expressed according to the relationships that we sustain to others as family members, as members of the body of Christ, as members of society, as members of the global village—all the communities of which we are a part by divine providence.

The distinctive thing about Christian love is that all of its objects are loved for God's sake. If it is objected that people should be loved for their own sakes, and not for some ulterior motive, the answer of Illtyd Trethowan is to the point:

> You are telling us, someone may say, that we ought to love people for God's sake. That is just what we do not want to do. We want to love them for their own sakes. And to that I reply that to love people because they are creatures of God, 'reflections' of God, is the only way to love them as they really are. To say that they are God's creatures is not just to mention an interesting fact about them. It is the essential truth about them. They have value indeed in themselves, but only because God gave it to them. Unless we see God in them as the source of value, we should not *really* see that they had it.[43]

The great commandment and the second like it are thus not to be understood as distributed between the first and second tables of the law, as though love for God were to be manifested only in obedience to the first four commandments of the decalogue. There is good reason to believe that the two tables referred to in Exodus and Deuteronomy are in fact duplicate copies of the covenant, one each for lord and vassal as was customary in those days. When God says, "Love me, and keep my commandments," the meaning is that all the commandments are to be performed out of love for him, the service of neighbor as well as the service of worship. The decalogue is the text of God's covenant with Israel; all ten "words" stipulate the way in which love and loyalty are to be expressed by the Lord's redeemed people.

Self-Love

The commandment to love my neighbor as myself implies that I love myself in some sense. The question is whether this self-love is sinful, natural, or moral.[44] Is the commandment "Love your neighbor as [you now sinfully

---

43. Illtyd Trethowan, *Absolute Value: A Study in Christian Theism* (London: Allen, 1970), 92.

44. Cf. Gene Outka, *Agape: An Ethical Analysis* (New Haven: Yale University Press, 1972), 55–74. Outka analyzes four judgments on self-love in the period 1930–1970 (plus a retrospective look at Kierkegaard): (1) wholly nefarious, (2) normal, reasonable, prudent, (3) justified derivatively from love to others, (4) a definite obligation in its own right.

love] yourself"? Or is it, "Love your neighbor as [you just naturally love] yourself" Or is it, "Love your neighbor as [you rightly love] yourself"? Historical precedence may be cited for each of these positions, although the ambiguity of "self-love" is such that it may appear in a single author—notably Augustine—now as the epitome of rebellion against God, then again as a motive for submission to him.[45] Consequently some disputes may be verbal rather than substantive.

Self-Love as Sinful

Agape, according to Nygren, excludes all self-love. "It is self-love that alienates man from God, preventing him from sincerely giving himself up to God, and it is self-love that shuts up a man's heart against his neighbor."[46] Self-love is the Christian's chief adversary, to be fought and conquered. Nygren appeals to Luther, who "has departed so far from the traditional idea, which discovers a *commandment* of self-love in the commandment of love to one's neighbor, that he finds this latter to contain a direct *prohibition* of every kind of self-love."[47] There is a similar strain in Calvin, who calls self-love "the parent of all iniquities" and refers to it as "that vicious passion which is born with us and dwells deeply in us."[48] Its appearance in the second great commandment does not give it an imperative force, Calvin argues.

> In the entire law we do not read one syllable that lays a rule upon man as regards those things which he may or may not do, for the advantage of his own flesh. And obviously, since men were born in such a state that they are all too much inclined to self-love—and, however much they deviate from truth, they still keep self-love—there was no need of a law that would increase or rather enkindle this already excessive love. Hence it is very clear that we keep the commandments not by loving ourselves but by loving God and neighbor; that he lives the best and holiest life who lives and strives for himself as little as he can, and that no one lives in a worse or more evil manner than he who lives and strives for himself alone, and thinks about and seeks only his own advantage.
>
> Indeed, to express how profoundly we must be inclined to love our neighbors, the Lord measured it by the love of ourselves because he had at hand no more violent or stronger emotion than this. And we ought diligently to ponder

---

45. Thomas Losoncy summarizes Augustine's complex teaching on self-love as follows: "(a) favourable—(*dilectio*). This is benevolent love when man discovers and promotes his true welfare in God; (b) neutral—the natural condition either of man's animal or rational nature; (c) wrongful—when man's love represents the root of all sin and rebellion against love—pride. Or this may also mean the disordered love of the body and material things and pleasures—lust or wrong desire." "St. Augustine," in *Ethics in the History of Western Philosophy*, ed. Robert J. Cavalier et al. (New York: St. Martin's, 1989), 77.

46. Nygren, *Agape and Eros*, 1.217.

47. Ibid., 2.713.

48. John Calvin, *Commentaries on the Four Last Books of Moses Arranged in the Form of a Harmony*, trans. Charles William Bingham, 4 vols. (1852; reprint, Grand Rapids: Eerdmans, 1950), 3: 195.

the force of this expression. For he does not concede the first place to self-love as certain Sophists stupidly imagine, and assign the second place to love. Rather, he transfers to others the emotion of love that we naturally feel toward ourselves. Hence, the apostle states that "love does not seek its own." . . . Indeed, the Lord has not established a rule regarding love of our ourselves to which charity toward others should be subordinate. But he shows that the emotion of love, which out of natural depravity commonly reside within ourselves, must now be extended to another, that we may be ready to benefit our neighbor with no less eagerness, ardor, and care than ourselves.[49]

The stature of Calvin notwithstanding, it is hard to see how a "violent emotion," especially when it arises out of our "natural depravity," can provide a sound canon by which to gauge our conduct toward others. There is nothing in the context of Leviticus that would lead one to the conclusion that an improper self-love is the measure of a proper love for others. What is called for is the same regard for others that one has for oneself, without the least hint that self-regard is depraved.

There is, of course, such a thing as a depraved and fatal self-love, mentioned by name (*philautos*) in Paul's characterization of human nature in the last days:

> But mark this: There will be terrible times in the last days. People will be lovers of themselves (*philautoi*), lovers of money, boastful, proud, abusive, disobedient to their parents, ungrateful, unholy, without love (*astorgoi*, "without natural affection"), unforgiving, slanderous, without self-control, brutal, not lovers of the good, treacherous, rash, conceited lovers of pleasure (*philēdonoi*) rather than lovers of God (*philotheoi*). [2 Tim. 3:1–4]

Philautos has the same negative connotations in Greek as the word *selfish* has in English. It is used here of such love of self as excludes all others, a self-love that lacks even the affection of natural human relationships, that puts pleasure in the place of God. Without doubt, selfishness is sinful; it is self-worship, *egolatry* if a word derived from Greek is needed. But just as the existence of idolatry does not cancel out the proper love of creation as God's handiwork, neither does egolatry mean that there cannot be a proper love of oneself as the image of God. Calvin's view admits no distinction between sinful self-assertion and lawful self-regard as a created being. The preacher's laudable zeal to provoke the faithful to love and good works and to be done with scholastic distinctions that blunt the sharpness of God's Word has nevertheless led wide of the mark in this case. Selfish love has no paradigmatic value, and this may explain why Calvin took little interest in the commandment as such.

49. Calvin, *Institutes*, 2.8.54.

Self-Love as Natural

A second way of understanding the love implied in "as yourself" is to take it in a nonmoral sense. On this view self-love is neither blameworthy nor praiseworthy; it is simply a fact of human nature that is assumed in the commandment. As John Stott puts it, "Self-love is not a virtue that Scripture commends, but one of the facts of our humanity that it recognizes and tells us to use as a standard."[50] As we naturally desire and seek our own good, so we are commanded to desire and seek the good of our neighbor. There is no need for a command to love ourselves because we do this naturally. Self-love, while not sinful, has no positive moral content.

Perhaps the strongest argument for this position is derived from Paul's instructions to husbands in Ephesians.

> Husbands, love your wives, just as Christ also loved the church and gave himself up for her. . . . So husbands ought also to love their own wives as their own bodies. He who loves his own wife loves himself; for no one ever hated his own flesh, but nourishes and cherishes it, just as Christ also does the church, because we are members of his body. [Eph. 5:23, 28–30]

At first this seems decisive. If no one ever hated his own flesh, doesn't it follow that self-love is a natural fact and not a moral obligation? Not necessarily. It might mean simply that human beings have a tendency to fulfill certain self-regarding moral duties when they are perceived to be in their own best interest. Care for one's flesh, that is, for one's bodily existence in the present life, is a duty that, generally speaking, people can be counted on to perform. But this is not the whole truth about human nature, and it would be a mistake to understand Paul to be speaking clinically or absolutely. It is not difficult to think of harmful practices—the abuse of alcohol, tobacco, and other drugs, for example—which people knowingly if compulsively persist in, and the personal habits of many who are familiar with the facts of nutrition and exercise are not correspondingly healthful.

Now if self-indulgence to one's harm is a moral concern, why isn't self-restraint to one's health also a moral issue? If abuse of the body is a morally culpable form of self-hatred, why isn't care for the body be a morally commendable form of self-love? Paul's very general statement that no one ever hated his own flesh should not be pressed to exclude the psychologically harmful self-loathing with which clinical psychologists frequently have to deal. Paul was not ignorant of human self-destruction, the suicide of Judas being a case in point. Whatever the skillful therapist determines is the best approach to the problem in a given case, there is a moral basis for the change

50. John R. W. Stott, "Must I Really Love Myself?" *Christianity Today*, 5 May 1978, 34–35.

in attitude toward oneself. It is right-mindedness to live according to God's moral norms, which include self-regarding as well as other-regarding duties. A recent textbook on healthcare ethics makes the point very well:

> It might seem that no special commitment [to life and health] needs to be made, since everyone has an instinct to live. No doubt the need to live, to grow, and to function well is innate; it is the very teleology of any organism. In the human person, however, whose inmost depth of being is not instinctive but free, this commitment is not a given; rather, it must be freely made by the person.[51]

It often passes without notice that to interpret self-love in a naturalistic fashion introduces an equivocation into the commandment as the word *love* is understood in two different senses. "Love your neighbor as yourself" on this reading is "Morally love your neighbor as you naturally love your self." But how can a natural phenomenon serve as the model for a moral imperative? It is unreal to think we can somehow translate an instinctive organic dynamism to a pattern of conduct toward others. The biblical commandment to love always exceeds our grasp as incompletely sanctified sinners, but it never lays on us requirements that are in principle beyond our reach as human beings (cf. Deut. 30:11).

Self-Love as Moral

The traditional view of self-love as a moral obligation has its roots in Augustine.

> It is impossible that one should love God and not love himself. In fact, he alone has a proper love of himself who loves God. Since a man can be said to have sufficient love for himself if he seeks earnestly to attain the supreme and perfect good, and this is nothing other than God, as what we have been saying shows, who can doubt that he who loves God loves himself?[52]

Thomas Aquinas continued the Augustinian perspective and presented the order of love as follows:

> Thus it is necessary that that affection of man be so inclined through charity that, first and foremost, each one loves God; secondly, that he love himself; and thirdly, that he love his neighbor. And among the fellow-men, he ought to give mutual help to those who are more closely united to him or who are more closely related to him.[53]

51. Benedict M. Ashley and Kevin D. O'Rourke, *Healthcare Ethics: A Theological Analysis*, 3d ed. (St. Louis: Catholic Health Association, 1989), 45.

52. Augustine, *The Way of Life of the Catholic Church*, in *The Catholic and Manichaean Ways of Life (De moribus ecclesiae catholicae et De moribus Manichaeorum)*, trans. Donald A. Gallagher and Idella J. Gallagher (Washington, D.C.: Catholic University of America Press, 1966), 39.

53. Thomas Aquinas, *On Charity (De Caritate)*, trans. Lottie H. Kendzierski (Milwaukee: Marquette University Press, 1960), 77.

Although Luther and Calvin reacted strongly against the idea of an "order of love" that placed self-love above or before love of neighbor, William Ames nevertheless found a place for it in Reformed theology.

> This is the order of love: God is first and chiefly to be loved and is, as it were, the formal reason of love towards our neighbor. After God, we are bound to love ourselves with the love of true blessedness, for loving God with love of union, we love ourselves directly with that greatest love which looks toward our spiritual blessedness. Secondarily, as it were, we ought to love others whom we would have to be partakers of the same good with us. . . . Hence it is that the love of ourselves has the force of a rule or measure for the love of others, *You shall love your neighbor as yourself.*[54]

Jonathan Edwards perpetuated the Augustinian tradition in the eighteenth century, but with a careful balance of two concerns. On the one hand, self-love is not wrong; human beings, including ourselves, are the image of God, and to be loved on that account. On the other hand, benevolence, the disposition to desire or delight in the good of others is "the main thing in Christian love, the most essential thing, and that whereby our love is most of an imitation of the eternal love and grace of God, and the dying love of Christ."[55] True Christian love creates a sympathizing and merciful spirit, and disposes a person to be public-spirited.

It should be noted that the Augustinian ground for self-love as a moral imperative is derived not from the second great commandment, though that confirms it, but from the commandment to love God, who himself desires what is in our best interest (see, e.g., Deut. 10:13; Matt. 6:33; 1 Pet. 3:10–12). Given the biblical frame of reference in which the goal is the glory of God and the norm is the will of God, the idea of self-regarding duties is not problematic. We belong to God and are responsible to him for the preservation of our own life, chastity, property, and good name, as well as that of others.[56] It is a theocentric self-regard that is assigned paradigmatic value in the commandment to love our neighbor as ourself.

Although it is true that there is no direct biblical command, "Love yourself," the Bible does expressly approve of godly self-love in Proverbs 19:8, "He who gets wisdom loves his own soul."[57] Nevertheless, the verb *to love* is more suitably used with reference to an object other than oneself, so it is natural for Paul to say, "The one who loves the other has fulfilled the law" (Rom. 13:8). To love oneself for the sake of God is surely virtuous, but it must be admitted that this is not the most obvious meaning of the term *self-*

54. Ames, *Marrow of Theology,* 302.
55. Edwards, *Charity and Its Fruits,* 213.
56. Cf. Westminster Shorter Catechism, qq. 68–78.
57. The Septuagint translates "loves himself," using the verb *agapaō.*

love. As with many of the compound words involving the noun *self,* there is a duality of positive and negative connotations. *Self-esteem,* for example, can mean either "self-respect" or "self-conceit"; *self-assertion* can mean "standing up for one's rights" or "putting oneself forward in an arrogant manner." So it is with *self-love;* it can mean "regard for one's own worth or happiness" or it can mean "inflated pride in oneself or preoccupation with one's own concerns."

Though popularly self-love may be practically equivalent to selfishness, in philosophy the historic meaning of the term is "regard for one's own well-being or happiness, considered as a natural and proper relation of a man to himself" (*Shorter Oxford Dictionary,* this usage dates from 1688). Contemporary psychology has taken over the philosophical use of the term, emphasizing such positive self-regarding attitudes as self-esteem, self-respect, self-acceptance, in the interest of promoting authentic selfhood, self-fulfillment, self-realization, self-actualization. Is this good or bad? It all depends on whether God is allowed into the picture as the one who determines what this "self" should look like when complete. As Richard Mouw remarks, "The Christian must be willing to say to God, 'Make me into the kind of self that you want me to be. Transform, if it pleases you, my understanding of what it is that will bring me happiness.'" [58]

Affirmation of the self God wants us to be necessarily involves denial of the self we would be content with given our old nature and its sinful desires (cf. Titus 2:12). Viewed in this light, "[s]elf-denial is not negative; it is positive re-direction of the total being."[59] Those who would follow Jesus must deny themselves and take up the cross daily (Matt. 16:24; Mark 8:34; Luke 9:23), must even "hate" themselves (Luke 14:26),[60] but the goal of self-denying, cross-bearing, Christ-following discipleship is not to become nothing but to be truly fulfilled: "For those who want to save their life will lose it, and those who lose their life for my sake, and for the sake of the gospel, will save it" (Mark 8:35 NRSV; cf. Matt. 10:39; 16:25; Luke 9:24). "The self-denial for which Christ calls," John Burnaby rightly concludes, "is a denial of the individual, personal, 'private' will, in so far as it falls short of the will of God."[61]

58. Richard J. Mouw, *The God Who Commands* (Notre Dame, Ind.: University of Notre Dame Press, 1990), 37.

59. G. C. Berkouwer, *Faith and Sanctification,* trans. John Vriend (Grand Rapids: Eerdmans, 1952), 139.

60. The parallel in Matt. 10:37 indicates that "hatred" is used in the common Semitic idiom as a comparative, meaning one must love Christ more than father or mother, son or daughter, even oneself (or "life itself" as the NRSV has it), to be his disciple.

61. John Burnaby, *Amor Dei: A Study of the Religion of St. Augustine* (London: Hodder, 1938), 123.

4

The Direction of the Christian Life

Show me your ways, O LORD,
    teach me your paths;
guide me in your truth and teach me,
    for you are God my Savior,
    and my hope is in you all day long.

—Psalm 25:4–5

Love for God includes the disposition to walk in his ways, to follow him out of reverence for who he is and gratitude for what he has done, to be obedient to what he is calling us to be and to do. The Christian life may be characterized as obedient love.[1] God's people have been chosen and cleansed and consecrated for loving obedience (1 Pet. 1:2). A run down through a concordance will quickly show how this theme pervades both Testaments.[2] Love submits to God's authority, desires to be guided by his instructions, and determines to carry out his will.[3]

So far from being antithetical to human nature, obedient love is integral to human fulfillment. The incarnate Son of God himself during his days on earth exhibited the reverent submission by which human nature is perfected. As the Scriptures say, "Although he was a son, he learned obedience from what he suffered and, once made perfect, he became the source of eternal salvation for all who obey him" (Heb. 5:8–9). The self-sacrifice of Christ for others was above

---

1. Cf. Paul Ramsey, "The central ethical notion or 'category' in Christian ethics is 'obedient love.'" *Basic Christian Ethics* (New York: Scribner's, 1950), xi. Also Henry Stob, "The Christian ethic [is] the systematic elaboration of the principle of obedient love." *Ethical Reflections: Essays on Moral Themes* (Grand Rapids: Eerdmans, 1978), 21.

2. In the Old Testament consult the usage of both *šama'* (to hear) and *shamar* (to keep). In the New Testament the basic words are *hypakouō* and *hypakoē*, but see also *phylassō* (e.g., Luke 11:28, "Blessed are they who hear the word of God and *keep* it") and *tēreō* (e.g., Matt. 28:20, "teaching them to *observe* whatsoever I have commanded you").

3. Helen Oppenheimer, noting that obedience cuts against the grain of contemporary moral ideals, offers this defense: "But if Christian obedience is allegiance and not subservience, then (since the worst is the corruption of the best) pseudo-religious oppression and capitulation can truly be understood as aberrations." "Obedience," *Westminster Dictionary of Christian Ethics*, ed. James F. Childress and John Macquarrie (Philadelphia: Westminster, 1986), 429.

all an act of obedient love (Phil. 2:8). Such was his commitment to doing the will of the Father that in the hour of the most dreadful crisis ever faced by any human being he prayed, "Yet not as I will, but as you will" (Matt. 26:39).

The initial and critical response to Christ is the submissive reception of him as he is offered in the gospel—"the obedience of faith" in Pauline terminology (Rom. 1:5; 16:26). This is the obedience that rests upon Christ alone for salvation and makes no pretense of being itself in any sense a basis for justification before God. It is through the obedience of the one—not one plus one—that the many are made righteous (Rom. 5:19). Christ's obedience is the one and only ground of justification; faith as obedient response to the proclamation of the gospel is simply the divinely bestowed instrument by which his obedience is counted as ours. Subsequent acts of obedience necessarily flow from the initial response of faith, but these are far from perfect and cannot be the basis on which we are pronounced righteous. Justification is by faith alone—by the obedience which is faith, not the obedience which is the result of faith.

The obedience of faith is therefore not to be confused with the obedience of love which follows faith in the order of salvation. The latter obedience is expressly said to be "faith working through love" (Gal. 5:6). The correct relationship between grace, faith, and good works in salvation is compactly and definitively expressed in Ephesians 2:8–10.

> For it is by grace you have been saved, through faith—and this not from yourselves, it is the gift of God—not by works, so that no one can boast. For we are God's workmanship, created in Christ Jesus to do good works, which God prepared in advance for us to do.

The divinely appointed way to good works is through the gracious gift of faith which unites us to Christ. The handiwork of God's new creation in Christ is exhibited in discipleship. Before faith our attitude was: "Nobody tells me what to do." Now the attitude of faith is: "Show me what you want me to do." Before faith we assumed our lives were our own to be lived as we pleased. Now with Jeremiah we confess, "I know, O LORD, that a man's life is not his own; it is not for man to direct his steps" (Jer. 10:23). Those whom God has bought with a price he does not leave on their own to figure out what to do with their new lives. God gives direction for the good works he has prepared in advance for believers saved by grace to do. The directing principle of the Christian life is the will of God as revealed in Christ and the holy Scriptures and illuminated by the Holy Spirit.[4]

---

4. The Westminster divines appropriately subsumed direction of the Christian life under the mediatorial office of Christ: "Christ executeth the office of a prophet, in his revealing to the church, in all ages, by his Spirit and Word, in divers ways of administration, the whole will of God, in all things concerning their edification and salvation." Westminster Larger Catechism, q. 43. Cf. Westminster Confession of Faith, 8.8; Westminster Shorter Catechism, q. 24.

The Word of God

"What rule hath God given to direct us how we may glorify and enjoy him?" The second question of the Westminster Shorter Catechism may be less well-known than the first (only the first made the *Oxford Dictionary of Quotations*), but it is hardly of less practical importance. The answer is classic evangelicalism: "The Word of God, which is contained in the Scriptures of the Old and New Testaments, is the only rule to direct us how we may glorify and enjoy him." The expression *Word of God* is used here in a sense equivalent to the Hebrew word *torah*. Though translated "law," *torah* in its widest sense means "divine teaching or revelation," including (but not limited to) instruction in the form of "commandments regulating conduct."[5] All Scripture is *torah* in the sense of being God's authoritative direction in the way of life.[6] The classic text is 2 Timothy 3:14–17.

> But as for you, continue in what you have learned and have become convinced of, because you know those from whom you learned it, and how from infancy you have known the holy Scriptures, which are able to make you wise for salvation through faith in Christ Jesus. All Scripture is God-breathed and is useful for teaching, rebuking, correcting, and training in righteousness, so that the man of God may be thoroughly equipped for every good work.

Most of the discussion of this text has understandably centered on its contribution to the doctrine of biblical inspiration, especially the implications of the term *theopneustos* (God-breathed) as an assertion of the divine origin of all scripture. We should observe that the text also asserts the divine purpose of Scripture—to make one wise for salvation through faith in Christ—and articulates the usefulness of Scripture in equipping the people of God for a life of obedient love, providing instruction, conviction, correction, and education in righteousness. Each Greek term deserves at least a brief note.

Didaskalia (teaching, instruction) is the comprehensive term for the communication of revealed truth. Romans 15:4 is a parallel text: "For

---

5. C. H. Dodd, *The Bible and the Greeks* (London: Hodder, 1935), 40. The specific Hebrew word for commandment is *miṣvâ* (plural *miṣvô*), as in Josh. 22:5, "But be very careful to keep the commandment (*miṣvâ*) and the law (*tôrâ*) that Moses the servant of the Lord gave you."

6. Cf. Richard J. Mouw: "The Bible is much more than a compendium of imperatives; the sacred writings contain historical narratives, prayers, sagas, songs, parables, letters, complaints, pleadings, visions, and so on. The moral relevance of the divine commandments found in the Scriptures can only be understood by viewing them in their interrelatedness with these other types of writings. The history, songs, predictions, and so on, of the Bible serve to sketch out the character of the biblical God; from this diversity of materials we learn what God's creating and redeeming purposes are, what sorts of persons and actions the Lord approves of, and so on. Divine commands must be evaluated and interpreted in this larger context." *The God Who Commands* (Notre Dame, Ind.: University of Notre Dame Press, 1990), 10.

whatever was written in earlier times was written for our instruction (*didaskalia*), that through perseverance and the encouragement of the Scriptures we might have hope." In 1 Timothy 4:13 Paul charges Timothy to devote himself as a minister of the word to reading (that is, the public reading of Scripture), to exhortation (*paraklēsis*), and to teaching (*didaskalia*). Scripture is useful for teaching all that we need to know about God and his will for our salvation.

Though the noun *elegmos* (reproof, conviction) occurs only here in the New Testament, the verb *elenchō* is used several times for the effective exposure of faults, and that is precisely the function of Scripture in view here. *Epanorthōsis* (correction) also occurs just this once in the New Testament. Though the related verb *epanorthoō* does not appear in the New Testament, it is used in the Septuagint meaning "to correct, restore." Scripture is thus useful for exposing our faults (*elegmos*) and setting us straight (*epanorthosis*).

Finally, Scripture is useful for *paideia* (training, education) in righteousness. In American English *education* largely refers to the process of developing knowledge or skill by formal schooling. In biblical Greek *paideia* refers to disciplined training in the practice of righteousness. Paul's climactic phrase underscores the critical role of Scripture in giving direction to the Christian life. Scripture is useful for education of character and conduct. The Spirit works by and with the Word to enable us to respond to what God is calling us to be and to do.

When it comes to particular actions, scriptural direction is given in a variety of forms, specifically prohibition, permission, mandate, counsel, precedent, and example.[7]

Prohibition

The most definitive form of scriptural direction is prohibition, as with the commandments not to commit murder, adultery, theft, perjury. The apostle Paul indicates that such actions are incompatible with love, for "love does no harm to its neighbor" (Rom. 13:10). The love commandment thus includes the general prohibition, Do no harm. Love may be more than not harming other people, but "nonmaleficence," as it is called, is a healthy part of love. Paul's immediate application of the law of love in Galatians is: "If you keep on biting and devouring each other, watch out or you will be destroyed by each other" (Gal. 5:15). Love may reach to the laying down of

---

7. John M. Frame in a parallel discussion uses a fourfold categorization: prohibition, permission, commandment, and praise. *Medical Ethics: Principles, Persons, and Problems* (Phillipsburg, N.J.: Presbyterian and Reformed, 1988), 12–18. Islamic ethics distinguishes five categories of acts: obligatory, recommended, indifferent, disapproved, and prohibited. Cf. Toshihiko Izutsu, *Ethico-Religious Concepts in the Qur'ān* (Montreal: McGill University Press, 1966), 20–21.

our lives for the sake of others in the body of Christ, but first it must come to grips with ecclesiastical cannibalism.

Though the Christian calling is fundamentally positive, we should not minimize the role of prohibitions as they relate to the goal of the Christian life. The negative commandments provide direction by giving "clear indications of what always and essentially contradicts the kingdom of God."[8] They even take precedence over the positive commandments in the sense that we are forbidden to do evil in order that good may result (Rom. 3:8). Biblical direction in the form of prohibition requires discernment as it is necessary to determine from Scripture as a whole—not isolated prooftexts—what God has actually forbidden. But properly interpreted, Scripture helpfully provides clear-cut limits for conduct that is pleasing to God.

Permission

It is sometimes assumed that "a morality of divine commands will be rigoristic, in the sense that it will allow no place for actions which are neither commanded nor forbidden, but permissive and morally indifferent."[9] This is a mistake; the biblical ethic leaves room for many actions that are neither prohibited nor mandated. As Gordon Clark notes, "The Bible recognizes a large sphere of morally indifferent choices."[10]

Clark's use of the technical term *morally indifferent* is correct, but the terminology is confusing to many, sometimes clouding even the discussion of professional ethicists. "Things morally indifferent" represents *ta adiaphora* in Greek, the third term in the Stoic classification of things as "good, bad, and indifferent."[11] The New Testament twice refers to *ta diaphora*, "the things that really matter, the values that excel" (Rom. 2:18; Phil. 1:10), but avoids the term *adiaphora* in discussing actions that are neither forbidden nor commanded. Both *adiaphora* and "morally indifferent" are too ambiguous and liable to misunderstanding to be really useful. A standard reference work, for example, says, "Actions neither required nor forbidden by the moral law, or which do not affect morality, are called morally

8. Bernard Häring, *Free and Faithful in Christ: Moral Theology for Clergy and Laity*, 3 vols. (New York: Seabury, 1978–81), 1:84.

9. D. A. Rees, "The Ethics of Divine Commands," *Proceedings of the Aristotelian Society*, n.s., 57 (1956–57), 100.

10. Gordon H. Clark, in *The Philosophy of Gordon H. Clark: A Festschrift*, ed. Ronald H. Nash (Philadelphia: Presbyterian and Reformed, 1968), 426.

11. Marcia L. Colish gives this account of Stoic ethics: "What is ethically relevant is what man can control. Through his *logos* man can control his subjective attitudes towards things. What lies outside man's control is ethically irrelevant. Thus, all things fall into one of three categories: the good, defined as virtue, and sufficient unto itself; the evil, defined as vice and all things conducive to it; and the *adiaphora*, or everything else. The *adiaphora* are morally neutral, since they lie outside man's rational control." *The Stoic Tradition from Antiquity to the Early Middle Ages*, 2 vols. (Leiden: Brill, 1985), 1:44. Augustine specifically rejected the Stoic doctrine of *adiaphora*. Ibid., 2:210.

indifferent."[12] The problem is that an action may be neither required or forbidden as such and yet affect morality when viewed from the point of view of motive or goal. In addition, circumstances may introduce morally significant factors so that it is no longer a question simply of an action permissible in itself.

Scripture does not require that we have an express warrant for everything that we do. The discussion of the strong and the weak in Romans and 1 Corinthians establish the principle that what God does not forbid, he permits, provided it does not conflict with some other principle of conduct and it is done for the glory of God. Responding to the issue raised at Corinth, Paul grants the principle: "Everything is permissible" (that is, everything is not forbidden), but at the same time he points out that not everything is beneficial or constructive, and he reminds believers of the overarching mandate of love: "Nobody should seek his own good, but the good of others" (1 Cor. 10:23–24). Thus, we are permitted to eat anything God has created for food (1 Cor. 10:25–26), subject to the glory of God and the good of our neighbor (1 Cor. 10:31–32). (How poorly does "morally indifferent" represent Paul's theology of permissive actions.)

Since the general rule permits what is not forbidden, express permission is exceptional in the Scriptures. Another instance in Paul's Corinthian correspondence concerns sexual abstinence within marriage. Paul concedes its permissibility, provided it is done only temporarily by mutual consent for a specific spiritual purpose, adding, "I say this as a concession (*syngnōmē*), not as a command (*epitagē*)" (1 Cor. 7:6). Couples are permitted this form of discipline, but Paul wants it clearly understood that it is not a requirement for a godly marriage.

Mandate

Scriptural direction for action largely takes the form of positive commandment or mandate, as in the original creation mandate to subdue the earth (Gen. 2:28) and the new creation mandate to disciple the nations (Matt. 28:19). These directives, commonly called the cultural mandate and the Great Commission, are the two foci of what God is calling us to do in this age. Together they encompass his purpose for humankind. Corporate responsibility is vital to their fulfillment, for obviously no individual can subdue the earth or disciple the nations alone. Individuals participate as they discern their God-given gifts and opportunities and are supportive of others in their specific calling.

John Murray makes some observations that are helpful on this point. The mandate to subdue the earth, he says, "means nothing if it does not mean the harnessing and utilizing of the earth's resources and forces" to bring them "into the service of [human] well-being, enjoyment, pleasure" for the glory of God. But human nature is richly diversified: "There is not only a diversity of basic need but there is also a profuse variety of taste and interest, of aptitude

---

12. *Dictionary of Philosophy and Psychology*, ed. James Mark Baldwin, 3 vols. (New York: Macmillan, 1901–1905), 1:533.

and endowment, of desires to be satisfied and of pleasures to be gratified."[13] These have to be taken into account in determining individual responsibility for carrying out the cultural mandate, as spiritual gifts have to be weighed with respect to the Great Commission.

The positive commandments, in contrast to the prohibitions whose function is to set limits, tend to be open-ended in their requirements. The affirmative counterpart of "Do no harm" is "Do good to all." Paul gives the principle its classic expression: "As we have opportunity, let us do good to all people, especially to those who belong to the family of believers" (Gal. 6:10). Doing good is limited only by opportunity, with the needs of fellow believers to be of paramount concern. The positive demands of love require discernment of what opportunities to do good are ours by divine providence and prudence in determining the means that are likely to be the most effective in action. The Christian life is thus not prescribed in great detail; the mandates require wisdom for their implementation.

Counsel

Scripture provides direction for all of life, but it is important to distinguish between command and counsel. If the question is, What is God's will for all people everywhere at all times; which actions are right and which wrong? Scripture commands. It prohibits some actions and mandates others; its direction in this case is universal or absolute. On the other hand, if the question is, What is God's particular will for me in my situation as a member of the body of Christ and a citizen of his kingdom? Scripture counsels. It gives principles and calls for prudential judgment; its direction in this case is relative to individual gifts and opportunities. Unlike command, counsel does not yield a definitive yes or no—otherwise each of us would have to be equipped with a personal Urim and Thummin. God calls us to use our biblically informed, spiritually illuminated judgment in carrying out his mandates.

Many of the choices we make daily are not the subject of great deliberation. What we become as persons determines our sense of priorities as we grow in our understanding of our calling as Christians and in our love for the Lord. Then, whatever our hand finds to do, we do it with all our might. This is as it should be. There are, however, a number of significant choices that do require serious reflection and conscious decision. Our answer to these, too, ultimately depends upon what we become as persons; yet there is a need in these cases for careful and deliberate choice. Whether to marry or not? Whom to marry? When to have children? Which church? Which profession? Which seminary? Which company? Which country? These involved deciding between competing options, all of which are lawful and good.

13. John Murray, *Principles of Conduct: Aspects of Biblical Ethics* (Grand Rapids: Eerdmans, 1957), 37.

In the area of such choices, Scripture does not give specific guidance, but it does give direction. It is not necessary for us to know infallibly that one course is absolutely better than any other. What is required is that we act to the best of our knowledge, based on sound understanding of the values of God's kingdom—his purposes for human life and the principles that promote them—and in dependence upon him in prayer. The principle is accurately stated by John Murray: "The Christian life involves in many cases choices between things which are good in themselves and the choice in such instances is dictated by intelligent evaluation of the circumstances, of the gifts God has given us, and of the calling to which he has called us."[14]

As with the category of permission, the classic discussion of counsel is found in Paul. Having already laid down the principle that those who lack the gift of continence should marry (1 Cor. 7:9), Paul has this counsel for virgins and widows who may be contemplating marriage:

> Now about virgins: I have no command (*epitagē*) from the Lord, but I give a judgment (*gnōmē*) as one who by the Lord's mercy is trustworthy. Because of the present crisis, I think it is good for you to remain as you are. . . . [However,] if a virgin marries, she has not sinned. But those who marry will face many troubles in this life, and I want to spare you this. [1 Cor. 7:25–26, 28]

> A woman is bound to her husband as long as he lives. But if her husband dies, she is free to marry anyone she wishes, but he must belong to the Lord. In my judgment (*gnōmē*), she is happier if she stays as she is—and I think that I too have the Spirit of God. [1 Cor. 7:39–40]

Paul's judgment is given as counsel to be weighed, but the virgin and the widow are free to marry if, having taken the apostolic counsel duly into account, they judge differently. The widow is free to marry "anyone she wishes—only in the Lord." If marriage is the path chosen, there are still Christian considerations to be taken into account. Garry Friesen puts it well: "The way of wisdom would point out that since believers are given no imperatives commanding or forbidding marriage, these decisions fall within the area of freedom. From that perspective, the goal of the Christian is to make wise decisions—decisions that will best enable him to obey God's commands and fulfill God's stated purposes for his life."[15]

---

14. Ibid., 77.
15. Garry Friesen, with J. Robin Maxson, *Decision Making and the Will of God: A Biblical Alternative to the Traditional View* (Portland: Multnomah, 1980), 285. The "traditional" view Friesen accurately critiques is the view, common in fundamentalist circles, that there is a detailed individual will of God that can be definitively known by extrascriptural means. Friesen's alternative, "the way of wisdom," is a biblically grounded call for responsible freedom in the Christian life (though his use of the term *nonmoral* suffers the same liabilities as the term *morally indifferent*).

The Lord's Prayer helps us to order our priorities in the Christian life. The first three petitions are God-centered: hallow your name, manifest your rule, accomplish your will. Prayer for daily bread, forgiveness of sins, protection from temptation, and deliverance from evil round out the essential concerns of the disciple of Christ. Making God's concerns paramount has a formative effect on the disciple's system of values.

Precedent

Normative direction for the Christian life is derived primarily from the didactic portions of Scripture, but biblical narrative may also provide such direction in the form of precedent. On one occasion at least Jesus appeals to the record of a historical incident for moral justification of conduct. When his disciples were accused of breaking the Sabbath when they picked some grain to satisfy their hunger, Jesus responded, "Haven't you read what David did when he and his companions were hungry? He entered the house of God, and he and his companions ate the consecrated bread—which was not lawful for them to do, but only for the priests" [Matt. 12:3–4]. Jesus presents this as a clear precedent for the principle that ceremonial regulations yield to fundamental human need. Had the Pharisees truly identified with God's concerns they, like David and Ahimelech in the original incident (1 Sam. 21:1–6), would have been able to see it, for Jesus goes on to tell them, "If you had known what these words mean, 'I desire mercy, not sacrifice,' you would not have condemned the innocent" (Matt. 12:7).

Since the apostles were given the role of laying the foundation of the Christian church, what they did in that regard is relevant to questions of church order as well as what they said. The Book of Acts thus records precedent-setting actions for the organization of the church as well as unrepeatable events. Such precedents (for example, governance by elders) are for the most part reiterated in the epistles, but they need not be to be normative. The first ecumenical council (Acts 15), called by the apostles but not reenforced by didactic exposition, stands as a precedent for the way Christ intends that the unity of his church be given visible expression.

Example

In addition to command and counsel, Scripture gives positive direction by way of commendatory example. No law required David's mighty men to risk their lives to bring their commander-in-chief water from the well by the gate of Philistine-occupied Bethlehem (2 Sam. 23:13–17). It was nevertheless an appropriate expression of their devotion to the Lord's anointed, and David graciously acknowledged it as such. No counsel advised Mary to break the alabaster jar of pure nard (estimated to be worth a year's wages) to anoint the Lord Jesus—some of those present in fact thought it highly imprudent (Mark 14:3–9; John 12:1–8). Jesus, on the other hand, called it a "beautiful deed" (*kalon ergon*) that will be told in her memory wherever the gospel is preached throughout the world. Love is not bound by strictly legal categories for its expression. It does the fitting thing in the responsible exercise of freedom—as did the widow who cast her whole livelihood into the temple treasury (Mark 12:44).

It is instructive to see Paul's use of commendation rather than command in soliciting contributions to the collection for the poor saints in Jerusalem. He holds up to the Corinthians the commendable example of the Macedonians: "Out of the most severe trial, their overflowing joy and these extreme poverty welled up in rich generosity. For I testify that they gave as much as they were able, and even beyond their ability. Entirely on their own, they urgently pleaded with us for the privilege of sharing in this service to the saints. And they did not do as we expected, but they gave themselves first to the Lord and then to us in keeping with God's will" (2 Cor. 8:2–5).

Having presented a model of Christian commitment, Paul calls the Corinthians to excel in the grace of giving. Then, rather than issuing a command (*epitagē*), Paul gives direction in the form of counsel (*gnōmē*) (2 Cor. 8:8, 10). He wants their generosity to be motivated by gratitude rather than by obligation so that their obedient response to the gospel will be evident to all (2 Cor. 9:13). Thus in the course of his appeal Paul recalls the most profound example of generosity to secure gospel (rather than legal) motivation: "For you know the grace of our Lord Jesus Christ, that though he was rich, yet for your sakes he became poor, so that you through his poverty might become rich" (2 Cor. 8:9). What is lost in precision by not prescribing the precise amount to be given is more than made up for in the affective power of Christ's example.

The Example of Christ

Paul's approach to Christian giving illustrates that the directing principle of the Christian life is the will of God as revealed in Christ and the holy Scriptures. To walk in God's ways means concretely to follow the example of Christ, particularly his model of serving and suffering. The classic call to follow his example in serving comes just after Jesus has washed the feet of his disciples:

> Now that I, your Lord and Teacher, have washed your feet, you also should wash one another's feet. I have set you an example (*hypodeigma*) that you should do as I have done for you. I tell you the truth, no servant is greater than his master, nor is a messenger greater than the one who sent him. Now that you know these things, you will be blessed (*makarioi*) if you do them. [John 13:14–17]

In serving his disciples by washing their feet, Jesus seeks to elicit a like humility in their service in response. The passage wants us to know who the

Footwasher is and that he does not wash feet out of lack of self-respect: "Jesus knew that the Father had put all thing under his power, and that he had come from God and was returning to God" (John 13:3). So what does he do? He interrupts his meal, gets up, takes off his coat, wraps a towel around his waist, pours water into a basin, and begins to wash and dry his disciples' feet. What for? To show the proper attitude of all service done in his name. The church's highest-ranking official—the teaching Lord—claims no privileged exemption from menial service. Happy are they who follow his example.[16]

The key passage on following Christ's example of godly suffering is found in Peter—the same Peter once given to taking sword against the opposition, so little disposed was he to the way of the cross (John 18:10–11). Now he knows better:

> For it is commendable (*charis*) if a man bears up under the pain of unjust suffering because he is conscious of God. But how it is to your credit (*kleos*) if you receive a beating for doing wrong and endure it? But if you suffer for doing good and you endure it, this is commendable (*charis*) before God. To this you were called, because Christ suffered for you, leaving you an example (*hypogrammos*), that you should follow in his steps (*ichnos*). [1 Pet. 2:19–21]

The words *charis* and *kleos* form an interesting contrast. *Charis* refers to God's favor that rests upon actions that are intrinsically attractive; *kleos* refers to the kind of fame that comes from projecting a macho image—doing wrong and taking the consequences. Peter asks, What kind of glory or prestige is that for a Christian to have? True fortitude is shown by following Christ, by tracing the pattern he has laid out: "When they hurled their insults at him, he did not retaliate; when he suffered, he made no threats. Instead, he entrusted himself to him who judges justly" (1 Pet. 2:23).

Christians are called to freedom (Gal. 5:13), to peace (Col. 3:15), and (as here) to suffering. The latter does not have quite the same appeal as peace and freedom, but Peter clearly tells us that Christ's vicarious suffering was exemplary as well as redemptive.[17] To follow in his steps is more precisely to follow his tracks. As J. N. D. Kelly points out, "The Greek *ichnos* signifies the actual footprint (in the case of game, the spoor), and in the plural the line of such footprints; to follow a man's footprints is to move in the direction he is going."[18] The way of Christ is through suffering to glory. It is the path he chose, and he bids us, "Follow me."

---

16. *Makarioi*, as in the other Beatitudes, means "happy" in the sense of being fulfilled as God intends us to be.

17. The original use of *hypogrammos* (example), of which this happens to be the only New Testament instance, was for a pattern to be copied in writing or drawing; by extension it took on the meaning of example in a behavioral sense.

18. J. N. D. Kelly, *A Commentary on The Epistles of Peter and of Jude* (New York: Harper, 1969), 120. The other instances of *ichnos* in the New Testament are Rom. 4:12 and 2 Cor. 12:18.

The directing principle of Jesus' example is summed up in the form of a new commandment: "A new command I give you: Love one another. As I have loved you, so you must love one another. By this all men will know that you are my disciples, if you love one another" (John 13:34–35). The newness lies in the model shown—as I have loved you. There is no greater love than this, and discipleship is recognizable in like treatment of others in the body of Christ. Paul furnishes a concrete instance: "Carry each other's burdens, and in this way you will fulfill the law of Christ" (Gal. 6:2). The principle that governed the life of Christ should now rule ours. As Paul writes elsewhere, "I am not free from God's law but am under Christ's law (*ennomos Christou*)" (1 Cor. 9:21), which the Spirit gives freedom to fulfill.

The Ministry of the Holy Spirit

As the apostle Paul knew from personal experience, what was missing in first-century Judaism was not *torah* but the Holy Spirit. "The *torah*," he says, "is holy, and the *mitzvah* [specifically the commandment not to covet] is holy and just and good" (Rom. 7:12, with Hebrew equivalents for *nomos* and *entolē*, "law" and "commandment"). So what's the problem? In a word, sin. The law, for all its divine authority and moral wisdom, cannot change the direction of the human heart, cannot overcome the impulse to sin. The law cannot give what it commands; it can only demand that its penal sanctions be enforced. Powerless to make alive, it mightily condemns to death. In this sense, "the letter kills, but the Spirit gives life" (2 Cor. 3:6). The glory of the new covenant is the ministry of the Spirit, bringing life, liberty, and the transformation of sinners into the likeness of Christ (2 Cor. 3:8, 17–18).

Twice Paul speaks of the ministry of the Spirit in terms of being led by the Spirit: Romans 8:14, "For all who are led by the Spirit of God are children of God" (NRSV); and Galatians 5:18, "But if you are led by the Spirit, you are not under law" (i.e., you are not in the condition of being bound to the law without being able to put it into practice). The leading of the Spirit is not a new source of guidance independent of the Word; it is rather a new impulse to walk in the paths of righteousness revealed in the Spirit-inspired Scriptures. The verb Paul uses for the leading of the Spirit is *agō*. Two contrasting texts where Paul uses the same verb clarify the meaning of "being led." The Corinthians formerly were drawn to idol worship; now by the Spirit they acknowledge Jesus is Lord (1 Cor. 12:2). More generally, persons without the Spirit are driven by all sorts of sinful desires (2 Tim. 3:6). In the application of redemption, the Spirit not only regenerates but takes up residence in believers to move them in the right direction. As Jonathan Edwards put it, the Holy

Spirit indwells believers "to influence their hearts as a principle of new nature, or as a divine supernatural spring of life and action."[19] Through the indwelling of the Spirit God enables believers both to will and to work that which is good (Phil. 2:13).[20]

The ministry of the Spirit not only enables the will; it also enlightens the mind. As Paul says in his classic call to Christian service, sinners are transformed into the likeness of Christ by the renewal of their mind (Rom. 12:2). It would be a mistake to take *mind* in an exclusively cognitive sense. Persons are too closely identified with their thoughts for their affections not to be included in them. This psychological truth about human nature is reflected in the biblical vocabulary of *heart* and *mind*; cognition and affection are both present in both terms, making them practically interchangeable with reference to a person's inmost being.[21] But today, as Mary Midgley points out, "many things on the current intellectual scene tend to make us disconnect feeling from thought, by narrowing our notions of both, and so to make human life as a whole unintelligible."[22] She continues:

> We are inclined to use words like 'heart' and 'feeling' to describe just a few selected sentiments which are somewhat detached from the practical business of living—notably romantic, compassionate and tender sentiments—as if nonromantic actions did not involve any feeling. But this cannot be right. Mean or vindictive action flows from and implies mean and vindictive feeling, and does so just as much when it is considered as when it is impulsive. In general, too,

19. Jonathan Edwards, *Religious Affections*, vol. 2 of *The Works of Jonathan Edwards,* ed. John E. Smith (New Haven: Yale University Press, 1959), 200. For a full treatment see Herman Ridderbos, "Life Through the Spirit," in *Paul: An Outline of His Theology,* trans. John Richard De Witt (Grand Rapids: Eerdmans, 1975), 214–23.

20. Cf. C. E. B. Cranfield: "The daily, hourly putting to death of the schemings and enterprises of the sinful flesh by means of the Spirit is a matter of being led, directed, impelled, controlled by the Spirit. Though the active participation of the Christian is indeed involved (*thanatoute*), it is fundamentally the work of the Spirit (hence the passive *agontai*)." *A Critical and Exegetical Commentary on the Epistle to the Romans,* 2 vols. (Edinburgh: Clark, 1975), 1:395.

21. See Gen. 6:5, "The Lord saw that the wickedness of humankind was great in the earth, and that every inclination of the thoughts of their hearts (*kāl yētzer māśĕbôt libbô*; LXX, *pas tis dianoeitai en tē kardia autou*) was only evil continually" (NRSV); Deut. 28:65, "Among those nations you will find no repose, no resting place for the sole of your foot. There the Lord will give you an anxious mind (*lēb*), eyes weary with longing, and a despairing heart (*nepeš*)"; Ps. 26:2, "Test me, O Lord, and try me, examine my heart (*kilyôt*) and my mind (*lēb*)"; Jer. 17:10, "I the Lord search the heart (*lēb*) and examine the mind (*kilyôt*), to reward a man according to his conduct, according to what his deeds deserve"; Jer. 31:33 (LXX, 38:33), "I will put my law (*tôrâ*; LXX, pl., *nomoi*) in their minds (*qereb*, inward part; LXX, *dianoia*) and write it on their hearts (*lēb*; LXX, *kardia*)"; Heb. 8:10, "I will put my laws in their minds (*dianoia*) and write them on their hearts (*kardia*)"; Heb. 10:16, "I will put my laws in their hearts (*kardia*), and I will write them on their minds (*dianoia*)"; Luke 10:27, "Love the Lord your God with all your heart (*kardia*) and with all your soul (*psychē*) and with all your strength (*ischus*) and with all your mind (*dianoia*)."

22. Mary Midgley, *Heart and Mind: The Varieties of Moral Experience* (New York: St. Martin's, 1981), 3.

ordinary prudent action flows from prudent feeling. . . . We are in fact so constituted that we cannot act at all if feeling really fails. When it does fail, as in
case of extreme apathy and depression, people stop acting; they can die in consequence.[23]

Midgley's conclusion lines up with the biblical psychology of human
action: "In general, feelings, to be effective, must take shape as thoughts, and
thoughts, to be effective, must be powered by suitable feelings."[24]

The knowledge and insight by which love abounds in the Christian life
(Phil. 1:9) is the fruit that the ministry of the Spirit. Moral illumination is
accomplished by and with the Word as the Holy Spirit guides us into the
truth, convincing us that the practices God has revealed are pleasing to him.
But the work of illumination involves more than simple cognition. As Richard Mouw rightly says, "It is the Holy Spirit who must instill the *longing* for
justice within us, a *love* for the poor, a *compassion* for the needy, a heart that
desires the good of the widow and orphan and prisoner and sojourner, a *felt*
hope for the reign of peace and righteousness."[25]

If it is the Spirit's ministry to lead, it is our responsibility to follow, to submit to his control, to yield to his impulses, to walk in his direction. Prayer is
a means of grace whereby the work of God's Spirit is furthered in our lives, in
love's increase both in knowledge of the directing principles of the Christian
life and in insight into their practical application.

The Role of Conscience

> Always let your conscience be your guide.
>
> —Jiminy Cricket in *Pinocchio*

> Conscience! That stuff'll drive you crazy.
>
> —Marlon Brando in *On the Waterfront*

Conscience plays to mixed reviews, and not just in the movies. Whether it
should be applauded or given the hook depends on how it performs, and its
performances are notoriously uneven. The New Testament itself speaks of a
good conscience (*agathē*, Acts 23:1, 1 Tim. 1:5, 19, 1 Pet. 3:16, 21; *kalē*, Heb.
13:18), a pure conscience (*kathara*, 1 Tim. 3:9, 2 Tim. 1:3), and a clear conscience (*aproskopos*, Acts 24:16), but conscience may also be evil (*ponēra*, Heb.
10:22), seared (*kekaustēriasmenōn*, cauterized, 1 Tim. 4:2), defiled (*memian-*

23. Ibid.
24. Ibid., 4.
25. Mouw, *God Who Commands*, 174.

tai, Tit. 1:15), or weak (*asthenēs*, 1 Cor. 8:7, 12). Conscience is therefore not above criticism, but to be discriminating critics we first have to ask, What is its assigned role?

The popular notion of conscience is that it is "a built-in human device for spot-checking right from wrong."[26] On this view conscience is not simply a necessary criterion for personal integrity but a sufficient criterion for morality itself. "My conscience is clear" thus becomes the ultimate moral justification. But the biblical ethic does not give conscience the role of a one-justice supreme court. Most of the New Testament references to conscience are found in Paul, and he himself says, "My conscience is clear, but that does not make me innocent. It is the Lord who judges me" (1 Cor. 4:4).[27] Neither does conscience have the last word when it condemns, as the apostle John (using the equivalent Old Testament language of the heart) indicates: "This then is how we know that we belong to the truth, and how we set our hearts at rest in his presence whenever our hearts condemn us. For God is greater than our hearts, and he knows everything" (1 John 3:19–20).

If conscience is not ultimate, what good is it? Mark Twain had one of his characters say that if he had a "yaller dog" that wasn't worth more than conscience he'd take it out and shoot it. Before we gun down conscience, however, we should consider how it might have a role subject to God, the Lord of the conscience. Luther's eloquent affirmation before the Diet of Worms at least gives us pause:

> Unless I am convinced by the testimony of Scriptures or by clear reason . . . I am bound by the Scriptures I have quoted and my conscience is captive to the word of God. I cannot and I will not retract anything, since it is neither safe nor right to go against conscience. I cannot do otherwise, here I stand, may God help me. Amen.[28]

Syneidēsis (conscience) occurs about thirty times in the New Testament and is found only in the Epistles and two instances in the mouth of Paul in the Book of Acts.[29] Sometimes the sense is close to "moral consciousness," as when Paul says, "We commend ourselves to every man's conscience in the sight of God" (2 Cor. 4:2), and "What we are is plain to God, and I hope it

26. Paul Lehmann, *Ethics in a Christian Context* (New York: Harper, 1963), 333.

27. Instead of *syneidēsis* Paul uses here *synoida* with the dative of the reflexive pronoun, an equivalent expression of which this is the only New Testament instance. The Septuagint uses the same construction in translating Job 27:6, which reads in Hebrew, "My heart does not reproach [me]."

28. Cited in Michael G. Baylor, *Action and Person: Conscience in Late Scholasticism and the Young Luther* (Leiden: Brill, 1977), 1. Baylor documents two principles consistently recognized in the medieval theology that justify Luther's stance: "that it is always a sin to act against conscience" and "that conscience ultimately derives it authority from God alone" (p. 3).

29. Plus a textual variant within the pericope of the woman taken in adultery, reflected in the KJV of John 8:9.

is also plain to your conscience" (2 Cor. 5:11). But for the most part *syneidēsis* refers to internal self-judgment, as when Paul "boasts," "Our conscience testifies that we have conducted ourselves in the world, and especially in our relations with you, in the holiness and sincerity that are from God" (2 Cor. 1:12). In this sense conscience is essentially a witness, excusing or accusing a person as to whether he or she has acted, or is about to act, according to his or her own moral consciousness. This is the force of Romans 2:15, "their consciences also bearing witness, and their thoughts (*logismoi*, internal deliberations) now accusing, now even defending them."

For conscience to function properly as a witness it must be cleansed by the blood of Christ (otherwise it will never rest in peace) and be informed by the Word of God. We must do what we think is right; otherwise there is no point in moral deliberation. But what we think must be made captive to Christ. Luther's conscience was not autonomous; he confessed that it was subject to correction by Scripture. As things stood, for him to go against conscience was to go against the Word of God. That he could not do and retain his moral integrity as one who had committed himself to Christ and the holy Scriptures. Thus he acted in good conscience.

Perhaps Calvin sums it up best when, in the final section of his great chapter on Christian freedom, he says, "A good conscience, then, is nothing other than inward integrity of heart." Noting Paul's references to faith and a good conscience (1 Tim. 1:5, 19), Calvin comments, "By these words he signifies a lively inclination to serve God and a sincere effort to live piously and holily."[30] The guide for a pious and holy life is Scripture, not conscience.[31] Many sorrows are theirs who look to their conscience rather than to the Word of God for direction, as Calvin was well aware.

> For when consciences once ensnare themselves, they enter a long and inextricable maze, not easy to get out of. If a man begins to doubt whether he may use linen for sheets, shirts, handkerchiefs, and napkins, he will afterward be uncertain also about hemp; finally, doubt will even arise over tow. For he will turn over in his mind whether he can sup without napkins, or go without a handkerchief. If any man should consider daintier food unlawful, in the end he will not be at peace before God, when he eats black bread or common victuals, while it occurs to him that he could sustain his body on even coarser foods. If he boggles at sweet wine, he will not with clear conscience drink even flat wine,

30. John Calvin, *Institutes of the Christian Religion*, ed. John T. McNeill, trans. Ford Lewis Battles (Philadelphia: Westminster, 1960), 3.19.16.

31. Peter Toon gives conscience a broader role as "judge and guide of the moral life," immediately adding that "to be such the conscience has to be formed, informed and educated in such a way that it contains the genuine possibility of making a distinction between right and wrong and of guiding into correct paths." *Your Conscience As Your Guide* (Wilson, Conn.: Morehouse, 1984), 14. Qualified in this way the broader view (traditional since Thomas Aquinas) is not indefensible, but it seems preferable in this instance to adhere strictly to the narrower biblical use of *syneidēsis*.

and finally he will not dare touch water if sweeter and cleaner than other water. To sum up, he will come to the point of considering it wrong to step upon a straw across his path, as the saying goes.[32]

The subordination of conscience to the word of God is fundamental to the freedom of the Christian life. The only extended treatments of conscience in the New Testament are Romans 14 and 1 Corinthians 8–10. Both passages are concerned with how believers with extrabiblical scruples may be accommodated within the body of Christ. In Romans the contrast is between the strong and the weak in faith; in 1 Corinthians between the knowledgeable and the weak in conscience.[33] Though the situational details differ, both passages address the same basic ethical problem. The exercise of liberty on the part of the strong may present a stumbling block (*proskomma*) or temptation (*skandalon*) to the weak in view of their tendency to yield to peer pressure and to go against conscience.

Paul does not go into the source of the opinions of the weak. Because they serve Christ they are to be cordially received, their conscientious scruples notwithstanding. At Rome they appear to be vegetarians (14:2), keepers of the religious calendar (14:5), possibly abstainers from wine (14:21)—all things God has neither commanded nor forbidden his people under the gospel. At Corinth they were those who felt bound for the sake of their Christian testimony to refrain from eating food that had been consecrated to idols (*ta eidōlothuta*) before being sold to the general public. In neither case was the problem legalism (as at Galatia) or dualism (as at Colossae). Paul offered no right hand of fellowship to rival systems of salvation, granted no concession to any who would overthrow Christian liberty by binding the conscience where God had left it free. But he did insist on charity toward those whose extrabiblical scruples put them in a vulnerable position.

Paul's concern is not that the weak might get their feelings hurt or otherwise be upset or take offense at the conduct of the strong; the cautionary words he uses in his appeal to the strong shows that he has in mind serious spiritual injury and potentially disastrous consequences: "Do not by your eating destroy (*apollumi*) your brother for whom Christ died" (Rom. 14:15; 1 Cor. 8:11); "Do not destroy [*kataluō*, overthrow] the work of God for the sake of food" (Rom. 14:20); "It is better not to eat meat or drink wine or to do anything else that will cause your brother to fall (*proskoptō*)" (Rom. 14:21); "When you sin against your brothers in this way and wound (*typtō*, beat) their weak conscience, you sin against Christ" (1 Cor. 8:12). Conscience-battering is a serious business; to pressure the weak to violate their scruples is to cause them to act contrary to what they believe is the will of God. At stake is nothing less than their personal integrity as Christians.

---

32. Calvin, *Institutes*, 3.19.9.
33. Nearly a third of the New Testament instances of *syneidēsis* are in 1 Cor. 8 and 10.

To risk this kind of grief is to no longer act in love (Rom. 14:15). The exercise of Christian liberty is thus subject to the ends of Christian charity: "Each of us should please his neighbor for his good, to build him up" (Rom. 15:2; cf. 1 Cor. 10:24). Paul's clincher in both passages is the example of Christ who put the spiritual good of others above pleasing himself (Rom. 15:3; 1 Cor. 11:1).

At the same time it must be recognized that a weak conscience is a liability and that it is better for the weak to become strong than to remain permanently exposed to temptation on account of their extrabiblical scruples. It is not good to have a conscience that is more strict than God. The weak therefore have a responsibility to allow their consciences to be informed by Scripture rather than remaining subject to the extraneous influences of background and culture.[34]

Summary

> The Lamb . . . will be their shepherd;
> he will lead them to springs of living water.
>
> —Revelation 7:17

As the goal of the Christian life is to be like Christ, and its motive is love for Christ, so the direction of the Christian life is the law of Christ, that is, "the whole tradition of Jesus' ethical teaching, confirmed by his character and conduct . . . and reproduced within his people by the power of the Spirit."[35] Christ, the rising sun, has come from heaven, "to shine on those living in darkness and in the shadow of death, to guide our feet into the path of peace" (Luke 1:79). "May the Lord direct your hearts to the love of God and to the steadfastness of Christ" (2 Thess. 3:5 NRSV).

34. William Ames, the great English Puritan divine, defined a scruple as "a rash fear without any ground." Scruples arise in various ways (e.g., from the company of scrupulous persons). What is to be done with them? Ames's advice is to avoid them in the first place, but if afflicted, to labor to remove them. What if they won't go away? "If they cannot be so removed, but that they do still molest, it is lawful, and the best course to do a thing against such scruples." One should, violently if necessary, refuse to consider them. *Conscience with the Power and Cases Thereof* (1639; reprint, Norwood, N.J.: Johnson, 1975), 1.4. Thus would Ames liberate the Christian conscience from the tyranny of false guilt feelings after determining that they have nothing to do with conscientious convictions grounded in the Word of God.

35. F. F. Bruce, *The Epistle to the Galatians: A Commentary on the Greek Text* (Grand Rapids: Eerdmans, 1982), 261.

5

The Primary Forms of Love

Make us eternal truth receive,
And practise all that we believe.

—John Dryden, *Veni Creator Spiritus*

Christian love, so far from being without shape or structure, is embodied in certain characteristic practices for the glory of God. The primary forms of love are what Jesus called the weightier matters of the law: justice, mercy, and faithfulness. "These," he said, "you ought to have practiced and the others [simply] not neglected" (Matt. 23:23).[1] In other words, "There are commandments in reference to which it is sufficient to say that they should not be left undone, such as the tithing of mint, anise and cummin, and there are commandments of such supreme and intrinsic importance as to demand . . . a positive and energetic determination to do them."[2]

The legalists of Jesus' day had it precisely reversed; they practiced the marginal and neglected the essential. It is a common failing, made worse by ethicists ("blind guides" in Matt. 23:24) assiduously filtering out gnats while casually serving up camels. Jesus restores a sense of proportion to love's obedience by marking out clearly those practices that God wants us above all to follow in the path of righteousness.

The question of the norm of the Christian life (as distinct from goal and motive) is thus properly, Which practices ought we to follow? rather than simply, Which actions are right and which wrong? The noun *practice* denotes frequent or usual action—habitual rather than sporadic conduct. God calls his people to a way of life, not isolated actions. He mandates practices that reflect his own character and righteousness, practices that are intrinsically good on

1. This rendering maintains the Greek word order; both the NIV and the NRSV translate *poiēsai* "practiced."

2. Geerhardus Vos, *The Teaching of Jesus Concerning the Kingdom and the Church* (Grand Rapids: Eerdmans, 1958), 62.

that account.[3] The rightness or wrongness of particular actions is properly addressed within the larger framework of what is or is not consistent with the Christian way of life as defined by the revealed will of God.[4] Thus the prophet Hosea presents cursing, lying, murder, stealing, and adultery as evidence that there is no faithfulness, no mercy, no knowledge of God in the land (Hos. 4:1–2).

The practices that Jesus identifies as the major concerns of the law (*krisis, eleos,* and *pistis* in Greek) figure prominently in the Hebrew Bible as *mišpāṭ, ḥesed,* and *ʾĕmûnâ* (and the overlapping *ʾemet*).[5] The three together—justice, mercy, faithfulness—comprise the essence of all that God is calling us to be and to do. Jesus' ringing declaration is in fact a reaffirmation of the great summary of the revealed will of God in Micah 6:8.

> He has shown you, *ʾādām,*[6] what is good.
> And what does the Lord require of you
> But to do *mišpāṭ,*
> And to love *ḥesed,*
> And to walk humbly with your God.

Although there is no noun in the final clause corresponding to *pistis* (faithfulness) in Matthew 23:23, "to walk with God" has the same import.[7] Two texts may be cited to illustrate the point, the Lord's promise to David, "If your heirs take heed to their way, to walk before me in faithfulness (*ʾĕmet*) with all their heart and with all their soul, there shall not fail you a successor on the throne of Israel" (1 Kings 2:4 NRSV; cf. 1 Kings 3:6), and Hezekiah's deathbed prayer, "Remember now, O LORD, I implore you, how I have walked before you in faithfulness (*ʾĕmet*) with a whole heart, and have done what is good in your sight" (2 Kings 20:3 = Isa. 38:3 NRSV). To walk with God implies loyalty and trust, in a word, faithfulness.

The threefold pattern of moral excellence appears also in the Lord's betrothal pledge to his people in Hosea 2:19–20 (21–22 in Hebrew).

---

3. Cf. the definition proposed in *Habits of the Heart:* "Practices are shared activities that are not undertaken as means to an end but are ethically good in themselves." Robert N. Bellah et al., *Habits of the Heart: Individualism and Commitment in American Life* (1985; New York: Harper, 1986), 335. Cf. Sir Walter Scott's famous line, "O what a tangled web we weave, / When first we practise to deceive!" (*Marmion,* chap. 6, l. 17).

4. Cf. Bernard Häring: "Moral theology . . . is not concerned first with decision-making or with discrete acts. Its basic task and purpose is to gain the right vision, to assess the main perspectives, and to present those truths and values which should bear upon decisions to be made before God." *Free and Faithful in Christ: Moral Theology for Clergy and Laity,* 3 vols. (New York: Seabury, 1978), 1:6.

5. For seminarians struggling with Hebrew vocabulary I have composed a cheer for the moral heavyweights: "*Mišpāṭ, ḥesed, ʾĕmûnâ*— / These things practice. / Hallelujah!"

6. No translation can reproduce the overtones of the Hebrew *ʾādām* (humankind) in personal address.

7. The Hebrew represented by "humbly" is an Old Testament *hapax legomenon,* the meaning of which is uncertain. The LXX renders it *hetoimon:* "and to be *ready* to go on with your God."

> I will betroth you to me forever;
> I will betroth you to me in righteousness and in *mišpāṭ*,
>   and in *ḥesed* and in compassion;
> I will betroth you to me in *ʾĕmûnâ*,
>   and you will know the Lord.

Here *mišpāṭ* (justice) is paired with *ṣādaq* (righteousness), a broader term in the same semantic domain, while *ḥesed* (mercy) is paired with *rahamim* (compassion), an emotional term (rendered "tender mercies" in the KJV of the Psalms) expressive of the feeling God has for his people. The third moral attribute appears separately and explicitly as *ʿemunah* (faithfulness).[8] In Hosea 12:6 (7 in Hebrew) the people of God are called to a threefold response that mirrors the moral qualities exhibited in the Lord's gracious initiative in salvation.

> But you, return to your God,
>   keep *ḥesed* and *mišpāṭ*
> and wait for your God continuously.

Those who have been bound to the Lord by his justice and mercy can truly appreciate the need for maintaining the same in their own practice, just as the Lord's great faithfulness calls forth a life of trust and commitment—waiting for God and walking with him. Justice, mercy, and faithfulness are thus the primary forms of obedient love and in principle its full and complete expression. They constitute the fundamental and irreducible moral norms that are always and everywhere to be maintained in practice.

Justice

What is justice? The short answer is, "To render to each his or her due."[9] As it says in the Book of Proverbs, "Do not withhold good from those to whom it is due, when it is in your power to do it" (Prov. 3:27 NRSV). When Paul says, "Owe no one anything, except to love one another" (Rom. 13:8 NRSV), he calls for justice as one of the forms of love—the first, though cer-

---

8. See also Ps. 89:14, "*sedeq* and *mišpāṭ* are the foundation of your throne; *ḥesed* and *ʾĕmet* go before you."

9. Cf. Cicero: "[Justice is concerned] with the conservation of organized society, with rendering to every man his due [*suum cuique*], and with the faithful discharge of obligations assumed." *De Officiis* (On Duties), trans. Walter Miller (Cambridge: Harvard University Press, 1913), 1.5.15. "The first office of justice is to keep one man from doing harm to the other, unless provoked by wrong; and the next is to lead men to use common possessions for the common interests, private property for their own." Ibid., 1.7.20.

tainly not the last, directive that love fulfills.[10] The only question is, What do I owe, and how do I know?

The epistemological question is logically prior. Where do I go to find out what I owe other human beings? Shall I search my conscience? Follow public opinion? Look to the civil law? Any and all of these may be seriously mistaken—the notorious practice of Jim Crow being a prime example of how justice can be mugged by all three at once. Conscience is subject to various environmental influences; public opinion is often no more than pooled ignorance; civil law is subject to change and thereby concedes that it is not identical with justice.

The higher norm of justice to which the civil law ought to conform is sometimes called natural law, but this terminology has a confusing history. Cicero, writing around 54 B.C., put it this way:

> True law is right reason in agreement with Nature; it is of universal application, unchanging and everlasting; it summons to duty by its commands, and averts from wrong-doing by its prohibitions. And it does not lay its commands or prohibitions upon good men in vain, though neither have any effect on the wicked. It is a sin to try to alter this law, nor it is allowable to attempt to repeal any part of it, and it is impossible to abolish it entirely. We cannot be freed from its obligations by Senate or People, and we need not look outside ourselves for an expounder or interpreter of it. And there will not be different laws at Rome and at Athens, or different laws now and in the future, but one eternal and unchangeable law will be valid for all nations and for all times, and there will be one master and one rule, that is, God, over us all, for He is the author of this law, its promulgator, and its enforcing judge.[11]

Cicero is talking about what we would call the moral law, which he correctly observes must have a supratemporal ground. But Cicero's god is Nature—not nature's God, not the personal Creator of heaven and earth. It is far from clear how "right reason" knows itself to be in agreement with impersonal nature—the whole cosmic order of things from which human beings must learn their place.

The doctrine of creation significantly alters the discussion of the question of "the law behind the laws." Chrysostom (d. 407), for example, confronts the moral relativism of his day with an argument that concludes, "It is evident that [the pagan legislators] derived their laws from the law which God

---

10. Cf. Henry Stob, "The Dialectic of Love and Justice," in *Ethical Reflections: Essays on Moral Themes* (Grand Rapids: Eerdmans, 1978), 137. Stob here seems to modify his earlier (1974) position that justice must be "distinguished from and contrasted to love, in order that so it may achieve its own unique identity." "The Concept of Justice," ibid., 124. The problem may be resolved by maintaining the distinction between *mišpāṭ* and *ḥesed*, but seeing both as manifestations of obedient love.

11. Cicero, *De Republica* (Concerning the Republic), trans. Clinton Walker Keyes (Cambridge: Harvard University Press, 1928), 3.22.33.

ingrafted in man from the beginning."[12] "Natural law" now refers not to the order of the universe but to the moral law governing human nature made in the image of God and responsible to him for doing his will. This revised version of natural law as innate knowledge of the moral law was articulated especially by Augustine.[13]

When Gratian, the father of canon law, enters the discussion in the middle of the twelfth century he begins his most famous work with the observation, "Mankind is ruled by two laws: Natural Law and Custom," adding (surprisingly to us), "Natural Law is that which is contained in the Scriptures and the Gospel."[14] He goes on to give this account of natural law: "[It] came into existence with the very creation of man as a rational being, nor does it vary in time but remains unchangeable."[15] Consequently, "Natural law absolutely prevails in dignity over customs and constitutions. Whatever has been recognized by usage, or laid down in writing, if it contradicts natural law, must be considered null and void."[16] The identification of natural and scriptural law, which at first takes us aback, becomes comprehensible when we understand that by "natural law" Gratian means the moral law revealed originally and constitutionally in human nature and republished verbally in the holy Scriptures.

Thomas Aquinas gives the discussion a new turn by taking "natural law" to refer to God's purpose for human nature, from which his directives (the moral law) could be inferred.

> It was Aquinas's view that by using our reason to reflect on our human nature, we could discover both the specific ends toward which we naturally tend (such as to live, to reproduce, to acquire knowledge, to have a role in an ordered society, to worship God) and the general end for which God created us, a blessed immortality. When we have discovered these ends, it is then possible for us to determine the means required to achieve them. This understanding of God's plan for us, built into our nature by his act of creation, Aquinas called natural law.[17]

The Reformers in the sixteenth century return to the original Augustinian position. Augustine had recognized an innate knowledge of the moral law, of

12. Chrysostom, *The Homilies on the Statutes to the People of Antioch*, trans. W. R. W. Stephens, in *A Select Library of the Nicene and Post-Nicene Fathers of the Christian Church*, ed. Philip Schaff (New York: Scribner's, 1903), 12.4.

13. Cf. Alasdair MacIntyre, "The Augustinian Alternative," in *Whose Justice? Whose Rationality?* (Notre Dame, Ind.: University of Notre Dame Press, 1988), 146–63.

14. Gratian, *Concordiantia Discordantium Canonum* (also known as *Decretum Gratiana*), cited in A. P. d'Entrèves, *Natural Law: An Historical Survey* (1951; reprint, New York: Harper, 1965), 33.

15. Ibid., 34.

16. Ibid..

17. Gerard J. Hughes, "Natural Law," in *The Westminster Dictionary of Christian Ethics*, ed. James F. Childress and John Macquarrie (Philadelphia: Westminster, 1986), 413.

which the fundamental precept is the golden rule in its negative form: Do not unto others what you would not have them do unto you. Calvin, following Augustine's lead, identified the the basic rule of natural law with the principle of equity: Do as you would be done by.[18] The Westminster standards continue this line of thought, teaching that God revealed the moral law to man at creation as the rule of his obedience. This law after the fall continues to be a perfect rule of righteousness, forever binding on all mankind. As such it was delivered upon Mount Sinai in ten commandments, making the Decalogue a re-presentation of the moral law originally revealed constitutionally in human nature. In the Reformed tradition "natural law" refers to the moral law of which all human beings have some awareness, including a basic sense of justice, by virtue of their being created in the image of God.

For all their differences, Thomas and the Reformers were agreed in relating natural law to the will of God. The secularization of the discussion was a post-Reformation development, in which Hugo Grotius played a leading role. "Grotius' aim was to construct a system of laws which would carry conviction in an age in which theological controversy was gradually losing the power to do so," and he attempted to prove "that it was possible to build up a theory of laws independent of theological presuppositions."[19] The problem is that every system of laws presupposes some view of human nature. Anthropological controversy is the Achilles' heel of Grotius' project inasmuch as philosophers "differ widely in their views about what human nature is and, as a result, about the moral theory that can be derived from it."[20] Exclusion of doctrine of creation left natural law without an adequate ground and exposed to the vagaries of some evolutionary "law of nature" (as in the case of social Darwinism), compounding the ambiguity of the term *natural law*.

The Bible does affirm a natural knowledge of the moral law, the key text being Romans 2:14–15. Although the Gentiles do not have the *torah*, they are not completely lacking in knowledge of the moral law. When they do "naturally" (*physei*), that is, without being instructed by special revelation, things that the law requires (*ta tou nomou*), they show the effect of the law (*to ergon tou nomou*) written on their heart. It does not follow, however, that general revelation alone is sufficient for constructing a natural-law ethic. Appeal to natural law alone for a knowledge of justice runs into difficulty on at least two major counts. First, the principle of equity, although it is useful as far as it goes, is too general to be decisive in situations of serious complexity. Second, as Aquinas himself observed, natural law is too easily accommodated to one's

18. John Calvin, *Institutes of the Christian Religion*, ed. John T. McNeill, trans. Ford Lewis Battles (Philadelphia: Westminster, 1960), 2.2.13, 4.20.16.

19. d'Entrèves, *Natural Law*, 52.

20. Hughes, "Natural Law," 413.

own interest at the expense of others; the epistemological problems are compounded by unregenerate hardness of heart.[21]

We are drawn finally to the Scriptures for our knowledge of justice. There we find both what is due human beings and why: God created us in his image and calls us to serve him. Justice means that every human being should be treated according to what it means to be human, and what it means to be human is to be one who bears the image of God and who has a divine calling to fulfill. In the biblical frame of reference a person's relation to God is always paramount, and freedom is preeminently being set at liberty to serve God (see, e.g., Luke 1:74–75). The first principle of justice is to maximize this liberty as something that is due human beings by divine right.

Although *mišpāṭ* is not a precise technical term, in general it is the term that is used to refer to God-given rules that embody proper relationships between persons and thus provides an index to the fundamental principles of justice in biblical ethics. The noun *mišpāṭ* makes its first appearance in the Lord's revelation to Abraham of the impending destruction of Sodom.

> The LORD said, "Shall I hide from Abraham what I am about to do? Abraham will surely become a great and powerful nation, and all nations of the earth will be blessed through him. For I have chosen him, so that he will direct his children and his household after him to keep the way of the LORD by doing what is right *(ṣĕdāqâ)* and just *(mišpāṭ)*, so that the LORD will bring about for Abraham what he has promised him." [Gen. 18:17–19]

Abraham proves to be a quick study; the second instance of *mišpāṭ* follows immediately as the key element of Abraham's remarkable intercession for the city of Sodom.

> Then Abraham approached [the Lord] and said: "Will you sweep away the righteous with the wicked? What if there are fifty righteous people in the city? Will you really sweep it away and not spare the place for the sake of the fifty righteous people in it? Far be it from you to do such a thing—to kill the righteous with the wicked, treating the righteous and the wicked alike. Far be it from you! Will not the Judge of all the earth do right *(mišpāṭ)*?" [Gen. 18:23–25)]

Discrimination between the righteous and the wicked is the first lesson of justice. If the Judge of all the earth cannot be counted on to do justice in this basic sense, the idea of a moral universe dissolves into chaos. Rather than treat the righteous and the wicked alike by destroying them both together, the Lord

---

21. Thomas Aquinas: "Now there had to be given a precept about the love of God and one's neighbour, because on this point the natural law was obscured as a result of sin; but not about the love of oneself, because on this point the natural law still prevailed." *The Old Law (1a2ae. 98–105)*, vol. 29 in *Summa Theologicae*, trans. David Bourke and Arthur Littledale (New York: McGraw-Hill, 1969), 1a2ae. 100, 5.

is prepared to spare even Sodom for the sake of a righteous remnant as few as ten. This does not mean, of course, that the wicked go unpunished forever; to note Peter's observation on the destruction of Sodom and Gomorrah (and also the flood), "the Lord knows how to rescue the godly from trial, and to keep the unrighteous under punishment until the day of judgment" (2 Pet. 2:9 NRSV).

Justice requires moral discrimination between the guilty and the innocent that each may be rendered forensically his or her due. "Aquitting the guilty and condemning the innocent—the LORD detests them both" (Prov. 17:15). A society that violates this basic principle sows the seeds of its own destruction, as the prophet Isaiah warned (Isa. 5:20–24):

> Woe to those who call evil good and good evil . . .
> who acquit the guilty for a bribe,
>   but deny justice to the innocent. . . .
> their roots will decay
>   and their flowers blow away like dust;
> for they have rejected the law of the LORD Almighty
> and spurned the word of the Holy One of Israel.

Because the Lord may be relied upon to vindicate the innocent over against the guilty, he is frequently called upon in Scripture for judgment, knowing that it will be discriminating and just. Thus David's eloquent speech to King Saul—who is unjustly pursuing him with murderous intent—concludes with the appeal: "May the LORD be our judge and decide between us. May he consider my cause and uphold it; may he vindicate me by delivering me from your hand" (1 Sam. 24:15). Solomon's prayer of dedication includes this petition for justice: "If someone sins against a neighbor and is given an oath to swear, and comes and swears before your altar in this house, then hear in heaven, and act, and judge your servants, condemning the guilty by bringing their conduct on their own head, and vindicating the righteous by rewarding them according to their righteousness" (1 Kings 8:31–32 NRSV).

God calls human judges to follow his example in aquitting the innocent and condemning the guilty. The guilty are liable to such punishment as they deserve, but they are not to be degraded by going beyond what justice requires (Deut. 25:1–3). That justice may be impartially administered, the Bible insists upon setting aside all forms of discrimination that tend to cloud moral judgment. Two texts, profound in their implications, may be cited by way of example: "You shall not render an unjust judgment; you shall not be partial to the poor or defer to the great: with justice you shall judge your neighbor" (Lev. 19:15 NRSV); "You must not be partial in judging: hear out the small and the great alike; you shall not be intimidated by anyone, for the judgment is God's" (Deut. 1:17 NRSV).

Judges must be blind to status for the sake of seeing the truth and doing justice; it must be close-handed to bribes so as to be even-handed in judgment.

> You shall appoint judges and officials throughout your tribes, in all your towns that the LORD your God is giving you, and they shall render just decisions for the people. You must not distort justice; you must not show partiality; and you must not accept bribes, for a bribe blinds the eyes of the wise and subverts the cause of those who are in the right. Justice, and only justice (Hebrew, *ṣedeq, ṣedeq*), you shall pursue, so that you may live and occupy the land that the Lord your God is giving you. [Deut. 16:18–20 NRSV]

Justice is impartial in discriminating between the innocent and the guilty, but the reality of the world is such that it must always be on its guard to preserve and protect the rights of the socially weak, specifically the poor, aliens, orphans, and widows.[22] Protective justice is mandated in the law of Moses (Exod. 23:6; Deut. 24:17; 27:19) and preached by the great writing prophets of Israel, as in Isaiah's profound call to repentance:

> [C]ease to do evil,
>   learn to do good;
> seek justice (*mišpāṭ*),
>   rescue the oppressed,
> defend the orphan,
>   plead for the widow. [Isa. 1:17 NRSV]

Jeremiah also was given this message for the king and people of Judah:

> Thus says the LORD: Act with justice and righteousness, and deliver from the hand of the oppressor anyone who has been robbed. And do no wrong or violence to the alien, the orphan, and the widow, or shed innocent blood in this place. [Jer. 22:3 NRSV]

Justice not only rectifies injustice by deciding cases (remedial justice); it has a structural dimension as well.

> Woe to those who make unjust laws,
>   to those who issue oppressive decrees,

---

22. Cf. James Barr: "[T]he cases which refer to the *mišpāṭ* of the poor, the orphan, the *ger* or dependent foreigner (e.g., Exod. 23:6; Deut. 24:17) seem clearly to refer to rights which these persons, because of their social weakness, will be unable to defend by their own action: their defense depends, therefore, on one side on God's action to protect them, on the other side on his prohibition against any taking advantage of the weakness of these persons." James Barr, "Ancient Biblical Laws and Modern Human Rights," in *Justice and the Holy: Essays in Honor of Walter Harrelson*, ed. Douglas A. Knight and Peter J. Paris (Atlanta: Scholars, 1989), 26.

> to deprive the poor of their rights
>   and withhold justice from the oppressed of my people,
> making widows their prey
>   and robbing the fatherless. [Isa. 10:1–2]

A just society seeks to provide structural guarantees of basic human rights. This will include not only remedial justice, the function of the judicial system, but also distributive justice, so that the benefits and burdens are fair. As Nicholas Wolterstorff puts it, "a person has a right to some good if (1) he or she has a *morally legitimate claim* that (2) the *actual enjoyment* of that good be (3) *socially guaranteed* against *ordinary, serious, and remediable threats.*"[23]

Wolterstorff suggests that human rights fall under a threefold classification: freedom rights (worship, speech, assembly, movement); protection rights (life, marriage, property, name); sustenance rights (food, clothing, shelter, health care). The first five commandments of the Decalogue establish the basic freedom rights: to worship and serve God in one's calling (1–4) and to exercise authority in God-given structures (5); the last five are concerned with protection and sustenance rights: life (6), sexual fidelity (7), property (8), reputation (9), nonaggression (10).

Mercy

Love is embodied in the practice of justice, but this is not its full or most characteristic manifestation. "Justice presupposes people pressing claims and justifying them by rules or standards."[24] Love does this and more. Rendering persons their due, securing and protecting their rights, is certainly one form of love. But to think of love in terms of obligations that can be specified with greater or lesser precision yields a minimalist ethic that takes no responsibility for going beyond the strict requirements of justice. Such a truncated ethic falls far short of what God is calling us to be and to do in response to his love.

On two occasions in the Gospel narrative Jesus faults the legalists of his day for not incorporating into their hermeneutic the principle of Hosea 6:6, "I desire mercy, not sacrifice" (Matt. 9:13; 12:6). The word in Hosea for "mercy" (translated *eleos* in Greek) is *ḥesed*, one of the key words in the Old Testament for its theological significance. In the King James Version *ḥesed* is predominantly rendered "mercy" (149 times), followed by "kindness" (38), "loving-kindness" (30), and "goodness" (12). This represents a consistent semantic domain of gracious or favorable disposition as manifest in action. In contrast to *mišpāṭ*, which may be demanded as a matter of right, *ḥesed* in all its forms (mercy, kindness, goodness) is free and often amazing.

---

23. Nicholas Wolterstorff, *Until Justice and Peace Embrace* (Grand Rapids: Eerdmans, 1983), 82.
24. Stanley I. Benn, "Justice," in *Encyclopedia of Philosophy*, ed. Paul Edwards, 8 vols. (New York: Macmillan, 1967), 4:298.

The King James Version follows the lead of the Septuagint in understanding the semantic domain of *ḥesed* as that of kindness. As C. H. Dodd points out:

Ḥesed is a characteristically Hebraic term for which we have no complete English equivalent. It is used of "kindness of men towards men, in doing favours or benefits" (B.D.B.). It is an attribute of God in relation to men, shown in delivering them from trouble, in forgiving their sin, in keeping covenant with them (and so closely allied with *'emet*). In this sense its natural translation is *eleos [mercy, compassion], which along with eleēmosynē* [mercy, almsgiving], *eleēmēn* [merciful], *poluleos* [rich in mercy] is its normal rendering in the LXX, whether it is used of God or of man.[25]

Equally important is Dodd's observation on the relation between *ḥesed* and *charis* (grace): "In the N.T. period *charis* would be felt to have a close relation with *ḥesed*, and it is evident that the associations of that word have had influence in moulding the characteristic New Testament use of *charis*, which is different from any ordinary Greek use."[26] This means that so far as the New Testament is concerned, *eleos* (mercy) and *charis* (grace) partially overlap in representing the meaning of *ḥesed*. Just how close the relationship is may be observed from Paul's usage in Ephesians 2:4–7. After making the point that before God intervened in our lives "we were by nature children of wrath, like everyone else," Paul describes what has happened to believers as follows.

But God, who is rich in mercy (*eleos*) out of the great love with which he loved us even when we were dead through our trespasses, made us alive together with Christ—by grace (*charis*) you have been saved—and raised us up with him and seated us with him in the heavenly places in Christ Jesus, so that in the ages to come he might show the immeasurable riches of his grace in kindness towards us in Christ Jesus. [NRSV]

The attribute of being "rich in mercy" finds its incomparable expression in God's love for sinners whom he saves by his grace—his freely bestowed favor on those who deserve only his wrath. The ages to come will show the incalculable riches of God's "grace in kindness" in extending mercy to the dead and condemned in trespasses and sin. The phrase "rich in mercy" is Old Testament; it represents *rab-ḥesed* in Exodus 34:6 and parallels.[27] The passage is thus very helpful to our understanding of *ḥesed*; it is "grace in kindness" toward sinners—in a word, "mercy."

25. C. H. Dodd, *The Bible and the Greeks* (London: Hodder, 1935), 59–60.
26. Ibid., 61–62.
27. In LXX *poluleos* translates *rab-ḥesed* in Exod. 34:6; Num. 14:18; Neh. 9:17; Ps. 85 (86 [Heb.]):15; 102 (103):8, and *gĕdāl-ḥesed* in Ps. 144 (145):8. Paul's *plousios en eleei* is equivalent but perhaps slightly more literal.

It would not be necessary to dwell on the linguistic correctness of the traditional rendering of *ḥesed* as lovingkindness or mercy were it not for the novel interpretation introduced by Nelson Glueck in 1927, now a commonplace of biblical studies. The following definition is typical: "*ḥesed* means proper covenant behavior, the solidarity which the partners in the covenant owe one another."[28] Similarly, Harry M. Orlinsky in a recent publication defends the "forensic essence" of *ḥesed*, giving this account of the revised understanding of the term:

> [S]cholarship, especially since Nelson Glueck's dissertation on this word appeared, has come to recognize in the term the basic element of 'loyalty, faithfulness, devotion' that derives from a legally recognized, contractual relationship, one that is inherent in the relationship between the head of a household and its members and among these members, between a master and a slave, between God and Israel.[29]

"To appreciate the forensic character of *ḥesed*," Orlinsky says, "one has but to note how it is used in association with such other legal terms as *mišpāṭ* (e.g., Mic. 6:8)." Other scholars point to the close association of *ḥesed* with *ʾĕmet* and proceed to merge *ḥesed* into faithfulness. Definition by (selective) "association" as a result deprives *ḥesed* of its distinct linguistic contribution and forces upon it the combined meanings of *mišpāṭ* and *ʾĕmûnâ* to get "stipulated covenant loyalty."[30] This takes *ḥesed* out of the semantic domain of grace, kindness, and mercy and relocates it in the domain field of law, justice, and obligation. It is hard to imagine a more radical linguistic shift or one with more profound theological implications. The question is: Does the linguistic data warrant reading *ḥesed* as covenant loyalty rather than free mercy? Is the quality of *ḥesed* after all strained?

Glueck's view of *ḥesed* was disseminated in English by N. H. Snaith in *The Distinctive Ideas of the Old Testament* (1944) and was eventually given the status of a lexicon entry by Koehler and Baumgartner. It has not passed, however, without scholarly challenge from an independent and critical minority, most recently by Francis I. Andersen, professor of studies in religion, University of Queensland.[31]

28. Hans-Helmut Esser, "Mercy, Compassion," in *New International Dictionary of New Testament Theology*, ed. Colin Brown, 3 vols. (Grand Rapids: Zondervan, 1976), 2:594.

29. Harry M. Orlinsky, "The Forensic Character of the Hebrew Bible," in *Justice and the Holy: Essays in Honor of Walter Harrelson*, ed. by Douglas A. Knight and Peter J. Paris (Atlanta: Scholars, 1989), 95–96.

30. An important exception is the article on *ʾĕmet* in *Theological Dictionary of the Old Testament*, ed. G. J. Botterweck and H. Ringren, trans. John T. Willis (Grand Rapids: Eerdmans, 1974–), 1:309–16. "Frequently God's *ʾemeth* is connected with his *chesedh*. It might be asked whether *ʾemeth* is only a characteristic of *chesedh*, or whether it stands independently of it. Parallelism and plural form of the verbs used with the two words as subject favor the idea of distinct attributes manifest in 'active kindness' and 'protective faithfulness'" (p. 314).

31. Francis I. Andersen, "Yahweh, The Kind and Sensitive God," in *God Who Is Rich in Mercy*, ed. Peter T. O'Brien and David G. Peterson (Homebush West NSW, Australia: Lancer-Anzea, 1986), 41–88. Andersen cites supporting articles by T. F. Torrance, "The Doctrine of Grace in the Old Testament," *Scottish Journal of Theology* 1 (1948): 55–56, and H. J. Stoebe, "*Die Bedeutung des Wortes Häsäd im Alten Tes-*

Andersen examines in context every Old Testament text in which *ḥesed* appears, showing convincingly that "the conjunction of *ḥesed* with grace and compassion [is] primal and constant."[32] He presents in evidence against the contrary thesis

> numerous instances in which (i) *ḥesed* denotes behaviour that copes with an emergency for which custom and contract provide no norms (*ḥesed* is not prescribed); (ii) *ḥesed* is an expression of love and generosity which a person need not have been expected to do (*ḥesed* is not obligatory); (iii) *ḥesed* behaviour is surprising, ingenious (the stories are told, and they are exciting, precisely because they are so unusual); (iv) the act of *ḥesed* is supremely meritorious, but the performer could not have been blamed for its omission; (v) *ḥesed* issues *in* covenant, rather than *from* covenant.[33]

The last point is particularly significant. It is God's mercy and grace—his *ḥesed*—that move him to enter into covenant with his chosen people in order to redeem them to himself. The covenant is the expression of God's everlasting love, freely bestowing *ḥesed* rather than turning it into a legal requirement that God is bound to perform. As the faithful God (*ʾēl ʾĕmûnâ*), the Lord promises to maintain the covenant and mercy he has graciously and sovereignly bestowed upon his people (Deut. 7:9). But note: "The obligation to keep a promise to do *ḥesed* does not mean that the *ḥesed* itself was obligatory."[34] "The Lord maintains *ḥesed* . . . on the ground of his own promise. . . . It is essentially an obligation to himself. It arises from his own nature and being."[35]

This is precisely the force of the description of the Lord as *ʾēl ʾĕmûnâ*: the faithful God, the God who makes and keeps his commitments, particularly his promise of mercy to his covenant people. Linguistically the problem with the modern view is that it assigns the meaning of *ʾēl ʾĕmûnâ* (fidelity) to *ḥesed* (mercy); the result is the loss of the distinctive contribution of both terms.

The supreme Old Testament revelation of the Lord as a God of *ḥesed* is given by the Lord himself in the definitive proclamation of his name (his nature and character) to Moses in Exodus 34:6–7. The following seeks to represent the Hebrew as closely as possible, leaving untranslated for the moment the two key nouns.

---

tament," *Vetus Testamentum* 2 (1952): 244–54. See also R. Laird Harris, "*ḥesed*," in *Theological Wordbook of the Old Testament*, ed. R. Laird Harris et al., 2 vols. (Chicago: Moody, 1980), 1: 305–7; and Katherine Doob Sakenfeld, *The Meaning of Ḥesed in the Hebrew Bible* (Missoula, Mont.: Scholars, 1978). Additional critical references may be found in Harris.

32. Andersen, "Yahweh," 42.

33. Ibid., 44. Andersen goes on to add, "(vi) there are even cases of *ḥesed* which arise from a conflict of love with loyalty, and involve the performer in acts of treachery or crime."

34. Ibid., 81.

35. Ibid., 50.

The LORD, the LORD,
God compassionate and gracious,
    slow to anger and rich in *ḥesed* and *ʾĕmet*,[36]
    maintaining *ḥesed* for thousands [of generations],
    bearing [taking away] iniquity, transgression, and sin;
But by no means will he clear [the guilty],
    visiting the iniquity of parents upon children,
    and upon children's children,
    upon third and upon fourth [generations].

This crucial text virtually provides the definition of *ḥesed* as a divine attribute. The revelation is given against the dark background of Israel's rapid apostasy (at Sinai!) and worship of the golden calf. Following his successful intercession for the people, Moses requests that the Lord show him his glory. In response the Lord says to Moses, "I will cause all my goodness to pass in front of you, and I will proclaim my name, the LORD, in your presence. I will have mercy [*ḥānan*, "show favor, be gracious"; cf. NRSV] on whom I will have mercy, and I will have compassion (*rāḥam*) on whom I will have compassion" (Exod. 33:19). God is free and sovereign in the bestowal of his grace; Israel survives because God so wills, not because he is obliged to show mercy to covenant-breakers. If anything he is obligated to carry out the stipulated punishment for apostates and rebels.

The revelation God proceeds to give Moses of the significance of his covenant name (YHWH) takes up the preannounced theme of sovereign grace. Echoing the verbs used in Exodus 33:19, the Lord proclaims himself to be *ʾēl-raḥûm wĕḥannûn*, the compassionate and gracious God. The next lines expand on God's grace and compassion, twice using the term *ḥesed*. This indicates that *ḥesed* belongs to the same semantic domain as *ḥannûm* (grace) and *raḥûm* (compassion), namely, that of kind or favorable disposition and action. The distinctive quality of the divine *ḥesed*, and that which warrants its normal translation as "mercy," is expressed in the climactic defining clause: "bearing [taking away] iniquity, transgression, and sin."

It is difficult to decide between "bearing" and "taking away" as the meaning of the final participle. The verb *nasa* is capable of either sense, and the ambiguity if not deliberate is at least felicitous in light of the full teaching of Scripture that the Lord takes away sins by bearing them himself (cf. Isa. 53:4–6, 12). Of course, this only becomes progressively clear as the history of redemption unfolds. The text as it stands contains a tension to the point

---

36. LXX has *makrothumos kai polueleos*, "longsuffering and rich in mercy." This euphonious phrase recurs in all the instances where Exod. 34:6 is repeated in the Old Testament.

of apparent contradiction. On the one hand, the Lord forgives all manner of sin; on the other hand, the Lord will never declare the guilty innocent. It will take the incarnation and crucifixion of the Lord of glory to show how God can justify the ungodly and still remain just. So great is God's mercy that he absorbs his own wrath, bears himself the punishment that sinners deserve.

Exodus 34:6–7 is cited several times in the Old Testament, though completely (mercy *and* judgment) only in Numbers 14:18.[37] Usually, as is theologically appropriate, it is the revelation of God's mercy that is recalled (Neh. 9:17; Ps. 86:15; 145:8; Joel 2:13), but once (Nahum 1:3) his judgment appears without mercy lest sinners think that forgiveness follows necessarily from the divine nature and begin to claim it as a matter of equal rights.[38] Mercy is not mercy if not free.

The New Testament opens with Mary, the mother of Jesus, and Zechariah, the father of John the Baptist, offering psalms of praise for God's mercy that is now to be fully revealed with the coming of Christ (Luke 1:54–55, 77–78).[39] The remembrance of mercy is not only for Israel; the Abrahamic covenant promised blessing to all nations. Of this the apostle Paul was intensely aware: "For I tell you that Christ has become a servant of the Jews on behalf of God's truth, to confirm the promises made to the patriarchs so that the Gentiles may glorify God for his mercy" (Rom. 15:8–9; cf. 11:30–32). How great is our indebtedness to God's mercy for salvation Paul shows in this telling paragraph:

> At one time we too were foolish, disobedient, deceived and enslaved by all kinds of passions and pleasures. We lived in malice and envy, being hated and hating one another. But when the kindness and love of God our Savior appeared, he saved us, not because of righteous things we had done, but because of his mercy. He saved us through the washing of rebirth and renewal of the Holy Spirit, whom he poured out on us generously through Jesus Christ our Savior, so that, having been justified by his grace, we might become heirs having the hope of eternal life. This is a trustworthy saying. And I want you to stress these things, so that those who have trusted in God may be careful to devote themselves to doing what is good. These things are excellent and profitable for everyone. [Titus 3:3–8]

37. Similar in presenting God as both merciful and just are Exod. 20:5–6 (= Deut. 5:9–10) and Deut. 7:9–10.

38. Anticipated by the apostle Paul: "What then shall we say? Is God unjust? Not at all! For he says to Moses, 'I will have mercy on whom I have mercy, and I will have compassion on whom I have compassion'" (Rom. 9:14–15).

39. Cf. John 1:14, where *plērēs charitos kai alētheias* (full of grace and truth) is the Johannine equivalent of *rab-ḥesed wĕʾĕmet*. (The LXX translation of this phrase is *polueleos kai alēthinos.*)

The full revelation of God's mercy brings with it the full responsibility to practice mercy, to glorify God by living lives that reflect his mercy. The note is sounded in the fifth Beatitude—"Blessed are the merciful, for they will be shown mercy" (Matt. 5:7)—and reverberates in the fifth petition of the Lord's prayer—"Forgive us our debts, as we forgive our debtors" (Matt. 6:12 KJV). It forms the climax of Jesus' exposition of love in the Sermon on the Plain: "Be merciful, just as your Father is merciful" (Luke 6:36).[40] The parable of the good Samaritan drives the point home; it concludes with a brief dialogue as a coda.

> "Which of these three do you think was a neighbor to the man who fell into the hands of robbers?"
> "The one who had mercy on him."
> "Go and do likewise." [Luke 10:36–37]

In one of the great passages of English literature, Portia (dressed like a doctor of laws), having established that Shylock is legally due his pound of flesh, suggests that he must then be merciful. To which Shylock responds, "On what compulsion must I? tell me that." Portia's reply captures the essence of the biblical practice of mercy.

> The quality of mercy is not strain'd;
> It droppeth as the gentle rain from heaven
> Upon the place beneath: it is twice bless'd;
> It blesseth him that gives and him that takes . . .
> It is an attribute to God himself;
> And earthly power doth then show likest God's
> When mercy seasons justice. Therefore . . .
> Though justice be thy plea consider this—
> That in the course of justice none of us
> Should see salvation: we do pray for mercy;
> And that same prayer doth teach us all to render the deeds
>   of mercy.[41]

The practice of mercy is constrained by the love of Christ. Those who have experienced the triumph of God's grace are called to like patterns of conduct: "Speak and act as those who are going to be judged by the law that gives freedom, because judgment without mercy will be shown to anyone who has not been merciful. Mercy triumphs over judgment!" (James 2:13).

---

40. Both the NIV and the NRSV translate *oiktirmōn* "merciful" here. The same word occurs at 2 Cor. 1:3, "Father of *mercies*" (NRSV), "Father of *compassion*" (NIV).
    41. William Shakespeare, *Merchant of Venice*, act 4, scene 1.

Faithfulness

In the great proclamation of his name to Moses the Lord revealed himself as ʾēl-raḥûm wĕhannûn, the compassionate and gracious God. Moses knew him also as ʾēl-ʾĕmûnâ, the faithful God, the God who keeps his covenant and his mercy with his chosen people who by his grace love and obey him (Deut. 7:6–10). Because of its crucial significance in the history of redemption, Moses makes the faithfulness of God the theme of his farewell song to the whole assembly of Israel.

> I will proclaim the name of the LORD.
>   O praise the greatness of our God!
> He is the Rock, his works are perfect,
>   and all his ways are just.
> A faithful God (ēl-ʾĕmûnâ) who does no wrong,
>   upright and just is he. [Deut. 32:3–4]

The metaphor of a rock is singularly appropriate. "A rock is stable and unmoving; therefore, it reminds us of the faithful God. Because He is faithful, He is upright and without flaw; therefore, He is reliable."[42] Systematic theology traditionally includes a discussion of immutability as one of the attributes of God. This is best understood as referring to God's absolute consistency of character.[43] If God were not the unchanging God, none of his moral attributes could be affirmed. What would it mean to say that God is just—some of the time, or that he is merciful to those who trust him—now and then.

God's stability of character is particularly manifest in his revelation as the faithful God—the God who makes and keeps his commitments. An instructive example is the Davidic covenant, in which the Lord promises that he will never take his ḥesed from David's offspring as he did from Saul (2 Sam. 7:15). David responds to the divine commitment thus: "O Sovereign LORD, you are God! Your words are trustworthy (ʾemeth), and you have promised these good things to your servant" (2 Sam. 7:28). These promises become known as "the sure mercies of David" that God invites all peoples and nations to embrace (Isa. 55:3–4). They find their ultimate fulfillment in Jesus, the Messiah, "the Root and Offspring of David and the bright Morning Star" (Rev. 22:16). "As surely as God is faithful, our word to you has not been 'Yes and No.' . . . For in him [the Son of God, Jesus Christ] every one of God's promises is a 'Yes.'" (2 Cor. 1:18, 20 NRSV).

42. John W. Sanderson, *Mirrors of His Glory: Images of God from Scripture* (Phillipsburg, N.J.: Presbyterian and Reformed, 1991), 52.

43. Cf. James Oliver Buswell, Jr., *A Systematic Theology of the Christian Religion*, 2 vols. (Grand Rapids: Zondervan, 1962), 1:53.

The Lord's faithfulness is the ground of Jeremiah's hope in the midst of judgment. In a passage that provides the theme for one of the most popular hymns in the English language, Jeremiah pens these words in praise of the Hope of Israel:

> Yet this I call to mind
> and therefore I have hope:
> Because of the Lord's great mercy we are not consumed,
> for his compassions never fail.
> They are new every morning;
> great is your faithfulness (ʾĕmûnâ). [Lam. 3:21–23]

In the New Testament the assertion that God is faithful appears regularly in connection with the perseverance of the saints. Thus believers are assured that "[God] will also strengthen you to the end, so that you may be blameless on the day of our Lord Jesus Christ. God is faithful; by him you were called into the fellowship of his Son, Jesus Christ, our Lord" (1 Cor. 1:8–9 NRSV). Union with Christ does not mean that believers will be free from temptation, but they do have this promise: "God is faithful; he will not let you be tempted beyond what you can bear" (1 Cor. 10:13). When believers yield to temptation, this is not the end of the relationship; "If we confess our sins, he is faithful and just and will forgive us our sins and purify us from all unrighteousness" (1 John 1:9). Paul's grounds his famous "sanctification" benediction in the divine faithfulness: "May God himself, the God of peace, sanctify you through and through. May your whole spirit, soul and body be kept blameless at the coming of our Lord Jesus Christ. The one who calls you is faithful and he will do it" (1 Thess 5:23–24).

Such reassurance, so far from condoning laxness in the Christian life, is rather a powerful motivation. The righteous live by trust in the faithful God (Hab. 2:4). Trust in God's faithfulness produces a corresponding quality of life. Believers are aptly described as "children of trust" (benai ʾĕmûnâ), persons characterized by faith and faithfulness, between which there is a close moral relationship: those whose entire salvation depends on the faithfulness of God are disposed to practice the same in their own relationships and responsibilities.[44]

44. Several recent works put fidelity in the forefront of ethical discussion: Katherine Doob Sakenfeld, *Faithfulness in Action: Loyalty in Biblical Perspective* (Philadelphia: Fortress, 1985); Margaret A. Farley, *Personal Commitments: Beginning, Keeping, Changing* (San Francisco: Harper, 1986); William E. Diehl, *In Search of Faithfulness: Lessons from the Christian Community* (Philadelphia: Fortress, 1987); Louis B. Smedes, *Caring and Commitment: Learning to Live the Love We Promise* (San Francisco: Harper, 1988); Gilbert C. Meilaender, *Faith and Faithfulness: Basic Themes in Christian Ethics* (Notre Dame, Ind.: University of Notre Dame Press, forthcoming). See also the seminal work by Gabriel Marcel, *Creative Fidelity*, trans. Robert Rosthal (New York: Noonday, 1964).

Within Scripture faithfulness is manifest in a variety of ways, from honesty in financial matters to fidelity in judicial office. "They did not require an accounting from those to whom they gave the money to pay the workers, because they acted with complete honesty" (2 Kings 12:15; Heb. *beʾĕmûnâ*).

> Jehoshaphat appointed some of the Levites, priests and heads of Israelite families to administer the law of the LORD and to settle disputes. And they lived in Jerusalem. He gave them these orders: "You must serve faithfully and wholeheartedly in the fear of the LORD. In every case that comes before you from your fellow countrymen who live in the cities . . . you are to warn them not to sin against the LORD. [2 Chron. 19:8–10; cf. Exod. 18:21]

"Think of us in this way, as servants of Christ and stewards of God's mysteries. Moreover, it is required of stewards that they be found trustworthy" (1 Cor. 4:1–2 NRSV). In the broadest sense, life itself is a trust from God, to be lived at last to hear his "Well done, good and faithful servant" and to enter into the joy of the Lord (Matt. 25:21, 23).

The Cardinal Personal Virtues

For love to be effective in the interpersonal practices of justice, mercy, and faithfulness, certain personal virtues are required, especially discernment, courage, self-discipline, and (in the proper biblical sense) humility. The importance of such personal characteristics for the moral life has long been recognized in the doctrine of the "cardinal virtues," traditionally justice, prudence, fortitude, and temperance.[45] Although the names by which they are known to us have come down through their discussion in Latin (*iustitia, prudentia, fortitudo,* and *temperantia*), the virtues first appeared in classical Greek philosophy as *dikaiosunē* (righteousness), *phronēsis* (understanding), *andreia* (courage), and *sōphrosunē* (self-control), thus providing a link with the ethical vocabulary of the Greek New Testament.

Cicero, writing in Latin in the first century B.C., represents the culmination of classical tradition of the cardinal virtues.[46] He follows the fourfold division of moral goodness, but in his scheme prudence (viewed epistemologically) comes first, followed by honor, fortitude, and temperance. Of particular interest is the second division, which bears the Latin name *honestum* ("honor" is closer in English than "honesty" but still inexact).[47] This virtue, Cicero says, is the most extensive in its application, being "the principle by which society

45. For a useful discussion see John Ferguson, "The Cardinal Virtues," in *Moral Values in the Ancient World* (London: Methuen, 1958), 24–52.

46. See John Casey, *Pagan Virtue: An Essay in Ethics* (Oxford: Clarendon, 1990). The term *cardinalis* was introduced by Saint Ambrose in the fourth century; it is used anachronistically with reference to the classical tradition.

47. According to one of Cicero's translators, "*honestum* is used to translate the Greek *kalon,* and denotes 'honour' in a broad sense; 'moral beauty' might be a more exact rendering." Cicero, *De Inventione,* trans. H. M. Hubbell (Cambridge: Harvard University Press, 1949), 326.

and what we may call its 'common bonds' are maintained."[48] He expands on
the content of *honestum* as follows:

> Of this again there are two divisions—justice (*iustitia*), in which is the crown-
> ing glory of the virtues and on the basis of which men are called 'good men';
> and, close akin to justice, charity (*beneficentia*), which may also be called kind-
> ness (*benignitatem*) or generosity (*liberalitatem*).[49]

Cicero's *honestum* is the equivalent of *dikaiosunē* in the broad sense of *righteousness*; it includes justice, but like the Hebrew *ṣĕdāqâ* it is used comprehen-
sively for all forms of morally right conduct—beneficence as well as justice.
This development was promising, but as Christian authors took over the tradition of the cardinal virtues, the narrow sense of justice (to each what is due)
prevailed over the broad sense of honorableness or righteousness. Obviously a
list of cardinal virtues that omits love is unsatisfactory on Christian premises.
Augustine's solution was to turn them all into love.

> Temperance is love preserving itself whole and unblemished for God, fortitude
> is love enduring all things willingly for the sake of God, justice is love serving
> God alone and, therefore, ruling well those things subject to man, and pru-
> dence is love discriminating rightly between those things which aid it in reach-
> ing God and those things which might hinder it.[50]

The more enduring Christian reconstruction was to add to the traditional
four cardinal virtues the distinctively Christian theological virtues of faith,
hope, and love. This scheme was worked out in great detail by Thomas
Aquinas, only to be abandoned by the Reformers and most Protestant theologians. An exception is William Ames, who found a biblical basis for the
scheme in 2 Peter 1:5–6.

> *Add to faith virtue* (i.e., justice or a universal rightness), *to virtue knowledge* (or
> prudence rightly directing all your ways), *to prudence continence* (the temper-
> ance by which you can resist the allurement of all pleasures which attract and
> draw men from the right way), *to continence patience* (fortitude with which you
> may outlast any hardship for righteousness' sake).[51]

Whatever the merits of this particular bit of exegesis, Ames was correct
in recognizing that prudence, fortitude, and temperance are personal virtues
without which the Christian moral life is ineffective. The inherent viability
of the doctrine of the cardinal virtues no doubt accounts for its perennial

---

48. Cicero, *De Officiis*, 1.7.20.
49. Ibid.
50. Augustine, *On the Morals of the Catholic Church*, trans. R. Stothert, in *Basic Writings of Saint
Augustine*, ed. Whitney J. Oates, 2 vols. (New York: Random, 1948), 1:331–32.
51. William Ames, *Conscience with the Power and Cases Thereof*, 3.15 (1639; reprint, Norwood, N.J.:
Johnson, 1975).

interest.[52] With the addition of humility to prudence, fortitude, and temperance (justice being considered as a part of interpersonal or social ethics), the presentation of the cardinal virtues provides a remarkably comprehensive approach to biblical personal ethics.[53]

Prudence (Practical Wisdom)

> If any of you lacks wisdom, he should ask God, who gives generously to all without finding fault, and it will be given to him.

> —James 1:5

The virtue of prudence is practical wisdom or moral discernment, not caution as the English term suggests. The Hebrew word is *hokmah*, "the skill or ability to make wise choices and to live in accordance with the moral norms of the covenant community."[54] Prudence is especially the wisdom to choose the best means to a good end, the wisdom not only to do the right thing but to do the right thing well, to excel in moral practice. The paradigm of prudence in the Gospels is the faithful and wise servant or steward who by prudent choices makes effective use of the divine trust (Matt. 24:45; Luke 12:42). So the apostle Paul urges believers, "Be very careful, then, how you live—not as unwise but as wise, making the most of every opportunity, because the days are evil" (Eph. 5:15–16).

Wisdom consists in understanding and living according to the Lord's will (Eph. 5:17), and God promises to give wisdom to those who know their lack and who really want to grow in moral discernment. But the gift of wisdom is not a mechanism that works automatically without engagement on our part and growth in grace. The key text is Hebrews 5:13–14: "All those who live on a diet of milk are inexperienced in the teaching of righteousness, for they are infants; but solid food is for adults, for those who have their senses trained by practice to discern both good and evil."[55]

The virtue of prudence is developed through exercise. As Richard Mouw points out, "character-formation requires the ability to place ourselves in

52. Josef Pieper, *The Four Cardinal Virtues* (Notre Dame, Ind.: University of Notre Dame Press, 1966); Peter Geach, *The Virtues* (Cambridge: Cambridge University Press, 1977); James D. Wallace, *Virtues and Vices* (Ithaca, N.Y.: Cornell University Press, 1978).

53. Moral theology traditionally follows Thomas Aquinas in subsuming humility under temperance. More recently its distinctiveness as a virtue is preserved by separate treatment. See Bernard Häring, "Humility as Christian 'Cardinal Virtue,'" in *The Law of Christ: Moral Theology for Priests and Laity*, trans. Edwin G. Kaiser (Westminster, Md.: Newman, 1966), 3:56–68.

54. Schubert Spero, *Morality, Halakha, and the Jewish Tradition* (New York: KTAV, 1983), 40. *Hokmâ* is the key word in the Book of Proverbs. In the vocabulary of the New Testament, "*s[ophia]* is *wisdom* primary and absolute; in distinction from which *ph[ronēsis]* is practical, *synesis* critical, both being applications of *s[ophia]* in detail." G. Abbott-Smith, *A Manual Greek Lexicon of the New Testament*, 3d ed. (Edinburgh: T. & T. Clark, 1937), 412.

55. Translation based in part on suggestions by Max Zerwick and Mary Grosvenor, *A Grammatical Analysis of the Greek New Testament*, rev. ed. (Rome: Biblical Institute, 1981), 663–64.

those settings where the appropriate virtues can begin to 'take' in our lives."[56]
There is no short-cut to moral discernment; it is taught by the Spirit in the
actual situations of life.[57]

Fortitude

> Keep alert, stand firm in your faith, be courageous, be strong. Let all that
> you do be done in love.
>
> —1 Corinthians 16:13–14 [NRSV]

Fortitude refers to strength of character manifest in conviction, courage, and perseverance in pursuit of what is right and good. It involves
firmness and boldness, endurance of hardship, and the willingness to face
opposition and to suffer rejection for the sake of righteousness. It is not
just for heroic Christians in extreme circumstances; fortitude is an everyday virtue necessary in every calling of life.[58] We will not see the kingdom
of God come without taking some risks, without in some way putting ourselves on the line.

Little wonder, then, that the Bible so often exhorts believers to be strong
and courageous. Deuteronomy 31:6 is typical: "Be strong and courageous. Do
not be afraid or terrified because of them, for the LORD your God goes with
you; he will never leave you nor forsake you."

The exhortation is accompanied by the ground for encouragement in the
promise of the never-failing presence of God. So also with David's exhortation
to Solomon after all the materials and personnel for the building of the temple
have been assembled: "Be strong and courageous, and act; do not fear nor be
dismayed, for the Lord God, my God, is with you. He will not fail you nor
forsake you until all the work for the service of the house of the Lord is fin-
ished." (1 Chron. 28:20 NASB)

As with prudence, fortitude is dependent upon the grace of God, as
the form of exhortation often bears out: "Be strong in the Lord and in
his mighty power" (Eph. 6:10); "Be strong in the grace that is in Christ
Jesus" (2 Tim. 2:1). The Spirit by which Christ dwells in his people is
the Spirit of wisdom and understanding, and of power (Isa. 11:2; cf.
Acts 1:8).

---

56. Richard J. Mouw, *The God Who Commands* (Notre Dame, Ind.: University of Notre Dame Press,
1990), 173.

57. Cf. Herman Ridderbos, *Paul: An Outline of His Theology*, trans. John Richard De Witt (Grand
Rapids: Eerdmans, 1975), 286.

58. For some illuminating modern examples, see Douglas N. Walton, *Courage: A Philosophical Inves-
tigation* (Berkeley: University of California Press, 1986).

Temperance (Self-Discipline)

> God did not give us a spirit of timidity, but a spirit of power, of love, and of self-discipline.
>
> —2 Timothy 1:7

Temperance is perhaps the least attractive of the traditional cardinal virtues, yet the self-discipline that is its primary focus is a prominent aspect of New Testament teaching on the Christian life, especially in the Pastoral Epistles.[59] As love requires the practical wisdom of prudence and the courage of fortitude to be effective, so it requires also the less visible, more intensely personal virtue of temperance, the discipline of oneself to live a more ordered life for the glory of God and the service of others.

It is well known that Calvin taught that the sum of the Christian life is self-denial. According to God's plan for our lives in Romans 12:1–2, "we are consecrated and dedicated to God in order that we may thereafter think, speak, meditate, and do, nothing except to his glory."[60] The individual parts of a well-ordered life are presented in Titus 2:12, where believers are called to live "sober, upright, and godly lives in the present age." Calvin comments:

> Now [Paul] limits all actions of life to three parts: soberness, righteousness, and godliness. Of these, soberness doubtless denotes chastity and temperance as well as a pure and frugal use of temporal goods, and patience in poverty. Now righteousness embraces all the duties of equity in order that to each one be rendered what is his own. There follows godliness, which joins us in true holiness with God when we are separated from the iniquities of the world. When these things are joined together by an inseparable bond, they bring about complete perfection.[61]

Thus soberness (= temperance), righteousness (= justice), and godliness (= piety) constitute the sum of virtue. As Calvin goes on with his exposition of the Christian life it becomes apparent that he is primarily concerned with matters traditionally associated with temperance. Thoroughly biblical and profoundly Christocentric in his approach, Calvin includes chapters on bearing the cross, meditation on the future life, and the use of the present life and its helps. By showing how self-denial is correlative to stewardship and helpfulness to others, he avoided the individualism that often attaches itself to the virtue of temperance.

---

59. Of the sixteen New Testament instances of *sōphroneō* and related terms, ten are found in the pastoral Epistles.

60. Calvin, *Institutes*, 3.7.1.

61. Ibid., 3.7.3.

Humility

> Clothe yourselves with humility toward one another, because "God
> opposes the proud, but gives grace to the humble."
>
> —1 Peter 5:5, citing Proverbs 3:34

Humility is even less attractive than temperance to the natural mind, and
it did not make anybody's list of virtues in the classical philosophical tradition.[62] Biblical religion, on the other hand, not only puts humility on the
list but ranks it at the top. Humility is the mark of the true servant of the
Lord, a point driven home in the scriptural tribute to Moses faced with the
sibling rivalry of Miriam and Aaron: "Now the man Moses was very humble, more so than anyone else on the face of the earth" (Num. 12:3 NRSV).
Above all, humility is the distinguishing characteristic of the promised
Messiah:

> Rejoice greatly, O daughter Zion!
> Shout aloud, O daughter Jerusalem!
> Lo, your king comes to you;
> triumphant and victorious is he,
> humble and riding on a donkey,
> on a colt, the foal of a donkey. [Zech. 9:9 NRSV]

This is the King who commands peace to the nations, whose dominion
extends to the ends of the earth (Zech. 9:10); our understanding of humility
must be adjusted accordingly. Not all that passes for "humility" is virtuous, as
the apostle Paul is alert to point out (Col. 2:23). Biblical humility is far
removed from the "servile self-abasement" that comes from a false low self-
esteem or self-loathing.[63] True and virtuous humility, of which Christ is the
supreme example, is rooted in a right understanding of one's nature and calling before God and is manifest in the self-confident service of others, the
opposite of self-centered pride (Phil. 2:3).

The imitation of Christ is preeminently an exercise in adopting his attitude of humility in being obedient to the will of God and offering oneself in
the esteemed service of others (Phil. 2:5–6). Its characteristic concrete manifestations are mapped out in Paul's great summary exhortation to true
humility:

---

62. Cf. Alasdair MacIntyre, *After Virtue: A Study in Moral Theory*, 2d ed. (Notre Dame, Ind.: University of Notre Dame Press, 1984), 136.

63. Helen Oppenheimer, "Humility," in *Westminster Dictionary of Christian Ethics*, ed. James F. Childress and John Macquarrie (Philadelphia: Westminster, 1986), 284.

Therefore, as God's chosen people, holy and dearly loved, clothe yourselves with compassion, kindness, humility, gentleness and patience. Bear with each other and forgive whatever grievances you may have against one another. Forgive as the Lord forgave you. And over all these virtues put on love, which binds them all together in perfect unity. [Col. 3:12–14]

6

The Universal Norms of Love

In the love for which Christ has freed us, we realize that the binding moral norms express the very structure of the human person.

—Bernard Häring, *Free and Faithful in Christ*

The traditional supernaturalistic moral commandments are especially repressive of our human needs. They are immoral insofar as they foster illusions about human destiny and suppress vital inclinations.

—Paul Kurtz, *The Humanist Alternative*

Love, the impelling motive of the Christian life, is embodied in the practice of justice, mercy, and faithfulness—the weightier matters of the *torah*, the scriptural revelation of the will of God. These in turn both inform and are informed by the universal norms of human conduct commonly called the moral law. For all human beings, whether they realize it or not, are created in the image of God and are subject to the same basic principles of moral obligation. These universal duties are summarily comprehended in the Ten Commandments, the law that love, and only love, fulfills.

The Ten Commandments

The Ten Commandments or the Decalogue[1] are listed first in Exodus 20 and repeated (with some variation of details) in Deuteronomy 5. Their unique place in the history of special revelation is formally recognized in the liturgical and catechetical traditions of both Judaism and Christianity. According to the Mishnah, the Ten Commandments (along with the Shema)

---

1. The Ten Commandments are referred to as "the ten words" in the Hebrew of Exod. 34:28; Deut. 4:13; and Deut. 10:4. Hence the Greek derivative *Decalogue* (from *deka*, "ten" + *logos*, "word"). For an exegetical treatment of the commandments as they appear in Exod. 20, see Brevard S. Childs, "The Decalogue," in *The Book of Exodus: A Critical, Theological Commentary* (Philadelphia: Westminster, 1974), 385–439.

were read daily in the temple at the time of Christ.[2] The catechetical tradition of the Christian church—continued and expanded by both Protestants and Catholics after the Reformation—puts the Ten Commandments (with some variations in enumeration) alongside the Apostles' Creed and the Lord's Prayer to provide the primary pedagogical tools for communicating the cognitive structure of the Christian faith.[3]

The use of the Ten Commandments for the organization of ethics predates its Christian expression. Philo of Alexandria, the most outstanding representative of Hellenistic Judaism at the time of Christ, provided for his Greek-speaking audience a commentary on the Pentateuch which included an *Exposition of the Laws*. The latter contains a treatise on the Decalogue, followed by four books on the "special laws" arranged under the Ten Commandments as "summary heads." A lengthy section on justice concludes the fourth book, followed by a separate treatise on the virtues, specifically courage, humanity (*philanthrōpia*), repentance, and nobility.[4]

Philo is notable in the history of the interpretation of the Decalogue for his use of the Ten Commandments as summary principles governing the whole

---

2. Moshe Weinfeld, "The Decalogue: Its Significance, Uniqueness, and Place in Israel's Tradition," in *Religion and Law: Biblical-Judaic and Islamic Perspectives*, ed. Edwin B. Firmage et al. (Winona Lake, Ill.: Eisenbrauns, 1990), 10. The Mishnah reference is *Tamid* 5:1. Weinfeld goes on to note that "the Decalogue is to be spoken daily in accordance with the Palestinian practice as reflected in the Cairo Genizah, and to this day pious Jews read the Decalogue daily at the end of prayer" (p. 10). Evidence for the liturgical use of the Decalogue and Shema is also provided by Qumran phylacteries and the Nash Papyrus (p. 34).

3. On the enumeration of the Ten Commandments the traditions diverge as follows:

Exodus	Reformed Anglican Orthodox	Jewish	Roman Catholic Lutheran
		1	
I am the Lord		1	
No other gods	1	2	1
No graven images	2	2	1
Name	3	3	2
Sabbath	4	4	3
Father & Mother	5	5	4
Murder	6	6	5
Adultery	7	7	6
Theft	8	8	7
False witness	9	9	8
Covet wife	10	10	RC 9/Luth10
Covet property	10	10	RC 10/Luth 9

The Roman Catholic, Lutheran, and Jewish traditions agree in taking "no other gods" and "no graven images" as one commandment; Roman Catholics and Lutherans divide the commandment not to covet, the former following the text of Deuteronomy, the latter the text of Exodus. The Reformed-Anglican-Orthodox division between the first and second commandments is found in Jewish authors as early as Philo and Josephus. Judaism is unique in taking "I am the Lord your God" (the opening word) as the first commandment.

4. Philo, *On the Decalogue, On the Special Laws, On the Virtues*, trans. F. H. Colson, in *The Loeb Classical Library*, ed. E. H. Warmington (Cambridge: Harvard University Press, 1937–39).

Mosaic legislation and also for his division of the Decalogue into two groups of five, directed respectively toward the service of God and human justice.

> The superior set of five treats of the following matters: the monarchical principle by which the world is governed; idols of stone and wood and images in general made by human hands; the sin of taking the name of God in vain; the reverent observance of the sacred seventh day as befits its holiness; the duty of honouring parents, each separately and both in common. Thus one set of enactments begins with God the Father and Maker of all, and ends with parents who copy His nature by begetting particular persons. The other set of five contains all the prohibitions, namely adultery, murder, theft, false witness, covetousness or lust.[5]

Only those who practice both tables are whole in virtue, being both lovers of God (*philotheoi*) and lovers of humankind (*philanthrōpoi*).[6] The early church took the same basic perspective in its use of the Ten Commandments for instruction in the Christian way of life.[7]

Within the Scriptures themselves, the special character of the Ten Commandments is immediately apparent from the mode by which they were given. The biblical record emphasizes that God himself spoke the Ten Commandments in the hearing of all the people at the great theophany at Sinai (Exod. 20:1, 22) and then wrote them on two tablets of stone and gave them to Moses. Thus Moses records: "The tablets [of the Testimony] were the work of God; the writing was the writing of God, engraved on the tablets" (Exod. 32:16), "inscribed by the finger of God" (Deut. 9:10).[8] The first edition was destroyed by Moses upon discovery of the worship of the golden calf, but the Lord graciously reinscribed them and directed that they should be deposited in the Ark of the Covenant (Deut. 10:1–5).[9] They were still there at the dedication of the temple during the reign of Solomon (1 Kings 8:9, 21).

The unique mode of production of the Ten Commandments is directly related to their status as constituting the covenant the Lord made with Israel. As Moses retells the event for the benefit of the generation ready to enter the Promised Land: "The Lord spoke to you out of the fire. You heard the sound of words

---

5. Philo, *On the Decalogue*, 50–51. Philo's order, "adultery, murder, theft," is also found in Luke 19:20 and Rom. 13:9, the Nash Papyrus, and the Codex Vaticanus of Deut. 5:17–20, and may be reflected in the chiasmus of Jer. 7:9 (Weinfeld, "The Decalogue," 13 n. 30).

6. Philo, *On the Decalogue*, 110.

7. See Robert M. Grant, "The Decalogue in Early Christianity," *Harvard Theological Review* 40 (1947): 1–17.

8. So also Deut. 4:13, "He declared to you his covenant, the Ten Commandments, which he commanded you to follow and then wrote them on two stone tablets," and Deut. 5:22, "These are the commandments the LORD proclaimed in a loud voice to your whole assembly there on the mountain from out of the fire, the cloud and the deep darkness; and he added nothing more. Then he wrote them on two stone tablets and gave them to me."

9. Cf. Exod. 34:1, "The LORD said to Moses, 'Chisel out two stone tablets like the first ones, and I will write on them the words that were on the first tablets, which you broke.'"

but saw no form; there was only a voice. He declared to you his covenant, the Ten Commandments, which he commanded you to follow and then wrote them on two stone tablets" (Deut. 4:13). The stone tablets on which the Ten Commandments are inscribed are "the tablets of the covenant that the Lord had made with you" (Deut. 9:9). That there are two tablets rather than just one is probably not to represent separate "tables" of duties toward God and neighbor, as attractive pedagogically as that has been over the centuries. Recent studies on covenants in the ancient Near East have shown that the two tablets may be actually duplicates of the covenant: one for the Lord and one for the people in symbolic recognition of the involvement and commitment of both parties.[10]

The covenant relationship is defined by the opening assertion, "I am the Lord your God, who brought you out of Egypt, out of the land of slavery" (Exod. 20:2). Although it is not the first word of command it is nevertheless the first word spoken and highly significant for all that follows. Theologically it establishes the proper order and connection between prevenient grace and obedient love.

Since the Ten Commandments constitute the Sinaitic covenant they are rightly viewed as the comprehensive summary of the covenant way of life, containing in principle the whole will of God for his redeemed people. The Ten Commandments are the covenant; the rest is commentary. This does not diminish the divine authority of the rest, the revelation mediated through Moses. As in the case of the divine voice from heaven and the divine inscription on tablets of stone, when Moses speaks what he has heard or reads what he has written, the proper response is: "All that the Lord has spoken we will do!" (Exod. 19:8; 24:3, 7 NASB). The scriptural expositions and applications of the Ten Commandments are also the Word of God for the direction of his covenant people and are as binding under the Mosaic administration as the ten words themselves.

But if the Ten Commandments are the covenant God made with Israel, how can they be universal norms of human conduct? How do Israel's obligations become the obligations of all humankind—including the Christian church whose very being depends on God's having made a new covenant to supplant the one made at Sinai?[11]

The answer to the second question throws light on the first. The continuing relevance of the Ten Commandments to the people of God may be determined by observing how they function in the New Testament. In a number of places the Ten Commandments are cited directly where the context requires a summary of the revealed will of God (Matt. 19:18–19; Rom. 13:8–

10. Cf. Meredith G. Kline, *Treaty of the Great King* (Grand Rapids: Eerdmans, 1963). Kline argues that the Decalogue contains the basic elements of a suzerainty treaty (historical prologue, demand for exclusive loyalty, stipulations, blessings and curses), which Deuteronomy manifests in extended form.

11. See Heb. 8:6–13.

10; James 2:8–11). In other places the Ten Commandments, though not cited directly, provide the framework for moral analysis and exhortation, as in the following examples from Jesus and Paul.

> For out of the heart come
> [6th] evil thoughts, murder,
> [7th] adultery, sexual immorality,
> [8th] theft,
> [9th] false testimony, slander. [Matt. 15:19]

> We know that the law is good if one uses it properly.
> We also know that law is made not for the righteous
> but for lawbreakers and rebels,
> [1st] the ungodly and sinful,
> [3d] the unholy and irreligious;
> [5th] for those who kill their fathers or mothers,
> [6th] for murderers,
> [7th] for adulterers and perverts,
> [8th] for slave traders [commerce in human beings]
> [9th] and liars and perjurers—
> and for whatever else is contrary to the sound doctrine that con-
> forms to the glorious gospel of the blessed God which he entrusted
> to me. [1 Tim. 1:8–11]

This use of the Ten Commandments follows the example of the Old Testament prophets in calling Israel to repentance.

> Will you
> [8th] steal,
> [6th] murder,
> [7th] commit adultery,
> [3d] swear falsely,
> [2d] make offerings to Baal,
> [1st] and go after gods you have not known
> and then come and stand before me in this house, which is called by
> my name, and say, "We are safe!"—only to go on doing all these
> abominations? [Jer. 7:9–10 NRSV]

That the ten words are still operative appears also from Jesus' exposition of the moral law in the Sermon on the Mount. In this royal proclamation of kingdom righteousness, Jesus cites directly the sixth and seventh commandments, "Do not murder" (Matt. 5:21) and "Do not commit adultery" (Matt.

5:27), and brings out their full import and reach to the thoughts and intents of the heart. The authority of the Decalogue is thus presupposed in Jesus' teaching; his emphasis on the heart does not set up an antithesis between an ethics of disposition and ethics of external command. Rather, Jesus' teaching "represents a proclamation of the full implications of these commandments in opposition to the casuistic and legalistic interpretations of the scribes."[12]

Also to the point is the manner in which Paul presents the fifth commandment as a matter of Christian responsibility: "Children, obey your parents in the Lord, for this is right. 'Honor your father and mother'—which is the first commandment with a promise—'that it may go well with you and that you may enjoy long life on the earth.' Fathers, do not exasperate your children; instead, bring them up in the training and instruction of the Lord" (Eph. 6:1–4).

Not only does Paul cite the fifth commandment directly as a norm of correct behavior for Christian children; he calls attention to its decalogical context by noting that it is the first commandment with a promise. The implication is that the Ten Commandments as a unitary code of conduct continue to structure the covenant way of life to which God's people are called "in the Lord," that is, in their identity as Christians. The only difference is that the promise, which in Exodus and Deuteronomy is "the land which the Lord your God is giving you," is universalized in recognition of the new covenant fulfillment of the typological element of the Ten Commandments as originally given to Israel. Still the promise as well as the norm of the fifth commandment still holds good, and the Ten Commandments provide a framework for the good works that God has prepared in advance for the people he has created in Christ Jesus to practice (Eph. 2:10).

The reason the Ten Commandments are directives for the people of God under the new covenant as well as the old is because they represent the essential will of God for human beings as such. Perhaps the clearest evidence of this is Paul's indictment of the whole human race as guilty before God for having broken the moral law (Rom. 1:18–3:20). The Gentiles, even without special revelation, know better than they do in either religion or morality (Rom. 1:20, 32). And when, however imperfectly, they do things that are specified in the law, "they show that the requirements of the law are written on their hearts" (Rom. 2:15). What law? As Paul continues his argument it becomes clear that it is the moral law as summarily comprehended in the Ten Commandments. The Jews, Paul says, have in the specially revealed law the embodiment of knowledge and truth, but he cites the Ten Commandments against them to demonstrate that there is also a gap between their knowledge and practice.

---

12. Ned B. Stonehouse, *The Witness of Matthew and Mark to Christ* (Grand Rapids: Eerdmans, 1958), 199.

[8th] You who preach against stealing, do you steal?

[7th] You who say that people should not commit adultery, do you commit adultery?

[2d] You who abhor idols, do you rob temples?

[3d] You who brag about the law, do you dishonor God by breaking the law? As it is written: "God's name is blasphemed among the Gentiles because of you." [Rom. 2:21–24]

The conclusion is that the whole world is held accountable to God for having broken the universal norms of righteousness as represented by the Ten Commandments. As Warfield aptly observed, "[T]here is no duty imposed upon the Israelite in the Ten Commandments which is not equally incumbent upon all men, everywhere. These commandments are but the positive publication to Israel of the universal human duties, the common morality of mankind."[13] The moral law is that which is universally and perpetually binding on human beings by virtue of their creation in the image of God. The substance of the moral law is the same whether revealed in human nature or in Scripture.

The Law of Moses

The Christian church, in keeping with the high view of inspiration held by Christ and his apostles, receives not only the Ten Commandments but also the whole Old Testament as the Word of God. Particularly relevant is Jesus' own word of caution with respect to the abiding validity of the *torah*: "Do not think that I have come to abolish the Law or the Prophets; I have not come to abolish them but to fulfill them. I tell you the truth, until heaven and earth disappear, not the smallest letter, not the least stroke of a pen, will by any means disappear from the Law until everything is accomplished" (Matt. 5:17–18).

As always Scripture must be compared with Scripture to avoid misinterpretation. From other Scriptures it is clear that Jesus brought to an end the observance of many of the laws of Moses—some by his teaching (Mark 7:19, "In saying this, Jesus declared all foods 'clean'"), others by his redemptive accomplishment. Thus, the entire sacrificial system and ceremonial washings were "external regulations applying until the time of the new order" (Heb. 9:10). Since the law of Moses was "only a shadow of the good things that are coming—not the realities themselves" (Heb. 10:1), its regulations are set aside once the realities have arrived in Christ (Heb. 7:18–19). The new covenant evinces a planned obsolescence in the history of redemption: "By calling this covenant 'new' he has made the first one obsolete; and what is obsolete and aging will soon disappear" (Heb. 8:13).

---

13. Benjamin B. Warfield, *Selected Shorter Writings of Benjamin B. Warfield*, ed. John E. Meeter, 2 vols. (Nutley, N.J.: Presbyterian and Reformed, 1970–73), 1:213.

The laws that foreshadowed the work of Christ are no longer to be observed because their fulfillment has rendered them obsolete. It must be emphasized, however, that the way in which they have been rendered nonbinding is by redemptive accomplishment rather than by legislative repeal. Had they been simply abolished would have called into question their validity, and they would indeed have "disappeared" without a trace of redemptive-historical significance. As it is, as laws which Christ fulfilled rather than abolished, they continue to be instructive even though they are no longer obligatory.

Augustine in addressing this issue subjected the law of Moses to a bipartite analysis (moral and symbolical). Asked how he could profess to believe the Old Testament and yet not observe it, Augustine replied: "The moral precepts of the law are observed by Christians; the symbolical precepts were properly observed during the time that things now revealed were prefigured."[14] For example, "Thou shalt not covet" is a moral precept; "Thou shalt circumcise every male on the eighth day" is a symbolical or a typological precept.[15] The moral precepts (generally identified with the Ten Commandments) are still binding; the symbolical precepts though they are no longer binding still have a spiritual use. Thus,

> while we consider it no longer a duty to offer sacrifices, we recognize sacrifices as part of the mysteries of Revelation, by which the things prophesied were foreshadowed. For they were our examples, and in many and various ways they all pointed to the one sacrifice which we now commemorate. Now that this sacrifice has been revealed, and has been offered in due time, *sacrifice is no longer binding as an act of worship, while it retains its symbolical authority.* "For these things were written for our learning, upon whom the end of the world is come."[16]

Besides circumcision and the sacrifices Augustine categorizes as symbolical precepts the tabernacle regulations, the dietary laws, the festivals, and the Sabbath.[17] He interprets the rules against blended clothing (wool and linen) and the mixed yoke (ox and ass) allegorically.[18] Finally, such precepts as the law of

---

14. Augustine, *Reply to Faustus the Manichaean,* trans. Richard Stothert, in *A Select Library of the Nicene and Post-Nicene Fathers of the Christian Church,* ed. Philip Schaff, (New York: Scribners, 1901), 10.2.

15. Ibid., 6.2.

16. Ibid., 6.5 (emphasis added).

17. "The rest of the Sabbath we consider no longer binding as an observance, now that the hope of our eternal rest has been revealed. But it is a very useful thing to read of, and to reflect on." Ibid., 6.4.

18. "To patch linen garments with purple, or to wear a garment of woolen and linen together, is not a sin now. But to live intemperately, and to wish to combine opposite modes of life . . . is always sin. So it is sin whenever inconsistent things are combined in any man's life." "There is no harm in joining an ox with an ass where it is required. But to put a wise man and a fool together . . . that both with equal authority should declare the word of God, cannot be done without causing offence." Ibid., 6.9.

retaliation "were suitable to the times of the Old Testament, and were not destroyed, but fulfilled by Christ."[19]

Augustine's moral/symbolical distinction eventually gave way to the more precise tripartite analysis first worked out in detail by Thomas Aquinas. The basic thesis is as follows:

> [I]t is necessary to divide the precepts of the Old Law into three classes: the moral precepts, arising from the dictates of natural law, the ceremonial precepts, which are concrete applications of the principle of divine worship, and judicial precepts, which are concrete applications of the principle that justice has to be observed among men.[20]

The moral precepts derive their force from "the dictate of natural reason," that is, from the way God has constituted human nature with the ends he has ordained. Some moral precepts, such as love for God and one's neighbor, are so clear and certain for authentic humanness that promulgation was not strictly necessary. The rationale for the definitive precepts of the Decalogue can also be easily grasped by ordinary intelligence, but since it is possible for human judgment to go astray on such matters, the promulgation of the Ten Commandments was necessary. The other moral precepts, which may be evident to the wise but not to everyone, are "superadded" to the Ten Commandments and are in principle reducible to them.[21]

Whereas the moral precepts derive their force from God's will for human nature and are thus universally binding, the ceremonial and judicial precepts "derive their force solely from their institution" and are thus only situationally binding. Of course, their performance is a matter of moral obligation for the people and time of their institution. But as applications of the principles of worship and justice they are subject to change in ways that the principles themselves (which reflect the unchanging nature and will of God) are not.[22]

Since the law of Moses was promulgated as a unitary whole without differentiating labels, how are the (universally binding) moral precepts to be distinguished from the (situationally binding) ceremonial and judicial precepts?

19. Ibid., 19.9. For an analysis of Augustine's multifaceted doctrine of Christ's fulfillment of the law see Harvey K. McArthur, *Understanding the Sermon on the Mount* (New York: Harper, 1960), 28–29.

20. Thomas Aquinas, *The Old Law (1a2ae.98–105)*, vol. 29 in *Summa Theologicae*, trans. David Bourke and Arthur Littledale (New York: McGraw, 1969), 1a2ae.99, 4.

21. Ibid., 1a2ae.100, 11.

22. Cf. Calvin: "[L]et no one be concerned over the small point that ceremonial and judicial laws pertain also to morals. For the ancient writers who taught this division, although they were not ignorant that these two latter parts had some bearing upon morals, still, because these could be changed or abrogated while morals remained untouched, did not call them moral laws. They applied this name only to the first part, without which the true holiness of morals cannot stand, nor an unchangeable rule of right living." John Calvin, *Institutes of the Christian Religion*, ed. John T. McNeill, trans. Ford Lewis Battles (Philadelphia: Westminster, 1960), 4.20.14.

Aquinas's hermeneutical principle is to consider the purpose of the precepts in light of the history of redemption. Since the ceremonial precepts regulating Israel's worship were ordained to prefigure Christ, fulfillment brings their practice to an end, though the truth they taught will always remain.[23] So far Aquinas follows Augustine; he breaks new ground in recognizing that the judicial precepts require a more nuanced approach. "[The judicial precepts] were not enacted in order to be figurative of anything, but to regulate the state of the people in accordance with justice and equity. Yet they were figurative as a consequence; inasmuch as the entire state of that people, which was regulated by these precepts, was figurative."[24]

The judicial precepts were for the special sanctification of the Jewish people in preparation for the coming of Christ. Their purpose having been accomplished, they no longer have any binding force. But unlike the ceremonial precepts, continued observance of the judicial precepts is not necessarily wrong. "For should any ruler order their observance in his territory, he would not be committing a sin, unless they were observed, or ordered to be observed, as binding through enactment in the Old Law."[25] To keep them on the ground that they are still binding would be sinful, but not otherwise.

By the time of the Reformation the tripartite division of the Mosaic law had become the standard hermeneutical tool for separating the universal precepts from the situational.[26] The Westminster Confession provides a classic statement of the ecumenical theological consensus.

> Beside this law, commonly called *moral*, God was pleased to give to the people of Israel, as a church under age, ceremonial laws, containing several typical ordinances, partly of worship, prefiguring Christ, his graces, actions, sufferings, and benefits; and partly, holding forth divers instructions of moral duties. All which ceremonial laws are now abrogated, under the new testament. (19.3)

> To them also, as a body politic, he gave sundry judicial laws, which expired together with the state of that people; not obliging any other now, further than the general equity thereof may require. (19.4)

For all its wide acceptance, the tripartite division of the Mosaic law has been seriously challenged in recent years by the theonomy movement in

23. Aquinas, *Summa Theologicae*, 1a2ae.101, 2.
24. Ibid., 1a2ae.104, 3.
25. Ibid.
26. See, e.g., Melanchthon, *Melanchthon on Christian Doctrine: Loci Communes 1555*, ed. and trans. Clyde L. Manschreck (New York: Oxford University Press, 1965), 83–85; John Calvin, *Commentaries on the Four Last Books of Moses Arranged in the Form of a Harmony*, trans. Charles William Bingham, 4 vols. (1852; reprint, Grand Rapids: Eerdmans, 1950), 1:417; Zacharias Ursinus, *The Commentary of Dr. Zacharias Ursinus on the Heidelberg Catechism*, trans. G. W. Williard (1852; reprint, Phillipsburg, N.J.: Presbyterian and Reformed, n.d.), 491–92.

Reformed social ethics.[27] Theonomists characteristically argue from the immutability of God's holiness to the immutability of God's law: "The law is a transcript—a writing out of the details—of God's moral perfection (Matt. 5:48; Ps. 19:7). As such, the law can no more be changed, abrogated, or improved upon than can God's perfection (Deut. 12:32; Ps. 119:160)."[28] But if Christians are not obliged to practice circumcision or to keep the passover or to abstain from pork and shellfish, hasn't the law been changed? The theonomists save their position by an equivocal use of the term *law*. On the one hand they say that the law is the "transcript" of God's perfection. On the other hand the law that is immutable is not the transcript; the principles embodied in the precepts are immutable, not the precepts themselves. "The *principles* of God's law are perpetual because they reflect the character of God, who is unchanging."[29]

Immutability is thus shifted from the laws to the principles behind the laws, which is not the point at issue. The question is whether or not some laws of God are binding in some situations but not in others. Since theonomists admit that whole categories of legislation are subject to change as circumstances require different "applications,"[30] the argument from immutability is without force. The issue is how the changes are made and the criteria by which they can be recognized.

Greg Bahnsen, who is the movement's chief apologist, argues for the presumptive continuity of the Mosaic laws on the principle that laws continue in force until revoked. Discontinuity must assume the burden of proof, but the New Testament does provide the basis for distinguishing between the universal and the situational in the law of Moses. Bahnsen himself favors a bipartite division between the moral law (consisting of general precepts and illustrative applications) and the ceremonial law (consisting of typological and separational precepts).[31] The ceremonial precepts were situational and are no longer obligatory. The judicial precepts, on the other hand, are part of the moral law and are uni-

27. See Greg L. Bahnsen, *Theonomy in Christian Ethics*, 2d ed. (Phillipsburg, N.J.: Presbyterian and Reformed, 1984). This basic work was first published in 1977; the second edition adds a preface in which the author replies to his critics (pp. xi–xxvii). Bahnsen provides a less technical introduction in *By This Standard: The Authority of God's Law Today* (Tyler, Tex.: Institute for Christian Economics, 1985). Theonomists—also known as reconstructionists—acknowledge the formative influence of R. J. Rushdoony; see especially his *Institutes of Biblical Law* (Nutley, N.J.: Craig, 1973). The most comprehensive evaluation of the movement to date is *Theonomy: A Reformed Critique*, ed. William S. Barker and W. Robert Godfrey (Grand Rapids: Zondervan, 1990). Bahnsen has responded in *No Other Standard: Theonomy and Its Critics* (Tyler, Tex.: Institute for Christian Economics, 1991).

28. Greg Bahnsen, "The Authority of God's Law," *The Presbyterian Journal*, 6 December 1978, 11. Cf. James B. Jordan, *The Law of the Covenant: An Exposition of Exodus 21–23* (Tyler, Tex.: Institute for Christian Economics, 1984), 9 n. 11.

29. Bahnsen, *By This Standard*, 141.

30. Ibid., 135, 136, 316.

31. Ibid., 135.

versally binding. This produces the movement's most distinctive thesis: "The civil precepts of the Old Testament (standing 'judicial laws') are a model of perfect social justice for all cultures, even in the punishment of criminals."[32] Bahnsen sums it up this way: "Just as the magistrate of the Older Testament had divine imperatives which he was responsible to carry out, so also magistrates in the era of the New Testament are under obligation to those commands in the Book of the Law which apply to civil affairs and social penology."[33]

Theonomy's most controversial proposition is that *"civil magistrates ought to mete out the punishment which God has prescribed in his word."*[34] Examples of standing laws or policy directives to classes of individuals that are universally binding are: "children, obey your parents; merchants, have just measures; magistrates, execute rapists." Christians in a democratic society should work through the (persuasive) political process to enact the Mosaic standing laws.

> [W]e are not advocating the forcible "imposition" of God's law on an unwilling society. "Theonomists" preach and promote biblical law's authority and wisdom praying that citizens will be *persuaded* willingly to adopt God's standards as the law of the land. As secularists campaign and debate to see their convictions influence civil law, so Christians should work to have God's word influence civil law instead. We do not advocate any modern "holy war" or use of force to compel submission to God's commands. . . .

> . . . What is proposed here is that all civil governments, whatever their structure, should be encouraged to submit to and apply the standing laws of Old Testament Israel.[35]

Why is this not a good idea?

Under the Mosaic administration of the covenant of grace God entered into a unique relationship with Israel as a theocratic nation, "a kingdom of priests and a holy nation" (Exod. 19:6). All citizens of Israel were members of the redeemed community, since all were baptized into Moses in the cloud and the sea (1 Cor. 10:2). Bearing in their flesh the sign of the covenant they were all "professed Jews" (cf. Rom. 2:28–29). King David reflects on the uniqueness of Israel in these words:

> And who is like your people Israel—the one nation of earth that God went out to redeem as a people for himself, and to make a name for himself, and to perform great and awesome wonders by driving out nations and their gods from before your people, whom you redeemed from Egypt. You have established

32. Bahnsen, *Theonomy*, xvii.
33. Ibid., 317.
34. Bahnsen, *By This Standard*, 271 (emphasis original).
35. Ibid., 322–23.

your people Israel as your very own forever, and You, O LORD, have become their God. [2 Sam. 7:23–24]

Bahnsen agrees, but emphasizes that Israel was not entirely unique in that it shares civil functions with all states. However, the uniqueness of Israel conditions the political use of the law in at least three ways. First, in the theocracy there was no need to distinguish sharply between the civil and the other uses of the law. As the covenant way of life, the law appears as an integrated unity in which the whole of life is subordinated to the will of God, Israel's Creator, Redeemer, and covenant Lord (cf. Deut. 15). Secondly, the social structures erected by the law are unique to the theocracy (cf. Lev. 25). The judges appeal to the priests when they are unable to decide hard cases (Deut. 17:9). The social organization of tribal elders gives way in the new form of the people of God, an ecclesial entity. Third, the standing laws of Israel are reflective of the special theocratic calling of Israel as the executor of God's wrath upon the reprobate (see Deut. 20).

The Bible is the constitution of the covenant community, the church, which is not coextensive with the nation as was the case in ancient Israel. The Bible is not the constitution of any nation-state today for the simple reason that God has not entered into a covenant relationship with any nation-state as he did with Israel. It is not the responsibility of any government to use the civil law so that "all idolatry and false worship may be destroyed." The function of the law within Israel was pedagogical—to teach what every sin deserved. It does not follow that God now commissions governments at large to exact the extreme penalty; the law of Moses was not given as a model penal code for the uncovenanted nations.

Laws are mutable or immutable relative to the intended situation. Thus, with the expiration of political Israel, the burden of proof is required for abiding obligation beyond general embody a moral principle of universal obligation.

The Ground of the Moral Law

"Can we be good without God?" That question made the cover of the *Atlantic Monthly* in December 1989, highlighting a feature article by Glenn Tinder, professor of political science at the University of Massachusetts in Boston.[36] Because the article is specifically about being good in a political sense, which it is widely agreed depends on recognizing the worth of the individual human being, the question is more precisely, "Can we affirm the dignity and equality of individual persons—values we ordinarily regard as secular—without giving them transcendental backing?"[37] Tinder argues that the

36. Glen Tinder, "Can We Be Good Without God?" *The Atlantic Monthly,* December 1989, 69–85.
37. Ibid., 70.

source of these values is biblical religion rather than secular rationalism, and he presses Nietzsche's logic: We cannot give up the Christian God and continue to hold on to Christian morality. The "incalculable worth" of every individual and a "responsible hope" for the political order require a transcendent ground; thus, we cannot be good without God.[38]

It is heartening to see the case for the theistic ground of morality made (and made well) in such a forum. If human beings are what the Bible says we are—created in the image of God—no account of morality will be adequate that stops short of its ground in the nature and will of the Creator. A believer and an unbeliever may agree that a particular act (murder, for example) is morally wrong and ought not to be done. The use of such terms (morally wrong, ought not to be done) is mutually intelligible; both understand the specific kind of judgment that is being made. But if the further question is asked, "Why is it wrong? What makes murder an immoral act?" the answers sharply diverge along theistic or naturalistic lines.

On biblical presuppositions, "all morality is grounded in the character, the acts, the purposes, and the instructions of the God of revelation."[39] Justice, mercy, and faithfulness are moral values because God is just and merciful and faithful; they are grounded in his character and acts. The Ten Commandments are universal moral norms because they represent the will of God for human nature as he has created it—to be fulfilled through his ordinances of worship, rest, authority, life, sex, property, and communication; they are grounded in his purposes and instructions for human beings always and everywhere.[40] The ceremonial and judicial precepts are situationally conditioned applications of the moral principles of worship and authority; they are grounded in God's particular purposes and instructions in the history of redemption.

The idea of morality as "obedient love" is sometimes thought to be successfully disposed of by posing the question, Are the precepts of the moral law commanded by God because they are right, or are they right because God commands them?[41] Here the believer appears to be caught on the horns of a dilemma, forced to choose between "commanded because right" or "right because commanded." To answer "commanded because right" seems to imply

38. Ibid., 85.

39. Henry Stob, *Ethical Reflections* (Grand Rapids: Eerdmans, 1978), 39.

40. Cf. John Murray: "[T]he ten commandments as promulgated at Sinai were but the concrete and practical form of enunciating principles which did not then for the first time come to have relevance but were relevant from the beginning. . . as they did not *begin* to have relevance at Sinai, so they did not cease to have relevance when the Sinaitic economy had passed away." *Principles of Conduct: Aspects of Biblical Ethics* (Grand Rapids: Eerdmans, 1957), 7.

41. The conundrum was first put by Socrates to Euthyphro. For a sample of the modern discussion, see William K. Frankena, "The Principles of Morality," in *Skepticism and Moral Principles: Modern Ethics in Review,* ed. Curtis L. Carter (Evanston, Ill.: New University Press, 1973), 71–73; James G. Hanink and Gary R. Mar, "What Euthyphro Couldn't Have Said," *Faith and Philosophy* 4 (1987): 241–61.

that morality is independent of and even superior to God. Being omniscient, he knows where the line is between right and wrong but he does not draw it; he only reveals to human beings the law that he himself must obey.

On the other hand, to answer "right because commanded" seems to imply that morality is arbitrary and that God could have commanded the opposite of the moral law as we know it. Lying, cruelty, and killing the innocent would then be right, and truthfulness, compassion, and protecting the innocent would be wrong.

C. S. Lewis found both horns intolerable and suggested that the fault lies with the categories. This seems to me to be the right tack. What God commands necessarily reflects who he is. The moral law is what it is because God wills human beings to be conformed to his nature. The binding force of the moral law is due to the will of God—the precepts are *obligatory* because commanded; but the content of the moral law is due to the holy nature of God— the precepts are commanded because (for want of a better word) *conformitory*. The notion of moral obligation is correlative to the creation of beings with moral responsibility. No law obliges God; he simply is—the holy God from whom all moral distinctions flow.

The objection to biblical theistic ethics sometimes takes the form that since a moral principle must hold true for all possible universes, the notion that morality is what God commands is clearly false for in a world created by an omnipotent demon morality would be the opposite of what we know it to be. The answer is that there are no possible worlds that could come into existence without the one Creator God who is. Unbelievers are thus imagining a situation that cannot exist, and then proceeding to criticize it on what they do not realize are biblical assumptions. The idea of an omnipotent demon can be thought up only by using criteria for the demonic that are derived from notions of morality implanted in the human heart by the true and living God. The situation is like Cornelius Van Til's illustration of a child sitting on his father's lap and reaching up to slap him in the face. The whole thing would be impossible if the lap were not there in the first place.[42]

The Use of the Moral Law

The question of the "use of the law" (*usus legis*) was introduced into theological discussion at the time of the Reformation. Precisely put, the question is: How does the moral law (summarized in the Ten Commandments) function in a fallen world? Better still: How does God use the moral law in the history and application of redemption?

42. The best current defense of divine command morality is Richard J. Mouw, *The God Who Commands* (Notre Dame, Ind.: University of Notre Dame Press, 1990).

It was Luther who first observed a "double use" of the law, for restraining crimes and for revealing crimes.[43] The first use is political or civil; the second is theological or spiritual. Commenting on Galatians 3:19 ("What, then, was the purpose of the law?"), Luther makes his key distinction: "[W]e reject not the law and works, as our adversaries do falsely accuse us: but we do altogether stablish the law, and require works thereof, and we say that the law is good and profitable, but in his own proper use: which is, first to bridle civil transgressions, and then to reveal and to increase spiritual transgressions."[44]

The civil restraint of the law is appointed by God for public peace and preservation of the social order so that the gospel may make its way unhindered by those in the grip of Satan. "God hath ordained magistrates, parents, teachers, laws, bonds and all civil ordinances, that, if they can do no more, yet at the least they may bind the devil's hands, that he rage not in his bondslaves after his own lust."[45] But the proper and principal use of the law is not to restrain sin but to expose it: "Another use of the law is theological or spiritual, which is (as Paul saith) 'to increase transgressions'; that is, to reveal unto a man his sin, his blindness, his misery, his impiety, ignorance, hatred and contempt of God, death, hell, the judgment and deserved wrath of God."[46]

Calvin builds on Luther's evangelical foundation. In the first place, he says, the law is like a mirror in which we can see ourselves as God sees us: "While [the law] shows God's righteousness, that is, the righteousness alone acceptable to God, it warns, informs, convicts, and lastly condemns, every man of his own unrighteousness." Though in itself the law can only accuse and condemn sinners, it is redemptively useful "in convicting man of his infirmity and moving him to call upon the remedy of grace which is in Christ."[47] This function eventually came to be called the pedagogical use of the law (from Galatians 3:24, "the law was our *paidagōgos* [disciplinarian] to lead us to Christ that we might be justified by faith").[48]

Secondly, the law is like a halter or bridle, "to restrain certain men who are untouched by any care for what is just and right unless compelled by hearing the dire threats in the law." Such coerced conformity to the law, though moti-

43. Cf. F. Edward Cranz, *The Development of Luther's Thought on Justice, Law, and Society* (Cambridge: Harvard University Press, 1959), p. 103. Thomas Aquinas made a different twofold distinction: "[E]very law is given to a particular people. Now a people contains two kinds of men: some prone to evil, and these need the law's coercion, as we have noted; others with a propensity to good by nature or habit, or rather grace, and these need to be instructed by the precepts of the law and urged on to what is better." *Summa Theologicae*, 1a2ae.101, 3. In post-Reformation terminology, these are the first and the third uses of the law.

44. Martin Luther, *A Commentary on St. Paul's Epistle to the Galatians*, ed. Philip S. Watson (London: T. & T. Clark, 1953), 302.

45. Ibid., 298.

46. Ibid., 298–99.

47. Calvin, *Institutes*, 2.7.6–9.

48. In the Hellenistic world the *paidagōgos* was not the schoolmaster (KJV) but the person put in charge (NIV) of supervising youths and conducting them to and from school.

vated by the fear of punishment, is necessary for the public community, its order and tranquility. It is this function of the law Paul has in mind when he teaches that "the law is not laid down for the just but for the unjust and disobedient" (1 Tim. 1:9–10).[49]

There is yet a third use of the law that does not appear so clearly in Luther (though it was expressly taught by his colleague Melanchthon). For Luther the proper and principal use of the law is to reveal sin, to convict and condemn sinners. Calvin, on the other hand, writes:

> The third and principal use, which pertains more closely to the proper purpose of the law, finds its place among believers in whose hearts the Spirit of God already lives and reigns. For even though they have the law written and engraved upon their hearts by the finger of God [Jer. 31:33; Heb. 10:16], that is, have been so moved and quickened through the directing of the Spirit that they long to obey God, they still profit by the law in two ways.[50]

The two ways are instruction and exhortation. As for the first, the law teaches believers the will of God to which they now aspire. Citing Psalm 119 (epitomized in verse 105, "Thy word is a lamp to my feet and a light to my path"), Calvin observes: "[H]ere the prophet proclaims the great usefulness of the law: the Lord instructs by their reading of it those whom he inwardly instills with a readiness to obey."[51] The law is a lamp for believers; the promise of grace accompanies the precepts and makes the law a delight for those who know the Mediator.

The instruction of the law is supplemented by exhortation. In Calvin's figure, "The law is to the flesh like a whip to an idle and balky ass, to arouse it to work."[52] At first sight this appears to contradict Calvin's doctrine of Spirit-inspired obedience to the will of God. If we are not moved by the overtures of the Spirit, what reason is there to think we will be moved by the exhortations of the law? Is the whip of the law more powerful than the grace of the Spirit? Calvin's figure may be ill-chosen, but in any case by the "whip" of the law he does not mean the threats or curse of the law. The hortatory power of the law for believers "is not a power to bind their consciences with a curse, but . . . to pinch them awake to their imperfection." It is the perfection of the law's positive demands, not the terror of its penal sanctions, that exhorts believers as "the law points out the goal toward which throughout life we are to strive."[53]

49. Calvin, *Institutes*, 2.7.10–11.
50. Ibid., 2.7.12.
51. Ibid.
52. Ibid.
53. Ibid., 2.7.13.

Eventually the different functions of the law became standardized as civil or political, convictional or pedagogical, and normative or didactic.[54] To summarize: The civil use of the law is as a bridle to restrain sin and to promote justice in society. The pedagogical use of the law is as a mirror to convict of sin and to show the need of a Savior. The third or directional use of the law is as a lamp to guide believers in their new obedience.

Although the Lutheran and the Reformed traditions share much in common on the doctrine of the law (including perennial internal debates on the proper understanding of the third use), in general the theological traditions reflect the different emphases of Luther and Calvin. In the Lutheran tradition the law always accuses (*lex semper accusat*); the law always exposes sin and threatens punishment—even to believers who live under a dialectic of law and gospel. The law is necessary for the regenerate as a guard against complacency in the Christian life—"lest the Old Adam go his own self-willed way. He must be coerced against his own will not only by the admonitions and threats of the law, but also by its punishments and plagues, to follow the Spirit and surrender himself a captive."[55]

In the Reformed tradition the law always informs; the law always reveals the moral will of God—especially to believers who are no longer under its threat of punishment. This way of looking at the law is best represented by the Westminster Larger Catechism, which refocuses the issue by looking at the different categories of persons addressed. It covers the ground by asking three questions.

Q. 95. Of what use is the moral law to all men?
A. The moral law is of use to all men, to inform them of the holy nature and will of God, and of their duty, binding them to walk accordingly; to convince them of their disability to keep it, and of the sinful pollution of their nature, hearts, and lives; to humble them in the sense of their sin and misery, and thereby help them to a clearer sight of the need they have of Christ, and of the perfection of his obedience.

Q. 96. What particular use is there of the moral law to unregenerate men?
A. The moral law is of use to unregenerate man, to awaken their consciences to flee from wrath to come, and to drive them to Christ; or, upon their continuance in the estate and way of sin, to leave them inexcusable, and under the curse thereof.

Q. 97. What special use is there of the moral law to the regenerate?

54. In Latin, *usus politicus sive civilis, usus elenchticus sive paedagogicus, tertius usus legis: usus didacticus sive normativus.* See Richard A. Muller, *Dictionary of Latin and Greek Theological Terms* (Grand Rapids: Baker, 1985), 320–21.
55. *Formula of Concord*, Epitome, article 6.

A. Although they that are regenerate, and believe in Christ, be delivered from the moral law as a covenant of works, so as thereby they are neither justified nor condemned; yet, besides the general uses thereof common to them with all men, it is of special use, to show them how much they are bound to Christ for his fulfilling it, and enduring the curse thereof in their stead, and for their good; and thereby to provoke them to more thankfulness, and to express the same in their greater care to conform themselves thereunto as the rule of their obedience.[56]

The evangelicalism of the Westminster divines is particularly evident in their doctrine of the special use of the law for believers. Neither the perfect demands of the law nor its penal consequences threaten those who rely on Christ for salvation. Christ has both obeyed the law and endured its penalty in their stead. In the words of John Newton's great hymn, "He has hushed the law's loud thunder, He has quenched Mount Sinai's flame."[57] The law can only deepen believers' understanding of the cost of their redemption and move them out of gratitude to serve their Savior according to his will.

The question of the use of the law is of more than historical interest; at issue are the opposite and equally ruinous errors of antinomianism and legalism. Antinomianism fosters moral laxity by denying the law its continuing normative relevance for the Christian life. From the correct assumption that believers are neither justified nor condemned by the law, it draws the false conclusion that the law can safely be disregarded as a revelation of the holy nature and will of God. Popularly it takes the form of dividing Christ's person (accepting him as Savior, but not as Lord) or dividing his work (trusting him for salvation from the consequences of sin, but not from its defilement and power). But Christ is not divided; he came into the world to save sinners, and those whom he justifies he also sanctifies by his word and Spirit. To trust in Christ as Savior is to trust in him not only for forgiveness but also for

56. Cf. the first three stanzas of Matthias Loi's splendid hymn (1863):

> The law of God is good and wise
> And sets his will before our eyes,
> Shows us the way of righteousness,
> And dooms to death when we transgress.
>
> Its light of holiness imparts
> The knowledge of our sinful hearts
> That we may see our lost estate
> And seek deliv'rance ere too late.
>
> To those who help in Christ have found
> And would in works of love abound
> It shows what deeds are his delight
> And should be done as good and right.

57. This is Newton's hymn that begins, "Let us love, and sing, and wonder," inspired by the same amazing grace that caused him to write his better-known favorite.

cleansing and renewal. This entails the principle of commitment to his lord-ship, to the law of Christ as the full revelation of the will of God.

The typical antinomian response is to raise the specter of legalism. Since the latter is a problem in many cases, it is well to take note of the varieties against which the complaint is legitimate.

Varieties of Legalism

What is legalism? First a word on what it is not. Adherence to God's precepts as the rule of duty is not legalism. Legalism, as defined in the *Shorter Oxford Dictionary*, is properly "adherence to law as opposed to the gospel; the doctrine of justification by works, or teaching which savors of it." However, revisionist definitions such as the following have become all too common: "The biblical legalist is one who finds security in the authoritative and revealed law of God to which he submits."[58] The negative connotations of legalism are here trans-ferred to historic divine-command morality by psychologizing the issue—thus begging the epistemological question. But the issue is not whether I find secu-rity in the law but whether God has authoritatively revealed the law. If the latter is true, to call the latter legalism is an abuse of language.[59]

Though it appears in more than one form, legalism (properly speaking) always involves bondage in ways that are opposed to Christian freedom. The basic form is justification by works, the idea that we can be righteous in God's sight by obeying the law. The purpose of the law is to show us that that route is closed, that "no one will be declared righteous in his sight by observing the law; rather, through the law we become conscious of sin" (Rom. 3:20; cf. 7:7–13). The law does not function as a standard by which we may show ourselves to be righteous but rather as the standard by which we know ourselves to be sinners. As a result of the law's proper functioning, "[W]e know that a person is not justified by the works of the law but through faith in Jesus Christ. And we have come to believe in Christ Jesus, so that we might be justified by faith in Christ, and not by doing the works of the law, because no one will be jus-tified by the works of the law" (Gal. 2:16 NRSV). So emphatic is Paul on this point that he says that "if justification comes through the law, then Christ died for nothing" (Gal. 2:21 NRSV).

Christ is thus the end of the law for all who believe (Rom. 10:4) in this sense. To be "under law" is to be under the obligation of perfect obedience without being able to comply, and consequently to be under the curse of the

58. James Whyte, "Protestant Ethics and the Will of God," *Theology* 76 (1973): 462.

59. Cf. Joseph Fletcher's psychologizing of the issue in his famous *Situation Ethics: The New Morality* (Philadelphia: Westminster, 1966). Legalists "wallow and cower in the security of the law" (p. 134), fol-low "childish rules" (p. 140), rely on the law as a "neurotic security device to simplify moral decisions" (p. 137).

law, the sanction of eternal punishment for disobedience. The work of Christ delivers believers from the bondage of both liabilities: Christ by his obedience and suffering has secured righteousness and forgiveness for all who trust in him. The law provides a necessary preparatory function in the application of redemption; its purpose is to direct to Christ the goal, through whom believers are no longer under law but under grace (Rom. 6:14).

Justification by works is the most conspicuous form of legalism, but there are other, more subtle varieties. Of these the most plausible perhaps is sanctification by law. Thus we are told: "Man's justification is by the grace of God in Jesus Christ; man's sanctification is by means of the law of God." But this obscures the gracious nature of sanctification and implies that the antidote to antinomian license is a good stiff dose of the law—a remedy vociferously rejected by the apostle Paul:

> You foolish Galatians! Who has bewitched you? Before your very eyes Jesus Christ was clearly portrayed as crucified. I would like to learn just one thing from you: Did you receive the Spirit by observing the law, or by believing what you heard? Are you so foolish? After beginning with the Spirit, are you now trying to attain perfection by human effort? [Gal. 3:1–3]

Paul's reaction becomes more intelligible when we observe that first-century Judaism ascribed a twofold redemptive function to the law. As Ridderbos represents the position, "The Law is the unique means to acquire for oneself merit, reward, righteousness before God, and the instrument given by God to subjugate the evil impulse and to lead the good to victory." [60] Paul's defense of the gospel contains a double polemic; the law is no more a weapon against the power of sin than it is a means of justification. This accounts for his saying, "For if a law had been given that could impart life, then righteousness would certainly have come by the law" (Gal. 3:22). Having begun the Christian life in faith by the grace of the Spirit, the Galatians were now in danger of relying on the law for making progress in sanctification. Paul brings them up sharply. Salvation is by grace through faith throughout—sanctification no less than justification.

Believers are not under law but under grace: not under the law's penalty for disobedience, and also not under its impotency for obedience. As the ground of justification is the work of Christ, so the dynamic of sanctification is the work of the Spirit: "If you are led by the Spirit, you are not under law" (Gal. 5:18). The leading of the Spirit does not consist in providing new information but rather in providing new motivation. The dominion of sin, which the law only confirmed and could not end, is overcome by God's grace through the

---

60. Herman Ridderbos, *Paul: An Outline of His Theology*, trans. John Richard De Witt (Grand Rapids: Eerdmans, 1975), 135.

ministry of the Spirit working by and with the Word. This not to denigrate
the law but to insist on its proper office: the law informs, the Spirit enables.

There is in this regard a relative contrast between the Mosaic and the Christian dispensations. Both are founded on the principle of salvation by grace
through faith, both are administrations of one covenant of grace through one
Mediator. Yet the time of the law had a special preparatory role in the history
of redemption. Its specific purpose was to demonstrate the spiritual inability
of sinful human nature, an inability that the law as law could not heal. Misinterpretation here was the great stumbling block: "Israel, who pursued a law
of righteousness, has not attained it. Why not? Because they pursued it not by
faith but as if it were by works" (Rom. 9:31–32). The promise of the Spirit
was rendered even more attractive through the law's preparatory ministry. The
contrast is not absolute between the time of the law and the time of the gospel;
what is new about the new covenant is the fullness of the Spirit.[61] The Spirit
does not reveal a new moral law but rather writes on the heart the one moral
law already revealed.

Another common form of legalism is that which binds the conscience where
God has left it free. This tendency shows up in a number of subvarieties. Sometimes extrabiblical rules, often trivial in nature, are elevated to canonical status
by formal or informal ecclesiastical tradition; sometimes suprabiblical rules are
self-imposed through excessive scrupulosity; sometimes biblical rules are mis-
understood or misapplied and imposed as absolute when the intent is otherwise. With regard to all such encroachments on conscience it is helpful to note
that rules are not righteous for being rigorous; it is not good to be more strict
than God. There is at least this to be said for divine command morality: it lib-
erates from all forms of will-worship. In the classic statement of the Westminster Confession, "God alone is Lord of the conscience, and hath left it free from
the doctrines and commandments of men" (20.2).

61. See Douglas J. Moo, "The Law of Moses or the Law of Christ," in *Continuity and Discontinuity: Perspectives on the Relationship between the Old and New Testaments*, ed. John S. Feinberg (Wheaton, Ill.: Crossway, 1988), 203–18.

7

The Resolution of Moral Conflicts

One of the liabilities of an ethic that fosters a strong commitment to duty and at the same time posits multiple universal norms such as the Ten Commandments is that of a perplexed conscience when in extreme circumstances the norms make conflicting demands—as in the obligation to preserve life and the obligation to speak truth. The Holocaust produced numerous instances of this particular conflict, but none so telling as the conduct of the villagers of Le Chambon-sur-Lignon in the mountains of southeastern France.[1] Led by the village's Huguenot pastor and his wife and assisted by several "Darbyist" (Plymouth Brethren) families in the surrounding countryside, the Chambonnais successfully rescued some six thousand persons—mostly Jewish children whose parents had already been murdered by the Nazis in central Europe—from the jaws of death.

As Philip Hallie recounts the story, from their first attempts to help Jewish refugees Pastor and Magda Trocmé learned that they would have to conceal their efforts from the authorities and others unsympathetic to what they were doing. "To reveal that help would be to betray the refugees, to put them in harm's way. Either conceal them or harm them—those were the alternatives."

> But in Le Chambon in the beginning of the 1940s, concealment meant lying—lying both by omission and by commission. It meant not conveying to the authorities any of the legally required information about new foreigners in Le Chambon, and it meant making false identity and ration cards for the refugees so that they could survive in Vichy France.[2]

Given their commitment to the duty of truthfulness, this presented a profound moral dilemma to the Trocmés and their co-conspirators.

> To this day, Magda remembers her reaction to hearing about the making of the first counterfeit card. . . . She remembers the horror she felt at that moment:

---

1. See Philip P. Hallie, *Lest Innocent Blood Be Shed: The Story of the Village of Le Chambon and How Goodness Happened There* (New York: Harper, 1979).
2. Ibid., 125.

duplicity, for any purpose, was simply wrong. . . . Even now, Magda finds her integrity diminished when she thinks of those cards. She is still sad over what she calls "our lost candor." . . . She still feels anguish for the children of Le Chambon who had to unlearn lying after the war, and who could, perhaps, never again be able to understand the importance of simply telling the truth. But usually when she says this, she suddenly straightens up her body, with typical abruptness and vigor, and adds, "Ah! Never mind! Jews were running all over the place after a while, and we had to help them quickly. We had no time to engage in deep debates. We had to help them—or let them die, perhaps— and in order to help them, unfortunately we had to lie."[3]

Were the falsehoods justifiable under the circumstances? If so, on what grounds? If not, can conscience rest in peace with the alternative? Such conflicts, being cases of conscience, require some kind of resolution one way or the other. It is therefore necessary to have at least in principle a method of dealing with them.

Prior to the debate over situation ethics in the 1960s evangelical ethicists seldom addressed the problem of moral conflicts head-on.[4] When pressed on the issue Gordon Clark responded, "No doubt it is a lacuna in my ethical theory; but perhaps it is not so serious philosophically . . . so long as the laws obviously apply to many ordinary situations."[5] Now there is something to be said for keeping borderline cases in perspective. Ethics courses constructed around hard cases easily give the impression that the moral life is just one big quandary, that there are no easy answers to any of its questions. But truthfulness under duress is a problem of conscience only for those for whom the practice of truthfulness is already well-established; persons who lie every day for personal advantage or simply for convenience are in no position to appreciate the dilemma faced by the villagers of Le Chambon. So Clark's point is well-taken.

Still the theoretical lacuna is perhaps more serious than Clark was prepared to admit. The conflict situation may be relatively rare, but that does not detract from its philosophical and practical significance. As the situation ethics debate brought to the fore, hard cases test the basic postulates of an ethical system, and different methods of resolution reveal widely divergent concepts of morality. It is neither wise nor safe to ignore the question of moral conflicts. Even if absolute certainty cannot be guaranteed in every case, at least a

3. Ibid., 126–27.
4. A notable exception is E. J. Carnell, *Christian Commitment: An Apologetic* (New York: Macmillan, 1957). Neither Carl F. H. Henry, *Christian Personal Ethics* (Grand Rapids: Eerdmans, 1957) nor John Murray, *Principles of Conduct: Aspects of Biblical Ethics* (Grand Rapids: Eerdmans, 1957) deals with the conflict situation as such.
5. Gordon H. Clark, in *The Philosophy of Gordon H. Clark: A Festschrift*, ed. Ronald H. Nash (Philadelphia: Presbyterian and Reformed, 1968), 425–26.

method can be proposed to reduce or to limit the amount of uncertainty for the sake of integrity of both conscience and system.

To clarify the question, two other kinds of moral conflict may be excluded. Not at issue is the internal conflict we feel when duty is difficult, as when doing right entails personal sacrifice or even suffering wrong. On this point the Socratic maxim is correct: It is better to suffer wrong than to do wrong. If the choice is "sin or suffer" there is no theoretical contest, though there may well be an existential one. The resolution in this case requires moral courage, not more knowledge. Also not at issue are the choices that have to be made because of limitations of time and resources. Such conflicts of duty, as between family, church, and vocation, are relative in nature; they require prudent decisions in distribution of time, money, and effort, but there is no question of breaking one commandment in order to fulfill another.

The basic options where the latter is an issue are to appeal to consequences, to choose the lesser evil, to choose the higher value, or to analyze the cases more carefully.[6]

Consequentialism

The supreme principle of a consequentialist theory of ethics is that an act is right if it is intended to produce a greater balance of good over evil than any available alternative.[7] In philosophical ethics consequentialism is best represented by utilitarianism; in theological ethics it was popularized by Joseph Fletcher as situation ethics; in Roman Catholic moral theology it is currently debated in the sophisticated form of proportionalism.[8] Since the situation ethics debate was in some respects a defining moment for evangelical ethics, it will be useful to begin with that particular version of consequentialism.[9]

In Fletcher's view there is only one biblical absolute, the law of love. "Only the summary of the law is law!" he says. The other commandments may be useful as generally valid illuminating maxims of conduct, but they are always subject to being overridden by the law of love. As Fletcher puts it, "In situation ethics even the most revered principles may be thrown aside if they conflict in any concrete case with love." The whole biblical ethic thus reduces to a single

---

6. For further analysis of resolution methodologies see Edmund N. Santurri, *Perplexity in the Moral Life: Philosophical and Theological Considerations* (Charlottesville: University Press of Virginia, 1987).

7. Cf. William K. Frankena: "An act is *right* if and only if it or the rule under which it falls produces, will probably produce, or is intended to produce at least as great a balance of good over evil as any available alternative." *Ethics,* 2d ed. (Englewood Cliffs, N.J.: Prentice-Hall, 1973), 14.

8. See John Finnis, "Utilitarianism, Consequentialism, Proportionalism . . . or Ethics," in *Fundamentals of Ethics* (Washington, D.C.: Georgetown University Press, 1983), 80–105.

9. The primary source is Joseph Fletcher, *Situation Ethics: The New Morality* (Philadelphia: Westminster, 1966). Fletcher's basic propositions were first published as "The New Look in Christian Ethics," *Harvard Divinity School Bulletin* 24 (1959): 7–18.

imperative: "Act responsibly in love." Conflicts between the other commandments are resolved by appealing directly to the law of love. "Apart from this,"
John Robinson argues along with Fletcher, "there are no unbreakable rules."

> In Christian ethics the only pure statement is the command to love: every other
> injunction depends on it and is an explication or application off it. There are
> some things of which one may say that it is so inconceivable that they could
> ever be an expression of love—like cruelty to children or rape—that one might
> say without must fear of contradiction that they are for Christians always
> wrong. But they are so persistently wrong *for that reason.*

In a formal sense, of course, it is perfectly true that the biblical ethic is one
of acting responsibly in love. Everything turns on whether love to be responsible must be embodied in actions that conform to the universal moral norms.
Although Robinson acknowledges that the whole class of actions prohibited
by the second table of the Decalogue are "fundamentally destructive of
human relationships," he goes on to say that this does not mean that any of
them cannot be right in certain circumstances. The new morality "starts from
persons rather than principles, from experienced relationships rather than
revealed commandments." Situation ethics posits an antithesis between persons and principles without considering whether principles may not in fact
embody personal concern—principles having to do with things like rape and
cruelty to children, which Robinson will not say are categorically wrong.[10]

Criticized for the lack of definition of *love* in *Situation Ethics* (one critic
remarked that it ran through the book like a greased pig), Fletcher subsequently provided this sharper formulation of the question: "Are there any
moral principles, other than to do the most good possible, which oblige us in
conscience at all time?" This question he answers in the negative; the law of
love, the sole absolute, is to do the most good possible. Situation ethics is a
variety of utilitarianism, as Fletcher himself points out. "Let's say plainly that
agape is utility; love is well-being; the Christian who does not individualize or
sentimentalize love *is* a utilitarian. . . . [W]hat remains as a difference between
the Christian and most utilitarians is only the language used, and their different answers given to the questions, 'Why be concerned, why care.'"[11]

---

10. Although situation ethics rigorously opposes exceptionless norms, from time to time they surface.
In defending abortion rights Fletcher allows the argument, "no unwanted and unintended baby should
ever be born" (*Situation Ethics,* 39). This is as universal and absolute as a rule can be, but the right rule is,
"No baby, born or unborn, 'intended' or 'unintended,' ought ever to be unwanted."

11. Joseph Fletcher in *Norm and Context in Christian Ethics,* ed. Gene H. Outka and Paul Ramsey
(New York: Scribner's, 1967), 332. Fletcher goes on to say, "The distance is not so great or so wide between
the secular humanist and the rational love-ethics of Christian situationists" (p. 349). It is not so surprising
to find him later dropping the Christian label altogether. See his article, "Humanist Ethics: The Groundwork," in *Humanist Ethics: Dialogue on Basics,* ed. Morris B. Storer (Buffalo, N.Y.: Prometheus, 1980),
253–60.

The utility of an act is the net balance of good over evil brought about as a consequence. As is commonly pointed out, "utilitarianism eliminates moral dilemmas in the final analysis by its appeal to the single principle of utility; there can (only) be uncertainties about which action in the situation would maximize welfare."[12] The problem is that these uncertainties, *which are created by the consequentialist theory itself,* are themselves impossible to overcome. In both situation ethics and utilitarianism the welfare to be maximized is not simply that of the individual (itself problematic), but the long-range welfare of humanity—the consequences for good over evil in the universe as a whole. One could never be sure of doing the right thing if it depended upon a balance of good over evil weighed in such a scale.

A prudent regard for foreseeable consequences is, of course, one feature of moral action that has to be taken into account, but only if the proposed action is not in itself unjust. Consequences not part of the action itself cannot be predicted with certainty, nor can they be controlled by the agent. The attempt to predict what will be for the greatest universal good and to act on that as the sole or supreme criterion of morality is an impossible demand. And if the utilitarian calculus were not enough of a problem, there is the added difficulty that the principle of utility or "love" without some limitation by a principle of justice is open to all sorts of obvious immorality. As Gordon Clark pointedly remarks: "The greatest good of the greatest number is a principle for tyrants." Hitler, Stalin, Mao (to name but three) all sacrificed millions of innocent people in the name of a greater long-range good.

Thus, not only does consequentialism fail as a method of resolving moral conflicts; by eliminating the category of intrinsic evil it exposes innocent human beings to all manner of unjust treatment—such as medical experimentation on unknowing or unwilling persons in the hopes of finding a cure for a disease. It is always prepared to frame and execute an innocent person in the interest of national security (cf. John 12:50). As Philippa Foot remarks, "There will in fact be nothing that it will not be right to do to a perfectly innocent individual if that is the only way of preventing another agent from doing more things of the same kind."[13]

"What is it," Foot goes on to ask, "that is so compelling about consequentialism? It is, I think, the rather simple thought that it can never be right to prefer a worse state of affairs to a better." "I believe," she continues, "that we go wrong in accepting the idea that there *are* better and worse states of affairs in the sense that consequentialism requires."[14] This is very much to the point.

---

12. James F. Childress, "Dilemma," in *Westminster Dictionary of Christian Ethics,* ed. James F. Childress and John Macquarrie (Philadelphia: Westminster, 1986), 156.

13. Philippa Foot, "Utilitarianism and the Virtues," in *Consequentialism and Its Critics,* ed. Samuel Scheffler (Oxford: Oxford University Press, 1988), 226.

14. Ibid., 227.

Though one can talk of numbers of lives saved, there is no way of calculating the innocent life taken; one can measure the financial legacy of a broken promise, but there is no way of factoring in the broken trust on human well-being. As Bishop Butler observed long ago: "The happiness of the world is the concern of him who is the Lord and Proprietor of it: nor do we know what we are about when we endeavour to promote the good of mankind in any ways but those which he has directed; that is indeed in all ways not contrary to veracity and justice."[15]

Tragic Morality

Another method of dealing with moral conflicts is to posit the idea of the tragic moral choice. In a fallen world, the theory goes, one may be faced with a choice between alternatives both of which conflict with some absolute principle of duty. Since it is impossible in such situations to avoid doing wrong, one should choose "the lesser of two evils."[16] Even so, guilt is incurred for the evil that is done and one must seek forgiveness for having done it. That it was the best thing one could do under the circumstances does not affect the need for confession of sin for having broken a universally binding commandment.

J. I. Packer, apparently hard-pressed by situation ethics, takes this approach. He asks, "[W]hat are we to think and do when we find ourselves in situations where we cannot move at all without transgressing a divine prohibition, so that the best we can do is evil from one standpoint?" His answer is to do the most good and the least evil, noting that "different principles come out on top in different situations."

> We may agree with the situationist that love for persons must arbitrate between the conflicting claims of moral principles, that doctrinaire decisions in such cases will not make the best of the bad job, and that unwillingness to face the situation's full complexities, and insensitivity to the variety of rules and claims that apply, will lead straight into ironclad Pharisaic legalism. But we shall reject Fletcher's grotesque idea that in such situations adultery, fornication, abortion, suicide and the rest, if thought the *best* course (which arguably in Fletcher's cases they might be—we will not dispute that here), thereby become *good*: which valuation, as Fletcher himself emphasizes, leaves no room for regret at having had to do them. Instead, we shall insist that evil remains evil, even when,

---

15. Joseph Butler, *Five Sermons Preached at the Rolls Chapel and A Dissertation on the Nature of Virtue* (Indianapolis: Bobbs, 1950), 89.

16. Thomas à Kempis is sometimes cited as an example, but only by ignoring the context: "Always choose the lesser of two evils; to avoid eternal punishment in the future, do all that you can to bear present troubles patiently." In other words, we may not sin to save our life. *The Imitation of Christ: A New Reading of the 1441 Latin Autograph Manuscript,* trans. William C. Creasy (Macon, Ga.: Mercer University Press, 1989), 3.12.2.

being the lesser evil, it appears the right thing to do; we shall do it with heavy heart, and seek God's cleansing of our conscience for having done it.[17]

Other evangelicals have taken the same tack. John Warwick Montgomery in public debate with Fletcher took the position that "when sinful human situations require a choice to be made between conflicting absolute moral demands, the trouble lies not with the demands but with the situations. In these cases, the 'lesser' of evils may have to be accepted, but it is still in every sense an evil and must drive the Christian to the Cross for forgiveness and to the Holy Spirit for restoration."[18] As an example he cites the case of whether it is right to shoot a sniper to save the lives of his targets. Montgomery argues, "To kill a human being, if Jesus is right, is a sin. It's morally wrong. Human beings are not to be killed. Thou shalt not kill."[19]

Montgomery goes on to say that it may be necessary to take the life of the sniper in view of the people who would otherwise be killed, but the person who makes that decision is still not morally vindicated.

> If the man is a Christian, this agonizing decision will cause him to look in the mirror and see himself as a member of a sinful society. His decision to shoot a fellow human being will compel him to seek forgiveness. There is a solidarity in human life that requires a person to see his own culpability in situations like this and therefore to seek forgiveness.[20]

Forgiveness for what? Montgomery seems to shift away from the culpability of the specific action to a more general and vague notion of guilt. Would not the latter mean that those who read about it in the newspaper are just as guilty as the police sharpshooter who pulls the trigger? The real problem, however, is not this confusion but Montgomery's assumption that the taking of human life is always wrong, no matter what the circumstances. His zeal for absolutes has led wide of the actual biblical teaching that forbids "all taking away the life of ourselves, or of others, except in case of public justice, lawful war, or necessary defence."[21] At least in this instance a more careful analysis of the case leads to a resolution of the sup-

---

17. J. I. Packer, "Situations and Principles," in *Law, Morality, and the Bible*, ed. Bruce Kaye and Gordon Wenham (Downers Grove, Ill.: InterVarsity, 1978), 164. Packer's argument is largely rhetorical: "doctrinaire decisions," "unwillingness," "insensitivity," and not just "legalism" but "*ironclad Pharisaic legalism*."

18. John Warwick Montgomery, in *Situation Ethics: True or False: A Dialogue between Joseph Fletcher and John Warwick Montgomery* (Minneapolis: Bethany, 1972), 46. Throughout the debate Fletcher tried to get Montgomery to face the logic of saying we ought to do what is wrong, but Montgomery would only say that a lesser evil is still evil. See pp. 53, 69–70, 82–83.

19. Ibid., 64.

20. Ibid., 65.

21. Westminster Larger Catechism, q. 136.

posed conflict. The police officer acting in the line of duty in taking the life of the guilty assailant does not commit sin, even though the consequences are tragic in the sense that a life sadly must be taken in the pursuit of justice.

The theory of the tragic moral choice derives some of its plausibility from the ambiguity of the word *evil*, which can refer to either physical evil or moral evil. To choose the lesser of two physical evils is not problematic from the moral point of view. To amputate a limb in order to save a life is not to maim but to heal by the only means available; so far from being morally blameworthy it is morally praiseworthy. But the idea of being compelled by (providentially governed) circumstances to choose the lesser of two moral evils, that is, the lesser of two sins, is highly problematic on Christian assumptions. It impugns the integrity of the Lawgiver by supposing he has issued conflicting commands, yet holds us responsible for obeying both of them. The idea of the tragic moral choice may be at home in the polytheistic world of Greek tragedy (where one risks disobeying one god in obeying another—since you're "damned if you do and damned if you don't," you disobey the god who can do the least damage), but it is incoherent in a world where there is only one Lawgiver and Judge (James 4:12).

Why is it that some evangelicals are attracted to the "tragic moral choice" option? Perhaps it is their sense of tragedy, their sensitivity to the calamities and ambiguities of living in a fallen world. But evil in the sense of tragic suffering and evil in the sense of moral transgression cannot be weighed in the same scale. Part of the problem is the assumption that actions with tragic consequences are necessarily sinful. The Bible does not make such an inevitable coordination. An act may have painful consequences but still be morally right, such as the forcible restraint of evil by lawful authority.

In making sin necessary under some circumstances tragic, that morality does not measure up to the biblical teaching that expressly rejects the idea of doing evil that good may come, and also affirms that God will not allow us to be tempted or tested above what we are able to bear. To hold that in a fallen world situations arise that make sin unavoidable renders the example of Jesus meaningless, for either he sinned, which is unthinkable, or else he never faced a really tough moral situation, and so was not tested at all points like us. The position further involves a psychological difficulty in requiring remorse for having done the only right thing under the circumstances. It tends also to short-circuit moral reasoning. Adopted for emergency use only, the principle has a way of expanding its sphere of application as emergencies multiply, until finally anything is possible, provided one feels half-guilty about it.

Hierarchicalism

One evangelical ethicist who vigorously rejects the idea of the tragic moral choice is Norman L. Geisler.[22] Rightly holding a priori on biblical grounds that moral conflicts must be capable of resolution without making sin inevitable, Geisler posits a hierarchy of graded absolutes so that in cases of conflict between God's commands (which conflicts are real, not just apparent) obedience to the higher absolute exempts from obedience to the lower absolute. The heart of Geisler's theory, alternatively called hierarchicalism or graded absolutism, is as follows:

> Ethical hierarchicalism is so named because it maintains a hierarchical arrangement or ordering of ethical norms based on the relative scale of values they represent. It implies a pyramid of normative values which *in and of themselves* are objectively binding on men. But when any two or more of these values happen to conflict, a person is exempted from his otherwise binding obligation to a lower norm in view of the pre-emptory obligation of the higher norm.[23]

In his most recent work on ethics, Geisler provides the following summary of the basic tenets of his position:

> The essential principles of graded absolutism are: There are many moral principles rooted in the absolute moral character of God; There are higher and lower moral duties—for example, love for God is a greater duty than love for people; These moral laws sometimes come into unavoidable moral conflict; In such conflicts we are obligated to follow the higher moral law; When we follow the higher moral law we are not held responsible for not keeping the lower one.[24]

Although Geisler's view of the matter is open to serious criticism, there is a legitimate role for hierarchy in biblical ethics. As Gerald Vann remarks, "Too often Christians have no idea of hierarchy within the moral law (minor principles being applicable, and therefore obligatory, only in function of the major principles) and think of all laws, even purely positive laws, as wholly unconditional, so that any breakage of the rules, even though innocent or perhaps mandatory, is regarded as sinful."[25] The classic case within Scripture is the permission granted David and his companions in their extremity to eat the consecrated bread that legally was for the priests alone. From this we infer that the ceremonial precepts could be relaxed for humanitarian reasons in cases of necessity *because their God-given purpose was to enhance human life, not to diminish it.*

---

22. Norman L. Geisler, *Ethics: Alternatives and Issues* (Grand Rapids: Zondervan, 1971); idem, *The Christian Ethic of Love* (Grand Rapids: Zondervan, 1973); idem, *Options in Christian Ethics* (Grand Rapids: Baker, 1981); idem, *Christian Ethics: Options and Issues* (Grand Rapids: Baker, 1989).

23. Geisler, *Ethics*, 114.

24. Geisler, *Options in Christian Ethics*, 132.

25. Gerald Vann, *Moral Dilemmas* (Garden City, N.Y.: Doubleday, 1965), 29.

The problem with Geisler's construction is that he sees this and all other conflicts between God's commands as real (not just apparent) conflicts between absolutes. He argues that since all God's commands reflect his holiness and require obedience, all are moral and therefore absolute. Though he uses the term *conflicting absolutism* to categorize tragic morality, he readily admits—in fact insists—that his own view presupposes conflicting absolutes. The difference is that whereas tragic morality posits irresolvable conflicts between absolutes, Geisler's system of graded absolutes provides for the resolution of such conflicts by exemption of the lower absolute by the higher. This solution, however, is not without problems of its own.

First, Geisler's use of the term *absolute* is peculiar if not equivocal. Webster's defines *absolute* as "having no restriction, exception, or qualification." Geisler insists that his exemptions do not constitute exceptions, but he does acknowledge that his theory is a "*qualified* absolutism," which sounds oxymoronic (akin to "boneless ribs"). Hierarchicalism still markets "absolutes" but they appear to be irregular, as we are told that "not all absolutes are absolutely absolute. Some are only relatively absolute, that is, absolute relative to their particular area."[26] The idea of an absolute as an exceptionless moral norm, Geisler argues, nevertheless remains intact. "Graded absolutism does not believe there are any exceptions to absolute laws, only exemptions." An exception would violate the universality and absoluteness of a command, but an exemption does not.

> The difference between an exemption and an exception can be illustrated as follows. When one kills another human being in self-defense, he is exempt from guilt (Exod. 22:2). Yet there is no exception made to the law which requires us to always treat another man—even a would-be murderer—as a human being with intrinsic value.[27]

Now it is true that human beings, even those who must be forcibly restrained from harming others, must be treated as persons with intrinsic value. But this is not the precise issue. The issue is rather whether God has absolutely forbidden the taking away of human life under all circumstances. If he has not, then clearly there is no conflict of absolutes in the kind of case (justifiable self-defense) that Geisler mentions. The moral absolute embodied in the sixth commandment is properly stated thus: Human life is sacred to God and may never be taken away without divine warrant. From Scripture we learn that such is warranted in the cases of public justice, lawful war, and necessary self-defense. If we state the universal norm governing the sanctity of human life negatively, "God forbids the taking away of human life except in the case of public justice,

---

26. Geisler, *Ethics,* 132. Geisler explains that "lower norms are not universal in the broadest sense of the word. . . . That is, lower ethical norms cannot be universally universal but only locally universal. They are valid *on their particular relationship* but not on all relationships" (p. 132, emphasis original). But even if we allow the oxymoronic "local universals" or "particular universals," these categories leave unresolved the problem of conflicts within spheres, as in the case of a life-threatening pregnancy.

27. Geisler, *Options in Christian Ethics,* 127.

lawful war, or necessary self-defense" these are not stating exceptions to absolutes (or exemptions, for that matter) but defining the absolute in such a way as to require the burden of proof that the taking away of human life is warranted by divine authority. They are instances of divine warrant, rather than either exceptions or exemptions from an absolute prohibition. Only a preconceived notion of an absolute imposed on the Scriptures leads to difficulty here.

Second, in his determination to show that there are conflicting absolutes Geisler makes no distinction between the universal moral law and the particular ceremonial and civil laws. It is this insistence that all God's commands are absolute that creates many problems where none exist—unnecessary in most cases. But rather than construe David and the shewbread as an exemption from a moral absolute, it is rather an indication that the ceremonial law was not intended to be absolute. As Cranfield notes, "the drift of the argument is that the fact that Scripture does not condemn David for his action shows that the rigidity with which the Pharisees interpreted the ritual law was not in accordance with scripture, and so was not a proper understanding of the Law itself."[28]

This is clear in the lesser-known incident in the days of Hezekiah.

> Although most of the many people who came from Ephraim, Manasseh, Issachar and Zebulun had not purified themselves, yet they ate the Passover, contrary to what was written. But Hezekiah prayed for them, saying, "May the LORD, who is good, pardon everyone who sets his heart on seeking God—the LORD, the God of his fathers—even if he is not clean according to the rules of the sanctuary." And the LORD heard Hezekiah and healed the people. [2 Chron. 30:18–20]

The hierarchy of human concerns over ceremonies thus works in this case, but only because the ceremonies are what they are—not absolute in themselves but for human welfare. The priests "violate" the Sabbath by not resting from their work only on a narrow interpretation of the Sabbath that God never intended. That intent is stated by Jesus in the overarching principle: The Sabbath was made for man—not man for the Sabbath (Mark 2:27). Deeds of mercy and necessity were never forbidden; they took precedence over the prescribed rest. By virtue of the purpose of the Sabbath to serve human beings these were not really Sabbath violations because the Sabbath was never intended to be absolute in that sense.

In the case of justifiable disobedience to the state, the conflict is not between what God commands, but between what God commands and what human authorities command. In such cases, we must obey God rather than the authorities. God does not require absolute obedience to the state; our duty

---

28. C. E. B. Cranfield, *The Gospel According to St. Mark* (Cambridge: Cambridge University Press, 1959), 165.

is to obey their lawful commands. When they command sin, there is not only no duty to obey them but our only duty is to obey God by our disobedience to the command to sin. To think of obedience to the state as a moral absolute is positively dangerous, even though qualified by exemption to a higher command. The fact is that God does not make it our duty to obey the state when it issues commands that conflict with the moral law. For more on this concern, see the comments about civil disobedience.

Third, as a method, Geisler's hierarchicalism is too open-ended. Such a theory requires that one know which value is intrinsically higher in the conflict situation. Geisler offers the following guiding principles (pp. 115–20):

Persons are more valuable than things.

Infinite Person is more valuable than finite person(s).

A complete person is more valuable than an incomplete person.

An actual person is of more value than a potential person.

Potential persons are more valuable than actual things.

Many persons are more valuable than few persons.

Personal acts that promote personhood are better than those that do not.

The unifying principle behind all of these is to promote the highest personal value, which Geisler understands to be the meaning of the command to love: "there is really only one thing which is ultimate and absolute—*love* (p. 134)." Geisler wants to restrict the preemption to the conflict situation, but the notion of an overriding personal value is so broad that the conflict it is liable to create hardly admits of any limitation. So long as one tends to do the most personal thing, he acts morally. In spite of protestations to the contrary Geisler's norms of obligation are not such that it is intrinsically wrong to do the opposite of what they require. There is no moral norm other than the law of love that may not be exempted under some circumstances. The practical result is not very different from situation ethics.

Prima Facie Duties

Other evangelical ethicists who reject tragic morality and appeal to the "higher value" solution make use of the concept of prima facie duties introduced into ethics by the British philosopher W. D. Ross. John Jefferson Davis, for example, acknowledges his affinity with Geisler but prefers the designation *contextual absolutism*. He explains, "The term 'contextual absolutism' contains the implicit reminder that the moral absolutes of Scripture need to be understood and applied within their proper context. Some normal or *prima facie* duties may not be actual duties when all things are taken into consideration."[29] More consistently, Stephen Mott remarks, "The term *absolute* or *universal* disguises the actual process of ethical decision making." Mott holds that "in practice even permanently binding values cannot always be the actual duty." Rather than speak in terms of "qualified absolutes," Mott sticks with the language of prima facie duties.

This moves in the right direction but is inhibited by being attached to the particular view of prima facie duties expounded by David Ross. According to Ross, reflection on what we "really think" about ethics yields a sixfold catalogue of duties: fidelity and reparation, gratitude, justice, beneficence, self-improvement, and nonmaleficence.[30] Anticipating the objection that such a plurality of norms would inevitably lead to conflict, Ross argues, "If we want to formulate universal moral laws, we can only formulate them as laws of prima facie obligation, laws stating the tendencies of actions to be obligatory in virtue of this characteristic or of that."[31] Prima facie duties are thus "conditional duties," "things that tend to be our duty."[32] Actual duty is determined by reference to the situation in its totality.

So far, so good—or at least not so far gone as to be beyond recovery by a better choice of language. But Ross goes on to insist that prima facie duties are still obligatory even in cases in which they are not our actual duty. By "prima facie" he does not mean simply "on first view, before further examination" (Webster's); he means that the duty still persists even after examination justifies another course of action. Thus, "it remains hard fact that an act of promise-breaking is morally unsuitable in so far as it is an act of promise-breaking, even when we decide that in spite of this it is the act that we ought to do."[33] In other words, Ross says that although promise-breaking may be our (actual) duty in a particular situation, promise-keeping remains our (prima facie) duty even in that situation. But to say that we both ought and ought not to break a promise is confusing to say the least. As a method of resolving moral conflicts, the appeal to prima facie duties looks a lot like wanting to have your cake and eat it, too.

29. John Jefferson Davis, *Evangelical Ethics: Issues Facing the Church Today* (Phillipsburg, N.J.: Presbyterian and Reformed, 1985), 14.

30. W. David Ross, *The Right and the Good* (Oxford: Clarendon, 1930), 19. Epistemologically Ross's view is a form of ethical intuitionism but this is not germane to the concept of prima facie duties as such. Ross is classified as a deontologist inasmuch as this theory includes obligations (admittedly "very few in number and very general in character") other than the duty to produce the greatest good. But the duty to produce the greatest good remains one of our chief duties, and in fact "eats up" the other duties which are to be followed in cases where there is only a slight preponderance of good at stake, but the principle of utility is supreme when a much greater good may be accomplished. The basis for this quantitative distinction is not clear.

31. W. David Ross, *Foundations of Ethics* (1939; reprint, Oxford: Clarendon, 1951), 86.

32. Ross, *The Right and the Good,* 18–19.

33. Ross, *Foundations of Ethics,* 85.

Mott follows Ross, holding that "[a] prima facie duty allows no exceptions. It has a claim upon us even in a situation in which we cannot fulfill it. It must always be taken into account. The prima facie duty is duty—other things being equal. The actual duty is duty—all things considered."[34] Thus, "right actions are those which have the greatest balance of prima facie rightness over their prima facie wrongness."[35] The advantage of this method, Mott says, lies in "the recognition that the duties which are not met remain as valid claims upon us."[36] He cites civil disobedience as an example: "The character of such an act of civil disobedience is conditioned by the realization that the obligation to government continues as an unmet claim and a wrong-making characteristic of the act."[37] But can we have it both ways? Can an act be right and still have wrong-making characteristics? The Rossian method confuses ethics by blurring the absolute distinction between right and wrong.

As with the idea of hierarchy there is a legitimate sense in which prima facie duties may be employed as a principle without mixing right and wrong. We may understand the sixth commandment in the sense that it is prima facie wrong to take away the life of another human being, meaning that the burden of proof always rests on the one who takes life to show that it is warranted by the Word of God. We agree that "we shall sometimes act with a sense of sorrow fitting to the difficult choices which we have to make."[38] But this regret stems from the abnormality that makes the action necessary, not from some remaining inherent wrong-making characteristic. So with civil disobedience. Since the civil government is an ordinance of God, civil disobedience always requires justification. But if it is justified, then to disobey is right—not partly right and partly wrong. God limits the authorities he has ordained; God does not require us to obey their immoral laws or directives.

Case Analysis

Historically the resolution of moral conflicts has proceeded by way of case analysis or casuistry, which is properly "the careful, devout effort to discover by reflection and discussion, the right course of action in typical circumstances," not (as is commonly thought and sometimes practiced) "the clever exercise of ingenuity to evade the inconvenient."[39] Since the pejorative meaning of casuistry ("rules for getting around the rules") is predominant, the term

---

34. Stephen Charles Mott, *Biblical Ethics and Social Change* (New York: Oxford University Press, 1982), 155.
   35. Ibid., 156.
   36. Ibid., 158.
   37. Ibid., 160.
   38. Ibid., 158.
   39. Albert R. Jonsen, "Casuistry," in *Westminster Dictionary of Christian Ethics*, ed. James F. Childress and John Macquarrie (Philadelphia: Westminster, 1996), 78–79.

is probably beyond resuscitation. But as a method of dealing with moral conflicts, serious casuistry or case analysis remains viable.[40] Before it was called casuistry (on the model of sophistry) the resolution of "cases of conscience" was called "casuistical divinity," and those who practiced it were "casuists," that is, "case-ists" (the Latin for "case" is *casus*). Whatever we call it, cases have to be dealt with; the choice is not between casuistry and no-casuistry but between good casuistry ("case-istry") and bad.[41]

We must, of course, proceed with caution; casuistry does not have a bad reputation for nothing. Given human depravity, what is presented as a resolution of a moral difficulty may turn out to be only an elaborate justification of sin. Pascal's *Provincial Letters* exposed a form of casuistry (*probabilism*) that deserved biting satire, and Pascal obliged in all the right places.[42] Proper case analysis or devout casuistry presupposes a sincere desire to know the will of God and a determination to resist accommodation to contemporary cultural

40. See Albert R. Jonsen and Stephen Toulmin, *The Abuse of Casuistry: A History of Moral Reasoning* (Berkeley: University of California Press, 1988). The authors' goal is "to rehabilitate not the *word* 'casuistry' but rather the *art* to which it disparagingly refers: the practical resolution of particular moral perplexities, or 'cases of conscience'" (p. 13). They give a sympathetic (yet critical) reading of the history of the method, including the century of "high casuistry" (1556–1656) and demonstrate its relevance to contemporary issues, especially in the field of bioethics. The title of their book reflects a play on words by the Anglican casuist, Kenneth Kirk (1886–1954): "The *abuse* of casuistry is properly directed, not against all casuistry, but only against its *abuse*" (p. 16).

41. See Richard Baxter, *A Christian Directory; or, A Sum of Practical Theology, and Cases of Conscience*, vol. 1 of *The Practical Works of Richard Baxter* (1673; Ligonier, Penn.: Sola Deo Gloria, 1990). Baxter's predecessors in the English Puritan tradition were the two Williams: William Perkins, *A Discourse of Conscience* (1595) and *The Whole Treatise of Cases of Conscience* (posthumous, 1606), and William Ames, *Conscience with the Power and Cases Thereof* (1639). In his prefatory "Advertisement," Baxter gives this account of the state of the art in 1673: "Long have our divines been wishing for some fuller casuistical tractate: Perkins began well; Bishop [Robert] Sanderson hath done excellently *de juramento*; Amesius hath exceeded all, though briefly. Mr. David Dickson hath put more of our English cases about the state of sanctification, into Latin, than ever was done before him. Bishop Jeremy Taylor hath in two folios [*Ductor Dubitantium; or, The Rule of Conscience*] but begun the copious performance of the work. And still men are calling for more, which I have attempted: hoping that others will come after, and do better than we all" (p. 4). The *Directory* or "Sum," as Baxter called it, runs to 904 double-column pages, which may help explain why no successor ever appeared.

42. The key thesis of probabilism ("probable-ism") was put forth by the Spanish Dominican Bartolomeo Medina in 1577: "If an opinion is probable [i.e., supported by argument, some evidence], it is licit to follow it, even though the opposite opinion is more probable [i.e., supported by better argument, more evidence]." In the Roman Catholic penitential system it allowed a confessor to take advantage of a reasonable doubt created by differing expert opinions in circulation, but in practice it fostered a minimalist ethic. As Jonsen and Toulmin observe, "[Pascal] saw and struck at the fatal flaw of extreme probabilism. He rightly recognized the inherent tendency of probabilism to slide toward moral skepticism, where every opinion is as good as any other, and into moral laxism, where all law falls before liberty." *Abuse of Casuistry*, 171. After Pascal's critique in 1656, probabilism gave way to probabiliorism ("probabler-ism"), which held that the more probable opinion must be followed, to which equiprobabilism ("equally-probable-ism") was added as a technical refinement in the eighteenth century (see *Westminster Dictionary of Christian Ethics* for details). Rejected as unnecessarily stringent and tending to scrupulosity was tutiorism ("safer-ism"), which held that only moral certainty can secure release from a doubtful obligation.

values. This dimension, calling as it does for vigilant self-examination, must never be lost sight of; only if our heart is right will our analysis of cases do us any good.

Another lesson from the history of casuistry is that the attempt to be exhaustive is misguided. What we primarily need is a method that will help us resolve for ourselves difficulties in the moral life as they arise. At the same time, there are many typical cases (artificial insemination in human reproduction, artificial nutrition and hydration for patients in a persistent vegetative state) which need to be addressed in advance of particular circumstances. It is here that the case analysis method offers the most promise.

The classical Christian approach to moral conflicts assumes that resolution is possible, is guided by, this governing principle: "That what God forbids is at no time to be done; what he commands is always our duty; and yet every particular duty is not to be done at all times."[43] Fulfillment of the positive commands is limited by circumstances (since we cannot do everything at once or anything all of the time) and by the prior restraint of the negative commands. If God forbids something, it may never be done, not even in pursuit of a positive command. A dutiful end will not justify a sinful means. Apparent conflicts between what God forbids and what he requires provoke a twofold analysis to determine what God actually commands and whether the circumstances alter a particular case.

Analysis of how the commandments apply in typical cases begins with careful consideration of the commandments themselves. Absolutes in the sense of objective, universal, exceptionless moral norms can only be formulated by attending carefully to the whole teaching of Scripture in a given area. Many of the dilemmas posed in the evangelical literature on moral conflicts are readily resolvable on this basic principle. The sixth commandment, for example, when interpreted in the light of Scripture as a whole, forbids "all taking away the life of ourselves, or of others, except in case of public justice, lawful war, or necessary defense."[44] The exceptions define the rule (rather than exempt it). The scriptural absolute is that human life is sacred to God and may not be taken without divine warrant, and it is warranted in these instances: public justice, lawful war, necessary defense. Otherwise the taking of human life is murder.[45]

43. Westminster Larger Catechism, q. 99, rule 5. Cf. Thomas à Kempis: "Never do what you know is wrong for anything in the world or to please anyone. Yet, to serve the needy a good work may be put aside or exchanged for a better one. In doing so, a good work is not lost; it is changed into something better." *Imitation of Christ*, 1.15.1.

44. Westminster Larger Catechism, q. 136.

45. The Book of Common Prayer retains Coverdale's correct translation of the sixth commandment: "Thou shalt do no murder." Cf. NIV, NASB, and NRSV, all of which have *murder* rather than *kill*, the familiar but misleading rendering of the KJV.

What about Abraham and Isaac? Did God overrule his own absolute and make an exception to murder? No, the "binding of Isaac" (*akedat yitzchak*), as the event is accurately called in the Jewish tradition, is a special instance of divine warrant for the taking of human life, designed to teach that *no human sacrifice other than the lamb of God could suffice to make atonement.* The place name is the key to the meaning of the event: "So Abraham called that place The LORD Will Provide. And to this day it is said, 'On the mountain of the LORD it will be provided'" (Gen. 22:14). As Abraham spoke prophetically to Isaac en route: "God himself will provide the lamb for the burnt offering, my son" (Gen. 22:8). The lamb, it turns out, is none other than God himself in the person of his Son.

The incident is not a "teleological suspension of the ethical" in Kierke-gaard's worried phrase. Strictly speaking we would have to say, murder is the unwarranted taking of human life and it is only warranted—the binding of Isaac aside—in cases of public justice, lawful war, and necessary defense. The exceptional warrant in the case of the binding of Isaac is unique and unrepeat-able. God teaches the primary lesson of substitutionary atonement (that only *he* can make the sacrifice) early in the history of redemption by special revela-tion to his friend, Abraham, to whom he had promised blessing through his only son, Isaac. All these features are unique to that single event, which in fact God allows to proceed only so far (Isaac is bound, not slain), and it would be pedantic to insist on making reference to it in the definition of murder.

Another example of a supposed conflict of duties that appears regularly in the evangelical literature has to do with vows. Erwin Lutzer puts the case as follows.

> A man may foolishly vow to kill another man. Now he is forced either to break his promise or become a murderer. In either case he is sinning. Here he must choose between the lesser of two evils. Hopefully, he will choose to break his vow. But he would not have been in this moral dilemma if he had not broken the scriptural instructions regarding vows (Eccl. 5:5). Having violated one instruction, he became entangled and therefore *had* to sin. In this case, two uni-versals were clearly in conflict, but only because one universal had already been broken.[46]

Lutzer rightly hopes that the choice won't be murder, but he doesn't explain why breaking a solemn vow to God is a lesser sin than killing a human being. The truth is, there is no sin in breaking such a vow. Lutzer's problem is that he has made vowing a moral absolute in the abstract apart from the content of what is vowed. A vow essentially calls upon God as one's witness, and God will not be made a witness to sin. A vow makes an action

---

46. Erwin W. Lutzer, *The Morality Gap* (Chicago: Moody, 1972), 107.

a religious duty, but it cannot be a religious duty to sin, and no vow can make it so. The historic teaching of the church is simple and clear: "[An oath] cannot oblige to sin."[47] There is no moral dilemma in Lutzer's example; there is only one right course of action: to repudiate the vow and to seek forgiveness for having made it.

What about Jephthah? Should he or should he not have kept his vow to sacrifice as a burnt offering to the Lord "whoever comes out of the doors of my house to meet me when I return victorious from the Ammonites" (Judges 11:31 NRSV)?[48] Is it not written, "When a man makes a vow to the LORD or takes an oath to obligate himself by a pledge, he must not break his word but must do everything he said" (Num. 30:2; cf. Deut. 23:21–23)? When the greeter turned out to be his daughter, wasn't Jephthah obligated to offer her as a burnt offering? No; it is also written, "You must not worship the LORD your God in their [the Canaanites'] way, because in worshiping their gods, they do all kinds of detestable things the Lord hates. *They even burn their sons and daughters in the fire as sacrifices to their gods*" (Deut. 12:31; cf. Deut. 18:10; Lev. 18:21; 20:2–5).[49] It was no more right for Jephthah to sacrifice his daughter (Judg. 11:39, "he did to her as he had vowed") than it was for Herod because of his foolish oath to deliver the head of John the Baptist on a platter (Matt. 14:1–12). Human sacrifice and murder are not acceptable forms of worship; the vows should have been penitently repudiated.

Paying attention to the whole teaching of Scripture in defining universal norms thus removes many supposed instances of conflicting absolutes. With respect to civil magistrates, it is the duty of the people "to obey their lawful commands"; the sixth commandment requires "all lawful endeavours to preserve our own life and the life of others"; among the requirements of the ninth commandment is the duty of "keeping lawful promises."[50] Of course, it still has to be determined whether or not a specific command or promise or life-preserving endeavor is lawful in a particular case,[51] so there is more to be done by way of analysis of the circumstances. But clarifying the universal norms is a necessary and valuable first step in relieving the perplexed conscience.

47. Westminster Confession of Faith, 22.4.

48. The English translations are evenly divided in taking the Hebrew particle of relation (*'asher*) impersonally (KJV, "whatsoever"; NIV, NASB, "whatever"; NEB, "the first creature") and personally (RSV, NAB, "whoever"; GNB, JB, "the first person"). The context ("out of the doors of my house to meet me") indicates the personal reading.

49. The closest biblical parallel is 2 Kings 3:27 where the king of Moab, losing the war against the coalition of Israel, Judah, and Edom, in desperation "took his firstborn son who was to succeed him, and offered him as a burnt offering on the wall" (NRSV).

50. Westminster Confession of Faith, 23.4; Westminster Shorter Catechism, q. 68; Westminster Larger Catechism, q. 144.

51. That a promise is costly does not make it unlawful; but it is unlawful if it involves sin or great temptation to sin (such as a vow of celibacy without the gift of continence).

In addition to the principle of *tota scriptura* (that is, the commandments are defined by the whole teaching of Scripture), case analysis recognizes the truth of the familiar maxim, "Circumstances alter cases." How a given act is to be construed depends upon the situation. Naaman's "bowing down" in the temple of Rimmon was not an instance of apostasy or idolatry despite appearances; the intention was not to worship but to provide physical support to the king (2 Kings 5:18–19). However, as Peter Geach who cites this example goes on to say, "It does not follow that there are not acts that unequivocally signify idolatry or a false god, nor does its follow that such are permissible merely because the man is tempted to apostasy by a threat that otherwise he, and his, will be thrown into a burning fiery furnace."[52]

In personal correspondence with the editor of an evangelical magazine on the "lesser of two evils" approach to moral conflicts, I was presented with the following case:

> A terrorist throws a hand grenade into a crowd. A man sees what is happening. He chooses to commit suicide by throwing himself upon the grenade and in so doing chooses what he thinks to be the lesser of two evils. The greater evil would be for the grenade to explode and kill five or ten others. Yet suicide is prohibited. What would you do with this kind of case?

This provides a good example of how circumstances alter the nature of a case. "Throwing oneself on a grenade" does not by itself give enough information to characterize the act morally; depending on the circumstances it could be either self-murder or self-sacrifice. The proper question is, Has God forbidden such an action as this? The most directly relevant text is the saying of Jesus: "No one has greater love than this, that one lay down one's life for one's friends" (John 15:13 NRSV). Heroic self-sacrifice in the necessary defense of human life is commended rather than prohibited in the biblical ethic. As we would not call Jesus' placing himself in certain jeopardy of his life suicide, neither is it a fair description of the action of someone's falling on a grenade in an emergency. Such a person's intention is not directly to end his or her own life but to spare the lives of others. The circumstances fundamentally alter the case.[53]

The issue of usury is a good historical instance.[54] The ancient Israelites were forbidden to charge interest on loans made to other members of the people of God. The circumstances were that in a subsistence economy such loans were a form of assistance to the poor of the community. To demand back more than was given was to exploit another's adversity for financial gain. The prin-

---

52. Peter Geach, *The Virtues* (Cambridge: Cambridge University Press, 1977), 89–90.

53. For a full discussion of how circumstances affect the moral characterization of an act, see Eric D'Arcy, *Human Acts: An Essay in their Moral Evaluation* (Oxford: Clarendon, 1963).

54. Cf. Jonsen and Toulmin, *Abuse of Casuistry,* 181–94.

ciple was recognized at the Council of Nicaea (A.D. 325), which directed one of its canons against priests who were charging interest on loans to the poor under their care. "Many clerics, motivated by greed and a desire for gain, have forgotten the scriptural injunction, 'He does not put out his money at interest' [Ps. 15] and instead demand a monthly rate of one percent on loans they make. . . . [T]hey shall be deposed from their clerical status."[55]

As economic and social life developed, it became apparent that not all loans are of this type. A distinction was made between interest-free assistance loans (the biblical paradigm) and interest-generating partnership loans which involved a shared risk. The church did not backslide on the issue of usury; the circumstances of mercantilism presented a fundamentally different case.

The keeping of promises receives a lot of attention in the literature on conflicting absolutes, but much anguish could be avoided by remembering that promises are made subject to divine providence. A couple pledges a large donation to the church building fund, but their business suddenly and unexpectedly goes bankrupt. There is no guilt in being providentially hindered from keeping a promise made in good faith. All the couple owes the church is an explanation of their changed circumstances. The old "faith-promise" method of supporting the mission of the church made the principle explicit by the preparatory phrase: "As the Lord enables . . ." (cf. James 4:15).

To summarize, the case analysis approach to moral conflicts and other perplexities of conscience is to reread the Scriptures and to review the case in the light of the circumstances on the assumption that resolution is at least theoretically possible without either having to choose the lesser of two sins or to abandon one universal in favor of another. Ethics is not like geometry, however. As Paul Ramsey (the poet) remarks, "Moral and aesthetic judgments do not consist exclusively of accurate and logically precise application of general principles to particular instances. Good judgment often requires the testing of principles against instances and vice-versa with no formula in advance guaranteeing an exact and sure answer."[56] Circumstances provoke reflection on the intention of the Lawgiver. Perplexities created by burgeoning medical technology require careful case analysis.

Excursus on Truthfulness

To return to the village of Le Chambon, were the falsehoods a lawful means of preserving human life? Debate over this type of conflict situation has a long history in both philosophical and theological ethics. Already in the fifth cen-

55. Ibid., 182.
56. Paul Ramsey, *The Truth of Value: A Defense of Moral and Literary Judgment* (Atlantic Highlands, N.J.: Humanities, 1985), 37.

tury Augustine observed, "Whether we should ever tell a lie if it be for someone's welfare is a question that has vexed even the most learned."[57]

The question is especially difficult since the Bible values truth not less than life. Truth matters; it has intrinsic value. And truthfulness is essential to human community. Deceit, like physical violence, is a form of coercive assault that robs us of our freedom and dignity. Little wonder, then, that the redeemed community of biblical prophesy is envisioned thus: "Then Jerusalem will be called the City of Truth, and the mountain of the LORD Almighty will be called the Holy Mountain" (Zech. 8:3). The vision provokes a present application: "These are the things you are to do: Speak the truth to each other, and render true and sound judgment in your courts; do not plot evil against your neighbor, and do not love to swear falsely. I hate all this, declares the LORD" (Zech. 8:16–17; cf. Eph. 4:25).

Case closed? Not quite. Scripture must be compared with Scripture to determine to what degree the obligation to speak truth may be extenuated by circumstances. Perhaps a series of questions will be useful in probing the extent of the biblical obligation.

Are We Always Obligated to Tell the Truth?

Jesus' own example answers this question in the negative. "[Herod] plied him with many questions, but Jesus gave him no answer" (Luke 23:9). There was no obligation to respond to Herod's inquisitive interrogatories, particularly at this late date; Jesus exercised his moral right to remain silent. See also John 19:8–9, "When Pilate heard this [that Jesus claimed to be the Son of God], he was even more afraid, and he went back inside the palace. 'Where do you come from?' he asked Jesus, but Jesus gave him no answer." Earlier Jesus had told Pilate that he had come into the world to testify to the truth, but Pilate had been in no mood to listen (John 18:37–38). It is now too late for Pilate to be asking Jesus who he is, and so Jesus maintains a just (and eloquent) silence.

Whatever may be the case with the obligation not to communicate what we know is false, clearly the obligation to communicate what we know is true is not absolute. Confidentiality and secrecy are biblical values that are justly guarded by silence. The biblical demand for truthfulness does not mean that

---

57. Augustine, *Against Lying,* trans. Harold B. Jaffee, in *Saint Augustine: Treatises on Various Subjects,* ed. Roy J. Deferrari (New York: Fathers of the Church, 1952), chap. 15. This volume also contains *On Lying.* As Jonsen and Toulmin describe the historical circumstances of the composition of the two influential treatises, "*De Mendacio* was probably prompted by St. Augustine's irritation at St. Jerome's exegesis of Galatians 2:11 [to the effect that Paul had lied about his disagreement with Peter], while *Contra Mendacium* was written in refutation of the Priscillianists [a heretical sect which justified lying for the cause]." Jonsen and Toulmin, *Abuse of Casuistry,* 381 n. 14. For the best modern treatment of the subject see Sissela Bok's wide-ranging and illuminating treatises, *Lying: Moral Choice in Public and Private Life* (New York: Vintage, 1979) and *Secrets: On the Ethics of Concealment and Revelation* (New York: Vintage, 1984).

everyone has a right to know what we know. When the authorities demanded to be informed of any strangers in their midst, the Chambonnais were under no obligation to convey that information to them.

Are We Always Obligated to Tell the Whole Truth?

Again, the question is answered in the negative by divine example. Consider the following dialogue between the Lord and Samuel (1 Sam. 16:1–3).

> The LORD said to Samuel, "How long will you mourn for Saul, since I have rejected him as king over Israel? Fill your horn with oil and be on your way; I am sending you to Jesse of Bethlehem. I have chosen one of his sons to be king."
>   But Samuel said, "How can I go? Saul will hear about it and kill me."
>   The LORD said, "Take a heifer with you and say, 'I have come to sacrifice to the LORD.' Invite Jesse to the sacrifice, and I will show you what to do. You are to anoint for me the one I indicate."

Under the circumstances Saul had no right to know the real purpose of Samuel's pilgrimage to Bethlehem. For Samuel's protection the Lord himself suggests a "cover" that was true—Samuel did come to sacrifice—but at the same time concealed the real point of his mission: the anointing of a successor to King Saul. A partial truth was permitted to circumvent full disclosure (cf. Jer. 38:24–27). This is not a plan for all seasons; the prior breakdown in relationship prevented the candor that should normally characterize human communication. Under ordinary conditions half-truths are no better than outright lies.

Are We Always Obligated to Tell the Plain Truth?

There is some evidence that the Bible approves the use of veiled speech under appropriate circumstances, speech that conceals more than it reveals by the use of ambiguous or equivocal expressions. The classic case is 2 Kings 6:19, where Elisha told the blinded Arameans who had been sent to capture him, "This is not the road and this is not the city. Follow me, and I will lead you to the man you are looking for." Then he led them to Samaria, Israel's capital (and enemy headquarters), and there they saw they had indeed been led to the man they had been looking for—by the man himself, Elisha, whose benign purpose becomes evident as he would not allow them to be executed but had them fêted instead.

Another instance of guileless equivocation appears in the narrative of Joseph and his brothers. On their departure from Egypt the first trip to buy grain, Joseph gave orders to have each of his brother's silver put back in his sack (Gen. 42:25). When they arrived in Egypt on the second trip, the brothers offered to return the money, but Joseph said to them, "It's all right. Don't be afraid. Your God, the God of your father, has given you treasure in your sacks; *I received your silver*" (Gen. 43:23). Joseph's words (literally, "your silver came to me") were true but ambiguous; Joseph's intent was to conceal for the moment that he had returned as well as received his brothers' payment for the grain. The motive and justification may be learned from the narrative as a whole, which moves through testing to complete reconciliation.

Intentional verbal ambiguity or equivocation, which may be appropriate under some limited circumstances, should be sharply distinguished from the doctrine of mental reservation that flourished briefly in the sixteenth century. The idea was that a statement contrary to fact could be qualified by an unexpressed condition in the mind and thus not be a lie; the statement would be true "as far as he [the speaker] and God were concerned."[58] The laxist doctrine was condemned by the Roman Catholic authorities in 1679, but its brief advocacy left casuistry with a bad name.

Mental reservation, of course, must be rejected as a method of resolving moral dilemmas involving truth-telling, for it is subversive of the very purpose of speech for interhuman communication. An utterance that requires a mental qualification to make it true is no different from a lie (that is, a false statement deliberately intended to deceive). The idea that a speaker is not responsible for "misinterpretation" by the hearer of his mentally qualified statement is absurd. A ministerial candidate is asked, "Have you ever committed adultery?" The answer (with mental reservation), "Never (on Sunday)" does not save it from being a lie.

Intentional ambiguity or veiled speech, on the other hand, is sometimes appropriate to divert the attention of an indiscreet inquirer away from a justly guarded secret. Such forms as the ambiguous, "Can't say," or the counterquestion, "Who knows?" are not so opaque that their intent is undiscoverable, which sets them apart from mere mental reservation. Roman Catholic moral theologians generally approve also of broad mental restriction based on conventions of language, such as "not available (to you)" or to a question impinging on the confidentiality of the confessional, "I know nothing (that I can communicate to you)." The argument is that such responses are based on recognized linguistic conventions and thus differ from "pure mental reservation."[59]

It needs to be emphasized, however, that although we are not always obligated to speak the plain truth, equivocation of whatever sort is wrong when mutual understanding is one of the relevant considerations. The Bible certainly places a higher premium on forthrightness than on cleverness in human communication.

58. Jonsen and Toulmin, *Abuse of Casuistry,* 202.
59. Bernard Häring cites the example of a group of nuns who were caring for handicapped children in Germany during the war. "Under Hitler's orders, the SS came to the orphanage and asked, 'How many children do you have who are afflicted by this or that kind of disease or are mentally retarded?' In a few cases, the nuns—in great distress but with literal 'truth'—answered the spoken question, and the unfortunate children were taken off to the gas chambers. Other nuns answered simply, 'We have no such children.'" That is, "No such children [as we will cooperate with you in sending to their deaths]," which the nuns saw as the real question they were being required to answer. *Morality Is for Persons* (New York: Farrar, 1971), 129–30.

Are We Always Obligated to Tell Nothing But the Truth?

So far there is wide agreement in the Christian tradition. Veracity is habitual truthfulness, and justly guarded secrets are best kept by silence. Diversion, evasion, and equivocation are permissible, but only when circumstances inhibit forthright communication and silence is not a viable option. At the point of telling something other than the truth, however, Augustine drew the line. Though some of the Greek fathers (notably Clement of Alexandria, Origen, and Chrysostom) allowed untruths when there was a just and necessary cause, Augustine held that "just lies" were no more possible than "chaste adulteries." His clincher was 1 John 2:21, "No lie is of the truth."[60] Even so, Augustine appeared uneasy with the absoluteness of his conclusion; though epistemologically satisfying, it remained ethically discomfiting.

Aquinas followed Augustine on the absolute prohibition against lying, but distinguished between malicious lies, which intend injury to another person, and officious ("dutiful") lies, which intend to help others or to save them from being injured. The former are mortally sinful, but the latter are only venial— wrong but forgivable. The absoluteness of the Augustinian position was thus mitigated somewhat. The Reformers gave up the mortal/venial distinction as being without biblical warrant, but the Dutch jurist Hugo Grotius found another mitigating factor in the nature of some cases.[61] As Sissela Bok notes, according to Grotius "not all intentionally false statements ought to count as lies from a moral point of view . . . a falsehood is a lie in the strict sense of the word only if it conflicts with a right of the person to whom it is addressed."[62] Grotius' argument was thus intrinsicalist rather than consequentialist; it rested on the correlation of rights and responsibilities in interpersonal relationships, not on the ability to predict or effect favorable outcomes. In the American Reformed tradition, Charles Hodge, Dabney, and Rushdoony follow Grotius, while Thornwell and John Murray defend the original Augustinian position.[63]

It is important to note that the Augustinian position, best represented by John Murray, approves of deception (not concealment alone) in appropriate circumstances, provided only that there are no statements contrary to fact. One may deceive by half-truths or equivocal expressions, but never by a delib-

---

60. Augustine, *Against Lying,* chap. 3.

61. Grotius, *The Rights of War and Peace [De Jure Belli ac Pacis, 1625],* trans. A. C. Campbell (Washington, D.C.: Dunne, 1901), 3.1. The treatise earned Grotius the appellation *father of international law.*

62. Bok, *Lying,* 39.

63. Charles Hodge, *Systematic Theology,* 3 vols. (1872; reprint, Grand Rapids: Eerdmans, 1952), 3:441–43; Robert L. Dabney, *Lectures in Systematic Theology* (1878; reprint, Grand Rapids: Zondervan, 1972), 425–26; R. J. Rushdoony, *Institutes of Biblical Law* (Nutley, N.J.: Craig, 1973), 542–49; James Henley Thornwell, *The Collected Writings of James Henley Thornwell,* 4 vols. (1871–73; reprint, Edinburgh: Banner of Truth, 1974), 2:538–42; John Murray, *Principles of Conduct: Aspects of Biblical Ethics* (Grand Rapids: Eerdmans, 1957), 131–48. Murray is criticized by Klaas Runia, "Situation Ethics in the Light of Scripture," *Vox Reformata* 9 (1967): 1–19.

erate falsehood. Consistency of mind and speech thus become the primary focus of the demand for truthfulness, giving an advantage to the clever who can deceive just as well with "truths" as with lies. This suggests that the moral weight of the command lies elsewhere.

According to the Westminster Shorter Catechism, the ninth commandment (Thou shalt not bear false witness against thy neighbor) "requires the maintaining and promoting of truth between man and man, and of our own and our neighbor's good name, especially in witness bearing" and "forbids whatever is prejudicial to truth, or injurious to our own or our neighbor's good name" (qq. 78–79). As Lewis Smedes puts it, "The primary reason for truthfulness . . . is in the point of view of truthfulness for the sake of the neighbor, in the relationship between the speaker and the listener. We should not think of truthfulness as consistency between our mind and our message so much as honesty between us and our neighbor."[64]

Certainly there is a prima facie obligation not to lie just as there is a prima facie obligation not to kill. As the burden of proof falls on one who takes a life to show that it was justifiable homicide, so the burden of proof falls on the one who tells a lie to show that it was justifiable falsehood. Two incidents in the biblical narrative may be cited by way of precedent.

The first of these is found in Exodus 1:15–22. The king of Egypt commanded the Hebrew midwives, Shiphrah and Puah, to kill any male they observed being born in the course of their duties. This order they refused to carry out; they let the boys live. When confronted with their disobedience, they told Pharaoh: "Hebrew women are not like Egyptian women; they are vigorous and give birth before the midwives arrive." The narrative continues with an indication of divine approval: "So God was kind to the midwives. . . . And because the midwives feared God, he gave them families of their own." There are two exegetical questions: Was the statement of the midwives false? If so, does the divine approval extend to their words as well as their deeds?

All that we know from the biblical record indicates that childbirth was just as difficult for Hebrew women as for women in general. Who can forget Rachel and the birth of Benjamin (Gen. 35:16–20)? Are we to suppose the prophets derived the powerful simile "as a woman in travail" from Gentile experience? Midwives had an established role in assisting the birthing process (Gen. 35:17; 38:28; cf. 1 Sam. 4:20); the term itself in Hebrew is a form of the verb *yālad*, "to bring forth." Shiphrah and Puah in making an excuse to cover their conduct simply took advantage of Pharaoh's crosscultural ignorance. Did God then approve their civil disobedience but not their deception? Nothing in the narrative points to such a division; the midwives stood up to Pharaoh by letting the boys live and, when challenged, by falsifying the report.

---

64. Lewis B. Smedes, *Mere Morality: What God Expects from Ordinary People* (Grand Rapids: Eerdmans, 1983), 222.

The murderous order of the king of Egypt signaled a radical breakdown in human relationships and hence in human communication; Pharaoh had no right to know the truth of the midwives' actions.

The second incident is the story of Rahab and the spies in the strategic walled city of Jericho (Josh. 2:1–24). Anticipating a dragnet, Rahab hid the spies on the roof. When the authorities arrived demanding that Rahab turn the spies over to them, she replied breathlessly, "Yes, the men came to me, but I did not know where they had come from. At dusk, when it was time to close the city gate, the men left. I don't know which way they went. Go after them quickly. You may catch up with them" (Josh. 2:4–5). No half-truth or equivocation or mental reservation, but a pure fabrication to put the hounds off the scent. In classic western, "They went that-a-way!"

That an action appears in the biblical record does not automatically mean that it is approved. In this case we are told later in the narrative that Rahab and her family were spared in the battle of Jericho "because she hid the men Joshua had sent as spies to Jericho" (Josh. 6:25). Certainly concealing the spies from the king of Jericho (treason from his point of view) is approved. Although it is not specifically mentioned in the New Testament retrospectives that extol Rahab's faith, the misdirection of the king's men would seem to be integral to the welcome and the protection for which she is commended (Heb. 11:31; James 2:25). The false lead is justifiable on the same grounds as providing aid and comfort to the spies: the king of Jericho had no right to know the truth of their presence inside the soon-to-be tumbling walls of his city.

The murderer in search of an innocent victim has no right to the truth of the victim's whereabouts and no reason to expect honesty from those who are aware of the situation. To insist on verbal truthfulness in such circumstances is manifestly against the purposes for which God has given us speech. The radical disruption of human relationships alters the nature of the case. Not even the Lord binds himself to uniform straightforwardness irrespective of circumstances. As David sang to the Lord when the Lord delivered him from all his enemies, particularly Saul (2 Sam. 22:26–27 = Ps. 18:25–26):

> With the loyal you show yourself loyal;
>   with the blameless you show yourself blameless;
> with the pure you show yourself pure;
>   and with the crooked you show yourself perverse.[65]

---

65. NRSV. More literally, "with the twisted you deal tortuously." For example, those who refuse to love the truth and be saved find that evangelistic pleading eventually gives way to judicial hardening. Since they have made themselves implacable to the generous offer of the gospel, "God sends them a powerful delusion so that they will believe the lie and so that all will be condemned who have not believed the truth but have delighted in wickedness" (1 Thess. 2:11–12).

When my son was a preschooler, I read to him the story of Rahab and the spies. Afterward he said to me, "Dad, Rahab told a lie, but it was a good lie, wasn't it, Dad?" Well, what is Dad to say? "Go ask your mother" can be used only so many times. The problem is that although falsehoods may be justified in extreme cases as a last resort in the protection of human life, they cannot be called good without qualification because they result from an abnormal situation and a breakdown of human relationships. As Hallie comments with respect to the Chambonnais, "[They] were as candid, as truthful with the authorities as they could have been without betraying the refugees. . . . The spirit of Le Chambon in those years was a strange combination of candor and concealment, of a yearning for truth and of a commitment to secrecy. They were as open as love permits in a terrible time."[66] They did the right thing, but regarded the deception as something regrettably necessary rather than unqualifiedly good.

66. Hallie, *Lest Innocent Blood Be Shed,* 127–28.

8

Marriage and the Family

> In the family of the just . . . even those who rule serve those whom they seem to command; for they rule not from a love of power, but from a sense of the duty they owe to others—not because they are proud of authority, but because they love mercy.
>
> —Augustine, *City of God*

Christians ethics, as we have seen, is the study of the way of life that conforms to the will of God. It asks the basic practical question: What is God calling us, his redeemed people, to be and to do? The direction the Bible gives in answer to that question concerns not only the personal virtues of the individual self and the interpersonal relationships between individuals, but also the social structures of human beings living in community, especially those institutions God has ordained with specific functions for the sake of human flourishing: marriage and the family, civil government, and the visible church.

Historically the Christian tradition in ethics subsumes these under the fifth commandment: Honor your father and your mother.[1] Parents are God's representatives in the primary social unit, the family. But rule in all spheres is similar in that it requires subordination to a divinely appointed office. Thus, Deborah, the prophet and judge, is referred to in her leadership role as "a mother in Israel" (Judg. 5:7), and elders in the apostolic church must have earned respect as fathers to be entrusted with ecclesiastical oversight (1 Tim. 3:4–5). The underlying principle of the commandment is the rightful exercise of authority in divinely ordained social structures. The principle may be applicable to voluntary associations in other social spheres (education, business,

---

1. The Westminster Larger Catechism, for example, takes the fifth commandment to refer to "especially such as, by God's ordinance, are over us in place of authority, whether in family, church, or commonwealth" (q. 124). The exposition of the Catechism, however, is limited to the rights and responsibilities of individuals, whereas the Westminster Confession of Faith, with chapters on the civil magistrate (23), marriage and divorce (24), and the church and sacraments (25–31), presents state, family, and church as social institutions with distinct purposes ordained by God, providing the broad outline of a Christian social ethic.

the arts, and so forth), but the biblical revelation addresses the issue directly only with reference to the communities of family, church, and state, each with its own God-given authority and irreducible function.

It is well to note at the outset the double-edged implications of the phrase *rightful exercise of authority.* On the one hand, the structural relationship by which some human beings have authority over others is divinely ordained by God; the rightfulness of the authority derives from the structure. On the other hand, the authority must be exercised rightfully, that is, in the manner and for the purposes that God intends. Institutional supra- and subordination is a matter of divinely given responsibilities, not superior and inferior human natures. As the epigraph from Augustine affirms, authority is transformed by the Christian understanding of servanthood following the example of Jesus (Matt. 20:25–28; John 13:12–17). Rebellion against authority and oppression by authority stand alike condemned in the biblical ideal.[2]

The apostle Paul points out that the fifth commandment is the first with a promise specifically attached: "that it may go well with you and that you may enjoy long life on the earth" (Eph. 6:2). Brevard Childs rightly observes that the promise "points to the rich blessing of the society which is in harmony with the divine order."[3] As hard as it is for Americans steeped in the radical individualism and egalitarianism of our culture to comprehend, human beings actually flourish in communities where responsibility for the common

---

2. The verb *hypotassō* (to be subordinate) provides an index to the recognition of authority and its rightful exercise as Christian virtues. The uses may be grouped as follows:

The supreme example:
    The Son to the Father—1 Cor. 15:28
    Jesus to Joseph and Mary—Luke 2:51
Believers to God—James 4:7; Heb. 12:9
    The church to Christ—Eph. 5:24
    Israel to the righteousness of God—Rom. 10:3
    The mind to God's law—Rom. 8:7
Believers to one another—Eph. 5:21
    Younger to elder—1 Pet. 5:5
    Prophets to prophets—1 Cor. 14:32
    Wives to husbands—Eph. 5:22; Col. 3:18
    Servants to masters—Tit. 2:9
Believers to civil government—Rom. 13:1

The institution of slavery, it must be said, was destined to be abolished on scriptural grounds, and its perpetuation was wrongly inferred from the New Testament household regulations. Both Testaments condemn the slave trade and chattel slavery, and both Testaments place a premium on being at liberty to serve God. Even indentured servitude is strictly limited in favor of the eventual economic independence of those who voluntarily enter such an arrangement. The early church fathers saw that the institution could not be consistently perpetuated in the gospel age, and the practice was largely discontinued. Its reintroduction and ecclesiastical defense in the New World on racial grounds was an apostasy of horrendous magnitude.

3. Brevard S. Childs, *The Book of Exodus: A Critical, Theological Commentary* (Philadelphia: Westminster, 1974), 419.

good is focused by divinely ordained structures. "Institutions," Robert Bellah reminds us, "are not only constraining but also enabling. They are the substantial forms through which we understand our own identity and the identity of others as we seek cooperatively to achieve a decent society."[4] All the more reason, then, since we both shape and are shaped by our social institutions, to seek to conform them to the will of God.

Simply put, "institutions are normative patterns embedded in and enforced by laws and mores (informal customs and practices)."[5] Although the social function of institutions is critical to public policy issues, it receives little or no attention in the political election rhetoric of "family values," leaving people with the understandable question, Why should the government concern itself with something that only families themselves can do anything about? Bellah focuses the problem exactly:

> There are certainly better families and worse, happier and more caring families and ones that are less so. But the very way Americans institutionalize family life, the very pressures and temptations that American society presents to all families, are themselves the source of serious problems, so just asking individual families to behave better, important though that is, will not get to the root of the difficulties.[6]

A comprehensive Christian strategy for social transformation will necessarily include three components: personal renewal, ecclesial example, and structural reform. This chapter is concerned primarily with the last of these as it regards the institution of marriage and the family. It seeks to deal with the importance and value of the family as a social structure, rather than "family values" in an individualistic sense.

The Structure of the Family

The basic social norm for the family is the creation ordinance stated at the beginning: "For this reason a man will leave his father and mother and be united [or, cleave] to his wife, and they will become one flesh" (Gen. 2:24). The commitment of a man and a woman to the unique relationship of marriage establishes a social unit that supersedes the existing parental structure and authorizes the couple to become themselves parents in fulfillment of the procreation blessing (Gen. 1:28). The biblical idea of the family is distinctly conjugal, consisting essentially of husband and wife and their dependent children, with kinship relations forming a secondary network of resources and

4. Robert N. Bellah et al., *The Good Society* (New York: Knopf, 1991), 12.
5. Ibid., 10–11. "In its formal sociological definition, an institution is a pattern of expected action of individuals or groups enforced by social sanctions, both positive and negative" (p. 10).
6. Ibid., 12.

responsibilities.[7] Already and apart from children, the married couple constitute a distinct social unit with its own unique structure. Children are God's added blessing by which the conjugal structure (marriage) takes on a new dimension (parenthood). The term *family* is generally reserved for this expanded structure, which includes actual (as distinct from potential) parental authority, but it may also be used with reference to a heterosexual married couple who either have never had children or whose children are no longer dependent upon them.

The conjugal-parental structure is commonly called the nuclear family to distinguish it from two other uses of the term: family in the sense of kinship and family in the sense of household.[8] The distinction is important, especially as it provides a way of steering between moral relativism (not recognizing the normative conjugal-parental structure when it exists in combination with other forms of kinship organization) and cultural absolutism (identifying the nuclear family with a particular form of domestic residential household, usually the Victorian or bourgeois model). The well-being of the nuclear family may indeed be served by its dissociation from composite family forms (certainly true in the case of polygamy, which was never the biblical ideal) and by its constitution as a separate residential household. Still these conditions for optimum well-being are distinct from the conjugal-parental structure itself, which appears in the Bible as a universal norm and in human society as a well-nigh universal practice.[9] Two parents are always desirable, but the family in the structural sense continues if one parent dies or (problematically) is sepa-

7. The conjugal-parental definition of the family stands in contrast to the new sociological prototype that is independent of either marriage or kinship: "The family is a relatively small domestic group consisting of at least one adult and one person dependent on that adult." David Popenoe, *Disturbing the Nest: Family Change and Decline in Modern Societies* (New York: Aldine De Gruyter, 1988), 5.

8. The Bible itself does not have a precise term for the conjugal-parental structure as such. *Oikos* and *patria*, the New Testament terms most commonly translated "family," have also (like the English term) wider referents (kinship, household), as do their Old Testament counterparts, *bayit* and *mišpāhâ*. The typical family unit occupying a village house in biblical times consisted of father, mother, and two to three dependent children, often placed in a compound of two to three houses with a shared courtyard, creating an extended family association of perhaps a dozen members. John Bimson, "Houses and the Family Unit," in *The Compact Handbook of Old Testament Life* (Minneapolis: Bethany, 1988), 56–58.

9. In a mid-century crosscultural study of 250 societies, Yale anthropologist George Peter Murdock concluded: "The nuclear family is a universal human social grouping. Either as the sole prevailing form of the family or [more commonly in his sample] as the basic unit from which more complex familial forms are compounded, it exists as a distinct and strongly functional group in every known society. . . . Whatever larger familial forms may exist, and to whatever extent the greater unit may assume some of the burdens of the lesser, the nuclear family is always recognizable and always has its distinctive and vital functions— sexual, economic, reproductive, and educational." *Social Structure* (New York: Macmillan, 1949), 2–3. Peter Laslett cites more recent research that confirms Murdock's conclusion and Marion Levy's parallel assertion "that most of humanity must always have lived in small families. By 1970, in fact, [Laslett says] demographers generally had come to recognize that the nuclear family predominates numerically almost everywhere, even in underdeveloped parts of the world." *Household and Family in Past Time*, ed. Peter Laslett (Cambridge: Cambridge University Press, 1972), 9. Cf. Jack Goody, *The Development of the Family and Marriage in Europe* (Cambridge: Cambridge University Press, 1983), 84 n. 2.

rated by divorce, and it may be conceded to exist (more problematically still) with nonconjugal parents. More on these issues later.

Given its early appearance in Scripture as a creation ordinance, it is not surprising to find the conjugal family assumed throughout as a normative structure for God's people at all places and at all times. "Honor your father and your mother" is one of the ten universal norms of love in which the moral law is summarily comprehended (Exod. 20:12 = Deut. 5:16). Filial respect for parents is reiterated in the great holiness chapter of Leviticus where it actually heads the list of moral duties by which the holiness of God's people is manifest (Lev. 19:3). Joint parental discipline is reflected in the Mosaic civil legislation (Deut. 21:18), and joint parental guidance is celebrated in the Wisdom Literature (Prov. 10:1; 30:17). Jesus, for his part, underscores the importance of the family as a divinely willed social structure by both teaching and example (Matt. 15:4; Luke 2:51), and his apostles affirm it repeatedly in the epistles as an enduring sphere of Christian practice.

The family thus appears throughout the Scriptures as a permanent institution ordained by God. Moreover its naturalness is such that married parents and their dependent children are recognized the world over as the basic social unit.[10] The family may be losing ground in the West as an autonomous sphere of social influence, but reports of its death (already one hears the phrase *post-nuclear family age*) have been greatly exaggerated. As Mary Jo Bane concluded from demographic information available in the mid-1970s, the family is *Here to Stay.* The reason is plain. Family commitments (marriage, child rearing, the ties that bind), Bane says, "are not archaic remnants of a disappearing traditionalism, but persisting manifestations of human needs for stability, continuity, and nonconditional affection."[11]

Even so, it would be naive to suppose that the family cannot be seriously undermined by hostile ideologies (radical feminism, Marxism, homosexualism) and practices (no-fault divorce, nonconjugal cohabitation, sexual license). The consequences of the new morality that Christopher Dawson warned about a generation ago loom ever more large:

> [If] marriage is transformed into a temporary arrangement for the satisfaction of the sexual impulse and for mutual companionship, which is not intended to create a permanent social unit, it is clear that the family loses its social and economic importance and that the state will take its place as the guardian and educator of the children. Society will no longer consist of a number of organisms, each of which possesses a limited autonomy, but will be one vast unit which controls the whole life of the individual citizen from the cradle to the grave.[12]

10. Cf. United Nations, *Universal Declaration of Human Rights* (1948): "Men and women of full age . . . have the right to marry and to found a family. . . . The family is the natural and fundamental group unit of society and is entitled to protection by society and the State" (Art. 16.1, 3).

11. Mary Jo Bane, *Here to Stay: American Families in the Twentieth Century* (New York: Basic Books, 1976), 141.

12. Christopher Dawson, *Enquiries into Religion and Culture* (New York: Sheed, 1933), 262–63.

Our question is, What is God's calling for the family? What directions does he give for his people to flourish in this sphere? What constitutes faithful family practice in the home and by the larger society? What social conditions are most conducive to the well-being of the family that God desires?

The Marriage Covenant

Marriage appears in the creation ordinance under a threefold aspect: leaving, marking the decisive establishment of a new social unit; cleaving, exhibiting the strong commitment to the new relationship (the Hebrew term denotes loyal affection); and becoming one flesh, being the purpose and goal of the leaving-cleaving complex (Gen. 2:24). The result of the marriage event, according to Jesus' definitive commentary (given in the context of condemning arbitrary divorce), is that the man and the woman are no longer two, but one, having been joined together by none other than God (Matt. 19:6 = Mark 10:8–9). In marriage, two heretofore discrete individuals (male and female) come together to form an interrelated social unit, a couple, a bonded pair.[13] It is understood that only a heterosexual couple constitutes a pair-bond in the biblical sense; Jesus explicitly includes Genesis 1:27, "God made them male and female," as part and parcel of the creation ordinance governing marriage (Matt. 19:4 = Mark 10:6).

Sexual intercourse belongs to marriage as a distinctive aspect of becoming one flesh, but the biblical expression conveys more than this. A man and a woman may be bodily joined through sexual intercourse outside of marriage (1 Cor. 6:16), but in marriage two whole persons are joined together by God and enjoy the mutually-given pleasures of sexual intercourse with his approbation. "One flesh" refers to the entire life-union of the couple, of which sexual intercourse is the unique realization and expression. The essential moral problem with nonmarital sexual intercourse is that it performs a life-uniting act without a life-uniting intent, thus violating its intrinsic meaning.[14]

Marriage is presented elsewhere in the Scriptures as a covenant whereby a man and a woman pledge themselves unreservedly to one another to be companions and partners in a common life and conjugal love. The most explicit text is found in Malachi (the context being once again condemnation of arbitrary divorce) where the Lord presents himself as witness against the husband who breaks faith with his wife—the wife of his youth, to be exact and evocative—"though she is your partner [ḥăberĕt, only used here] the wife of your marriage covenant" (Mal. 2:14). Similarly, Proverbs 2:17 warns against the adulteress who deserts the "intimate friend" (ʾallûp, cf. Jer. 3:4) of her youth

13. According to the dictionary, a pair is "a single thing made up of two corresponding parts that must be used together," as a pair of scissors or, less helpfully, a pair of pants.

14. Cf. Lewis B. Smedes, *Sex for Christians: The Limits and Liberties of Sexual Living* (Grand Rapids: Eerdmans, 1976), 128, 130, 203.

and forgets the covenant of her God. Though the allusion in this instance may be to the covenant between God and his people rather than to the marriage covenant as such, still the connection is very close inasmuch as fidelity to God's covenant is eminently mirrored in fidelity to one's own covenant of marriage. To forget the one is to forget the other.[15]

So much is the covenantal perspective on marriage a part of Old Testament religion and culture that God's covenant with Israel is often pictured in such terms. In Ezekiel 16:8 the marriage covenant forms the climax of the rehearsal of God's tender mercies in the salvation of his people: "I gave you my solemn oath and entered into a covenant with you, declares the Sovereign Lord, and you became mine." The great restoration covenant in Hosea, which the apostle Paul interprets as reaching beyond Israel to embrace the elect of all nations, is presented as the new betrothal:

> I will betroth you to me forever;
> I will betroth you in righteousness and justice,
>   in love and compassion
> I will betroth you in faithfulness,
>   and you will acknowledge the LORD.[16]

The difference between covenant and contract is highly illuminative—even critical—for understanding the true nature of the marriage bond. As the authors of the first of a new Harvard series on the family and public policy note: "the very idea of a contract is inimical to our notion of marriage."[17] All of the interhuman covenants in the Bible are characterized by sworn fidelity as the paramount feature. John Murray profoundly observes:

> It is not the contractual terms that are in prominence so much as the solemn engagement of one person to another. To such an extent is this the case that stipulated terms of agreement need not be present at all. It is the giving of one-self over in the commitment of troth that is emphasized and the specified conditions as those upon which the engagement or commitment is contingent are not mentioned. It is the promise of unreserved fidelity, of whole-souled commitment that appears to constitute the essence of the covenant.[18]

---

15. The verb *dābaq* (to cleave) in the marriage ordinance (Gen. 2:24) is used frequently for loyalty to God's covenant. See Deut. 10:20; 11:22; 13:4; 28:60; 30:20; Josh. 22:5; 23:8.

16. Hos. 2:19–20; cf. Rom. 9:24–26, citing Hos. 2:23 and 1:10.

17. Frank E. Furstenberg, Jr., and Andrew J. Cherlin, *Divided Families: What Happens to Children When Parents Part* (Cambridge: Harvard University Press, 1991), 26.

18. John Murray, *The Covenant of Grace* (London: Tyndale, 1954), 10. For a vivid illustration of the difference between the covenantal and a contractual approach to marriage, see Lenore J. Weitzman, *The Marriage Contract: Spouses, Lovers, and the Law* (New York: Free, 1981). Weitzman presents twenty-five topics to be addressed with detailed provisions: general purpose, legalities, parties, aims and expectations,

Thus, while prenuptial contracts may have been in vogue elsewhere in the ancient Near East (at least among the rich—some things never change), they are incompatible with the biblical ideal of marriage as a total personal commitment in which divorce becomes thinkable only in the wake of such radical breaches of fidelity as adultery and malicious desertion.

The marriage covenant has been brought to eloquent liturgical expression in the English vernacular tradition, tracing back to the fourteenth century and becoming a fixed part of the language in its Elizabethan form.[19] The couple is first asked in what amounts to the remnants of a betrothal ceremony (the questions are technically called the "espousals") whether they each will have the other as their wedded partner to live together after God's ordinance in the holy estate of matrimony. Having answered that they are willing to forsake all others and to keep only to each other as long as they both shall live, the couple then make the following pledges (the "nuptials") which constitute the marital vow and covenant betwixt them made.

> I N. take thee N. to my wedded wife, to have and to hold from this day forward, for better, for worse, for richer, for poorer, in sickness, and in health, to love and to cherish, till death us depart, according to God's holy ordinance: And thereto I plight thee my troth.

> I N. take thee N. to my wedded husband, to have and to hold from this day forward, for better, for worse, for richer, for poorer, in sickness, and in health, to love, cherish, and to obey, till death us depart, according to God's holy ordinance: And thereto I give thee my troth.[20]

---

duration, work and careers, income and expenses, current property, acquired property, debts, domicile and living arrangements, responsibility for household tasks, surname, sexual relations, personal behavior, relations with family and friends, decision to have or not to have children, plans for raising children, religion, health and medical care, inheritance and wills, liquidated damages, resolving disagreements, changing and renewing the contract, and (naturally) dissolution. The list is endless. "I'll do the cooking, darling, you pay the rent." "O.K. Now what about kids and the TV remote?" Only a lawyer could see this as progress.

19. Cf. Order of Matrimony according to the Manual of the Church of Salisbury, *Monumenta Ritualia Ecclesiae Anglicanae*, ed. William Maskell, vol. 1 (London: William Pickering, 1846), 46. The service is in Latin except for the nuptuals, which stand out in middle English:

> I N. take the N. to my wedded wyf to haue and to holde fro this day forwarde for better: for wors: for richere: for poorer: in sykenesse and in hele: tyl dethe vs departe if holy chyrche it woll ordeyne, and thereto I plight the my trouthe.

> I N. take the N. to my wedded housbonder to haue and to holde fro this day forwarde for better: for wors: for richere: for poorer: in sykenesse and in hele: to be bonere and buxum in bedde and at the borde tyll dethe vs departe if holy chyrche it woll ordeyne, and thereto I plight the my trouthe.

The vows are identical except for the woman's promise to be "bonere and buxum in bed and at board," comprehended by Cranmer in the single *obey*, losing the alliteration and color but retaining in sixteenth-century vernacular the middle English sense of "bonair and buxom" (i.e., submissive).

20. *The Book of Common Prayer, 1559: The Elizabethan Prayer Book*, ed. John E. Booty (Washington, D.C.: Folger, 1976), 291–92. The marriage vows were taken over unchanged from *The First and Second Prayer-Books of King Edward the Sixth, 1549, 1552* (London: Everyman's, 1910) composed by Archbishop Cranmer. "Depart" in the sense of "separate" was already obsolete when the prayer book was issued. The

The classic form of the marriage covenant has thus endured for centuries. Only whether or not to include the woman's promise to obey has been an issue. With the approval of the Alternative Services Book in 1980, wedding vows taken in the Church of England may be either identical (omitting the woman's promise to obey as recommended by the synod of bishops in 1928 and approved as an option by Parliament in 1965) or symmetrical (retaining the traditional promise to obey but adding the man's promise to "worship"). The covenant endures in this form:

> I, N, take you N,
> to be my wife/husband
> to have and to hold
> from this day forward;
> for better, for worse,
> for richer, for poorer,
> in sickness and in health,
> to love and to cherish
>   [or to love, cherish, and obey/worship]
> till death us do part,
> according to God's holy law;
> and this is my solemn vow.[21]

Marriage in God's design is a permanent and exclusive union, binding a man and a woman to each other in an exclusive lifelong companionship of common life and conjugal love. What is the purpose of marriage in God's design, and how does he will for it structurally to be carried out? These questions relate respectively to marriage as a vocation and marriage as an estate with sex-related offices.

The Marriage Vocation

Marriage as a divine calling encompasses several purposes. First and foremost is the union of the couple in a sexually complementary companionship, designed for emotional and erotic fulfillment. In the biblical narrative that gives us the prototype of marriage (Gen. 2:18–24) God, observing that it is

---

1662 update—"til death us *do part*"—retains the cadence of the original but, being somewhat forced, has become fixed in the popular mind as "til death *do us part*." Still, the point does remain fixed in the collective memory, even if not in practice.

21. *The Alternative Service Book 1980* (London: Clowes, 1984), 290. *Worship* is used (oddly, one would think, for a modernization) in the obsolete sense of *honor.* Cf. R. C. D. Jasper and Paul F. Bradshaw, *A Companion to the Alternative Service Book* [1980] (London: SPCK, 1986), 385. For a comprehensive history of the marriage liturgy see Kenneth Stevenson, *Nuptial Blessing: A Study of Christian Marriage Rites* (London: Alcuin Club/SPCK, 1982).

not good for Adam to be alone, indicates his purpose to make "a help (*ʿēzer*) corresponding to him." Contrary to a popular presentation, the Hebrew *ʿēzer* does not mean "assistant"; its use here and elsewhere in the Old Testament indicates that it is, like the English word *help*, a much stronger term. The noun *ʿēzer* is most often used of God as our help, as in the monument *Ebenezer* ("stone of help"), so named because, Samuel says, "Thus far has the LORD helped us" (1 Sam. 7:12; cf. Ps. 70:5; 121:1–2; 124:8; 146:5).

It is to succor Adam in his aloneness rather than to assist him in his busyness that God makes Eve "corresponding to him." This Hebrew phrase when analyzed according to its components comes out "according to what is in front of him." The meaning appears close to "mirror-image" in English—corresponding as the right hand corresponds to the left: fundamentally alike yet significantly different (as anyone who can find only two right gloves on a cold morning can attest). Sexual differentiation is obviously an important feature of the narrative, but the leading emphasis falls on the nature common to both male and female humans. None of the animals even begins to correspond to Adam. Only another being in God's image could possibly be a help in the sense intended. The man is alone. God makes a woman and brings her to the man. The man says, "At last! Here is someone like me—bone of my bones and flesh of my flesh" (Gen. 2:23).

The background for understanding the import of Adam's joyful response—the first human words on record—is provided by the general creation account in the first chapter of Genesis. There we are informed that "God created man in his own image, in the image of God he created him; male and female he created them" (Gen. 1:27).[22] Sexual differentiation is announced as one of the fundamental truths about human nature, second only to our creation in the image of God, the basic identity of human beings, men and women alike and equally. After the pattern of what God is uniquely and transcendently, humans are free, rational, affectional, moral agents: in a word, persons, capable of relating meaningfully to others, in particular those who are sexually other, most profoundly within marriage.

The Christian church at least since the mid-sixteenth century has included the "mutual help" of husband and wife—"mutual society, help, and comfort (= encouragement)" in the full prayer book phrase—as one of the three prime ends of marriage, the others being procreation and purity.[23] This represents a

---

22. Cf. Gen. 5:1–2, "When God created man (*ʾādām*), he made him in the likeness of God. He created them male and female and blessed them. And when they were created, he called them 'man' (*ʾādām*)." Besides being the personal name of "the [first] man," Adam, the Hebrew *ʾādām* is used as a generic term for the human race inclusive—here explicitly—of male and female.

23. Both *Edwardian Prayer-Books* and the *Elizabethan Prayer Book* put the ends of marriage in the order (1) procreation, (2) purity, (3) mutual help. Bucer's (not taken) advice to Cranmer on this point following the first edition is worth noting: "The address which stands at the beginning of this order is excellently godly and holy: nevertheless at about the end of it three causes for matrimony are enumerated, that

sound insight into the import of Genesis 2:18. If being alone is not good for the man, neither is it good for the woman. Being a helpmate is just as much a husband's role as it is a wife's. Husbands and wives are "helps-meet" (to adapt an archaism derived from the language of the King James Version), as has long been recognized in the church's teaching. Mutuality of help within marriage is not a new doctrine; it lies at the heart of the biblical revelation that marriage is for companionship.[24]

The companionship of marriage finds expression in the cohabitation and the conjugal love of the couple. In the Scriptures marriage is presented as an ardent sexual relationship (Prov. 5:18–19; Song of Songs 8:6–7). Christian couples should not deny themselves the erotic expression of their love, as though sexual intercourse and true spirituality are incompatible (1 Cor. 7:1–5; Heb. 13:4). Sexual delight within marriage is one of the good gifts of God's creation to be received with thanksgiving by those who believe and know the truth (1 Tim. 4:3–5), and Paul directs the heaviest artillery in his verbal arsenal against those who would teach otherwise (vv. 1–2). Jesus himself affirmed marriage by his presence at the wedding in Cana of Galilee, where (with a little maternal prompting) he showed himself to be the bountiful Lord of creation in whose kingdom there are no shortages of blessed gifts. As everything good in God's creation is redeemed by Christ, sex finds its true liberation and fulfillment in his kingdom.

The sexual union of the couple, meaningful in itself as an act of self-giving love and mutual pleasure, is also the God-intended way of bringing children into the world. According to the original creation mandate, human beings—male and female—are called to "fill the earth and subdue it" (Gen. 1:28). Husband and wife are not only intimate companions in life and in love but also cooperative partners in the broad cultural calling of humankind. Procreation and dominion over the earth for the glory of God, including the new dimension of redemptive mission, is the joint labor of the couple as heirs together of the grace of life (1 Pet. 3:7). As the Archbishop of Canterbury remarked in his sermon at the royal wedding in 1981: "There is

---

is children, a remedy, and mutual help, and I should prefer that what is placed third among the causes for marriage might be in the first place, because it is first." Martin Bucer, *Censura* (A Critical Examination), 1551, in E. C. Whitaker, ed. and trans., *Martin Bucer and The Book of Common Prayer* (Great Wakering: Mayhew-McCrimmon/Alcuin, 1974), 120. Compare the order later adopted by the Westminster Confession of Faith: "Marriage was ordained for the mutual help of husband and wife, for the increase of mankind with a legitimate issue, and of the church with a holy seed; and for preventing of uncleanness" (24.2). This is also the order of the Roman Catechism (1566), though its emphasis is still clearly procreation. *Catechism of the Council of Trent for Parish Priests*, trans. John A. McHugh and Charles J. Callan (New York: Wagner, 1934), 343–44.

24. So important is the unitive purpose of marriage in the Bible that the Mosaic civil legislation provided that a man newly wed should be excused from military and civil service to be free at home for a whole year to "cheer" the wife he had married (Deut. 24:5). The husband had a responsibility for the well-being and happiness of his wife as they began their life together.

an ancient Christian tradition that every bride and groom on their wedding day are regarded as a royal couple. To this day in the marriage ceremonies of the Eastern Orthodox Church crowns are held over the man and the woman to express the conviction that as husband and wife they are Kings and Queens of Creation."[25]

The procreation mandate is repeated as a blessing to Noah after the flood (Gen. 9:1) and is given also to Jacob as God begins in earnest to fulfill the Abrahamic promise of a great nation (Gen. 35:11). Of course, the processes of conception and birth remain ultimately in the Lord's hands, and providentially childless marriages are not without God's blessing and purpose (certainly ruling out divorce for infertility). Still the normal responsibility and natural hope of the married couple is for children who look expectantly to the Lord of life, knowing that "the fruit of the womb is his reward" (Ps. 127:3 KJV).

As with the dominion and mission mandates, the procreation mandate calls for thoughtful and rational obedience. Responsible parenthood may entail the limitation or spacing of children for various physical, economic, psychological, or social reasons. It is not the case that birth control springs invariably from selfish or hedonistic motives. Though the Bible places a high value on having children as one of the prime blessings of marriage, the decision to procreate is rightly weighed in relation to the other intrinsic goods of the couple's companionship and partnership. The preferential option of the Bible is clearly for children, other things being equal, encouraging generosity toward the procreation mandate. The biblical guidance in this respect takes the form of counsel rather than command, leaving it to the couple to discern how they may best fulfill the will of God in their particular circumstances.

There is wide agreement across Christendom on the principle of rational and responsible family planning. The intramural debates between Christians largely concern the legitimacy of contraception as a method of birth control. Those who argue that any method interferes with divine providence or usurps divine prerogatives are up against the apostle Paul, who explicitly permits temporary abstinence from sexual intercourse within marriage for devotion to prayer (1 Cor. 7:5).[26] God's providence embraces the acts of free moral agents, so there is no question of sinning against God's decree of par-

---

25. Stevenson, *Nuptial Blessing*, 211. The Byzantine, Armenian, Coptic, Ethiopic, and old Syriac rites all use the crowning ceremony, "investing it with various kinds of symbolism, according to local tradition and liturgical flair" (p. 120).

26. The disgraceful episode of Onan (Gen. 38:8–10) has no bearing on the question of birth control (other than to establish the antiquity of withdrawal as a known method). Onan's sin was to mock the institution of levirate paternity and to show contempt for Tamar, his sister-in-law. The circumstances are, to say the least, peculiar.

ticular children who are being denied existence by the couple's agreement to temporarily suspend sexual relations.

Since 1951 the Roman Catholic Church has officially endorsed the practice of continence (periodic abstinence, restricting sexual intercourse to the woman's infertile cycles) as a natural method of birth control, but has remained opposed to contraception. Pope Paul VI in the 1968 encyclical *Humanae Vitae* ("On Human Life") acknowledged that the function of sexual intercourse within marriage is unitive as well as procreative, but argued that these functions are inseparable so that the conjugal act must always be "open to the transmission of life." This position was reaffirmed by Pope John Paul II in *Familaris Consortio* (On the Family) in 1981, to the disappointment of many Catholics who question "whether it makes sense to say that acts deliberately chosen during the sterile period are 'open to the transmission of life' in some morally significant sense that contraceptive acts are not."[27] The Vatican argument is that sexual intercourse need not be for procreation but it must always be open to procreation. This is based on an appeal to natural law. The idea is that God's purposes are discoverable by right reason, and that purpose may be deduced from function. Since the sexual organs are by nature generative, to close off the possibility of transmission of life in their use is to go against nature. However, the function of the sexual organs is not exclusively procreative. They are a source of pleasure and a means of mutual self-giving expressive of the love and union of the couple. They are always relational, whereas they are not always generative. If it is permissible for a couple to have sexual intercourse while consciously intending to avoid pregnancy, it seems arbitrary not to allow the most effective means to that end.

Nor should a method be rejected on the grounds that it is artificial as opposed to natural. What is called artificial means might just as well be called human means; it is an application of the art of medicine to enable the couple to carry out their morally legitimate intent. There is a rational use of freedom both in the calculation of the fertile cycles and in the development of artifices for contraception. There is no biblical reason why human beings may not make use of scientific knowledge in this area; it is natural for human beings to do so in that it accords with their nature as free rational agents. For a marriage to be open to the transmission of life does not require that each act of sexual intercourse have the same openness. Contraceptive acts may be regarded as partial acts within the total sexual life of the couple oriented toward both union and procreation.[28]

27. Benedict M. Ashley and Kevin D. O'Rourke, *Healthcare Ethics: A Theological Analysis*, 3d ed. (St. Louis: Catholic Health Association, 1989), 263. Ashley and O'Rourke uphold the Vatican position but provide an excellent summary of the course and the status of the debate.

28. Cf. the (rejected) majority report of the Papal Commission (1969), *Healthcare Ethics*, 263–64.

The Married Estate

In the traditional marriage covenant a man and a woman commit themselves unreservedly to each other to live together in the holy estate of matrimony—a definite social institution with an existing normative structure. They take each other, not to just any relationship, but to the specific relationship of "wedded wife" and "wedded husband" (never mind the redundancy of the adjective in modern English). The relational terms *husband* and *wife* denote marital subvocations by which conjugal responsibility is equitably distributed between the marriage partners in view of their gender complementation. There is no need for the couple to start from scratch in determining the structure of the marital relationship; to live together according to God's ordinance entails recognition of a divinely appointed and mutually beneficial order for male and female in the marriage estate. Brigette Berger's comment on the importance of institutions is relevant here:

> Human beings could not survive without institutions. . . . If it were not for institutions, the world would have to be reinvented every day. . . . If a man and a woman, mutually attracted to each other, had no institutional patterns to have recourse to in their efforts to act on the basis of the attraction, they would have before them a vast number of thinkable options.[29]

Hardly anything provokes more controversy in contemporary American culture than the idea of gender roles, whether in marriage or elsewhere. This is understandable given the history of male oppression and women's struggle for justice as equal human beings. But to be equal is not to be identical, and justice requires taking relevant differences into account. Procreation is part of the marriage vocation, but only one of the partners can bear children. The subvocation of giving birth is inescapably gender specific and requires as a matter of justice recognition as a relevant difference calling for special consideration and protection. Child-bearing would seem to be sufficient by itself to establish the reality of sexually distinct responsibilities or offices within marriage. The question is how to make gender-related roles equitable and mutually fulfilling for the couple.[30]

29. Brigette Berger and Peter L. Berger, *The War Over the Family: Capturing the Middle Ground* (Garden City, N.Y.: Anchor/Doubleday, 1983), 145.

30. Evangelicals are profoundly divided on the issue of gender roles, as may be seen by the following representative works: Letha Dawson Scanzoni and Nancy A. Hardesty, *All We're Meant to Be: Biblical Feminism for Today*, 3d rev. ed. (Grand Rapids: Eerdmans, 1992), with supporting bibliography, 391–409; John Piper and Wayne Grudem, eds., *Recovering Biblical Manhood and Womanhood: A Response to Evangelical Feminism* (Wheaton, Ill.: Crossway, 1991). John Stott appears to provide something of a bridge between the two camps (at least I like to think so since I identify largely with him). See his chapter, "Women, Men and God," in *Decisive Issues Facing Christians Today* (Tarrytown, N.Y.: Revell, 1990), 254–84.

Often we are presented with a false choice between rigid sex roles and no sex roles at all. But the worse-case scenario implied by the adjective *rigid* distorts the biblical perspective. God has ordained two complementary ways of being his image, of being human, neither of which is superior to the other. Role relationship in marriage does not imply natural superiority and inferiority. As we reject white supremacy (the right to dominate based on the dogma of racial superiority), so we reject male supremacy (the right to dominate based on the dogma of sexual superiority). Neither hierarchicalism nor egalitarianism does justice to the biblical perspective of husbands and wives as companions and partners in marriage, having the same humanity, sharing the same salvation, serving the same kingdom, but holding distinct offices for the sake of the joint marriage enterprise.

An office is a God-given responsibility with reference to one of his ordained social institutions, in this case marriage and the family, for the sake of its proper functioning. The key text on the mutual responsibilities of husbands and wives is Ephesians 5:21–33, where the husband is said to be the head (*kephalē*) of the wife. It has been vigorously argued that *kephalē* is used here in the sense of origin, which is a lexical possibility, but the context seems rather to require the sense of leader, a meaning that is clearly established in Septuagintal Greek.[31] But what kind of leadership is this? Paul does not say, "Husbands, rule your wives," but "Husbands, love your wives." Whatever responsibility he is given as "first among equals," it is to be exercised in sacrificial love for the well-being of his wife, to ensure her marital happiness. This means attentiveness to the psychological ingredients of a happy marriage, namely, "kindred minds, sexual warmth, social intimacy, equitable giving and receiving of emotional and material resources."[32] Surely it is a transformed "patriarchy" that has these values, and especially equity, as its goal.

The wife is asked reciprocally to respect her husband in his office by being subordinate (*hypotassō*) to him. Again we must ask, What kind of "followship" is this? It certainly does not invite a chain-of-command analogy that unfortunately continues to be the mentality in some conservative Christian circles. Paul avoids the direct imperative, "Wives, obey your husbands." Wives are not to be treated as children or as servants who don't know what their master is doing (John 15:15). Such treatment would be fundamentally out of accord with the companionship and partnership of marriage. Thus, omission of the wife's promise to obey from the marriage ceremony does not imply rejection of the biblical structure. *Hypotassō* occurs in the New Testament in a variety of contexts dealing with ordered human relationships, but the nature of the

31. E.g., Judg. 11:11, "They appointed [Jephthah] over them for a *kephalē* in order to lead." See also 2 Sam. 22:44; compare Eph. 1:22; Col. 2:10.

32. David G. Myers, *The Pursuit of Happiness: Who Is Happy—and Why* (New York: Morrow, 1992), 174.

responsibility depends on the nature of the relationship. The husband-wife relationship differs qualitatively from all the others; it has an intrinsic dynamic all its own, and as such becomes a fitting analogy for the relationship of Christ and his church.

Understood from a biblical and Christian perspective, role relationship within marriage serves to focus responsibility so that the ends of marriage may be effectively attained. The office of headship is given to the man, not on the grounds of superiority of nature, but because it serves God's creative design—provided it is exercised in the manner in which God intends. Holding the husband accountable for the overall provision and direction of the marriage secures for the wife the freedom necessary to fulfill the uniquely feminine role of child-bearing with all its attendant hazards and demands. Beyond this, the Bible is actually quite reticent when it comes to descriptive criteria of masculinity and femininity. Instead of a definitive cognitive answer to the question of what it means to be male or female, the Word of God ordains relationships in which sexual complementation is learned by experience. The presumed correlation between gender roles and nature may be corroborated by scientific research, but fidelity to the subvocations of the marital estate does not depend on empirical verification of gender being determined by nature rather than by social construction.[33]

The traditional structure of the marriage estate should not be confused with the "cult of domesticity" in which "wife" is equivalent to "housewife." In discussions on the family, Jack Goody rightly complains, "Everything 'traditional' gets lumped together in one undifferentiated mass."[34] The genius of the traditional concept of the marriage estate is accurately expressed by Lenore Weitzman (even while calling for its replacement):

> Traditional legal marriage created a unity that transcended the parties' individual interests. While the marital partnership was certainly not egalitarian (it was based on different and unequal roles for men and women), it nevertheless assumed that the spouses were engaged in a joint enterprise, were responsible for each other, and would share the fruits of their united endeavors.[35]

Weitzman's own view is that "legal marriage impedes egalitarian relationships because it imposes sex-based rights and responsibilities on husbands and wives."[36] But couples committed to the traditional structure, in which the

33. This is not to minimize the significance of the accumulating corroboration. See the extensive supporting literature cited in Anne Moir and David Jessel, *Brain Sex: The Real Difference Between Men and Women* (New York: Carol, 1991), 207–24.

34. Goody, *Development of the Family*, 3.

35. Lenore J. Weitzman, *The Divorce Revolution: The Unexpected Social and Economic Consequences for Women and Children in America* (New York: Free, 1985), 4–5.

36. Ibid., 417. Significantly, the first issue of *Ms.* magazine (1972) carried an article by Susan Edmiston on "How to Write Your Own Marriage Contract."

husband plays a distinctive gender role in providing for and directing the family and the wife plays a distinctive gender role in bearing and caring for the children, still find abundant freedom for creativity in determining the shape of their own companion-partnership.[37] On the other hand, for those who reject the traditional structure, legal marriage has become problematic. Speaking of no-fault divorce, Weitzman rightly observes that the new rules shift the criteria for marriage "from fidelity to the traditional marriage contract to individual standards of personal satisfaction," thereby redefining marriage as "a time-limited, contingent arrangement rather than a life-long commitment."[38] "Traditional family law," she says, "established a clear moral framework." Are couples really better off without one? And what about the children?

Parental Responsibility

> Children need *a world* to grow into. . . . The meaningful question is not *whether* there will be an institution of the family in the future but, rather, *what kind* of institution is likely or desirable.
>
> —Brigette Berger and Peter Berger,
> *The War Over the Family*

Children are God's gift to parents. Through the sexual union of the couple God creates new life and entrusts that life to their care as his added blessing upon their married estate. Marriages providentially without children are not without God's blessing and may be abundantly fruitful in many other respects; they are certainly not to be stigmatized as barren. Still it is natural for the couple to hope for the second blessing of children—God's *dona super-addita* (gifts over and above) to their companionship, partnership, and conjugal love.

The biblical idea of parenthood is hardly exhausted in the transmission of biological life. This is only the beginning. As God uses the sexual union of the couple to create new life, so he ordains the family to be the sphere in which that new life is protected and nourished. Nonconjugal parenting places children in an extremely disadvantaged condition, depriving them of the right of a structure God has ordained specifically for their welfare, economically, emotionally, and above all spiritually.

The children of believing parents in particular are brought into a special relationship by virtue of the covenant of grace in which God promises to be God to us and to our children (Gen. 17:7). Their baptism is a sign to them and to others that they too are reckoned among the people of God, that the kingdom

---

37. Cf. Arlie Hochschild, with Anne Machung, *The Second Shift: Working Parents and the Revolution at Home* (New York: Viking, 1989), 15–16.

38. Weitzman, *Divorce Revolution*, 367–68.

of heaven belongs to them as well as adult disciples (Luke 18:16). The widening missionary horizon of the Abrahamic covenant under the New Testament does not undercut its familial significance, as God continues to work salvation within the solidarity of the family relationship (Acts 2:39). Not that physical descent is an unbelief-proof guarantee of salvation; the faithfulness of parents figures in the fulfillment of the promise. God's salvific purpose is fulfilled in no way other than reliance upon his grace and obedience to his will, as God's remarkable assertion about Abraham makes clear: "For I have chosen him, so that he will direct his children and his household after him to keep the way of the LORD by doing what is right and just, so that the LORD will bring about for Abraham what he has promised him" (Gen. 18:19).

For our part, we dare not underestimate the capacity of little children for a knowledge of the Savior, nor underrate the value and reality of their religious experience. King David testifies: "You brought me out of the womb; you made me trust in you even at my mother's breast" (Ps. 22:9). The apostle Paul reminds Timothy that "from infancy you have known the holy Scriptures, which are able to make you wise for salvation through faith in Christ Jesus" (2 Tim. 3:15). We may never forget that faith is the gift of God, itself part of his wonderful salvation. Larry Christenson notes that "the conscious, intellectual aspect of faith comes with maturing understanding. But the essential element of faith—the personal trust-resting-in-spiritual-life-union—this depends upon the gracious condescension of God, not upon a person's mental grasp of the process."[39] The key for parents is to seek to elicit the response appropriate to the level of development of the child, sowing the seed of the Word in faith, knowing that it is the Holy Spirit who prepares the heart in his own time and way.

The classic biblical passage on the responsibility of parents for the spiritual nurture of their children is Deuteronomy 6:4–7.

> Hear, O Israel: The LORD our God, the LORD is one. Love the LORD your God with all your heart and with all your soul and with all your strength. These commandments that I give you today are to be upon your hearts. Impress them on your children. Talk about them when you sit at home and when you walk along the road, when you lie down and when you get up.

Notice the prerequisites for effective instruction in the way of the Lord. God's people are called first to recognize his lordship as the ultimate source of authority and truth, then to love him with all their heart and soul and strength, then to have his commandments upon their heart, that is, to internalize God's precepts and be committed themselves to obeying them, then to impress them on their children. How? Instruction of a more or less formal nature plays a part (compare vv. 20–25 with Exod. 12:21–27), but the nur-

39. Christenson, *The Christian Family,* 150.

ture called for here is more comprehensive. It is related to everyday activities so that the total home environment becomes a means of bringing children up in the training and instruction of the Lord (Eph. 6:4). Table talk, family prayers, reaction to current events, attitudes toward other people, recreation and general lifestyle—all these shape the child's fundamental perspective on life. Children gather what parents really think is important less from precept than from example.

As joint heirs of the grace of life, husband and wife are jointly responsible for child care conducive to the physical, and emotional, and spiritual development of the child. Parenthood is a divine vocation for both fathers and mothers, with overlapping (but not completely interchangeable) roles.[40] To be a father in the biblical sense is to be a begetting and nurturing father, after the pattern of the heavenly Father who pities and spares his children (Ps. 103:13; Mal. 3:17).[41] The thought is captured in the familiar hymn:

> Children of the Heav'nly Father
> Safely in his bosom gather . . .
> God his own doth tend and nourish
> In his heav'nly courts they flourish.

Making provision for one's family is an important part of being a father (1 Tim 5:8; 2 Cor. 12:14 speaks more inclusively of *parents* saving up for their children, highlighting marriage as an economic partnership). But children do not live on bread alone. Paternal responsibility goes beyond "making a living" to taking an active role in bringing children up in the Lord (Eph. 6:4). "Training and instruction" in the way of the Lord includes the element of discipline, and Paul, knowing very well that authority and power can be abused, cautions against frustrating children. "Fathers, do not embitter your children, or they will become discouraged" (Col. 3:21).[42] Children need correction, for they are sinners; but they need to be corrected in love, even as our heavenly Father corrects us (Heb. 12:9). The loving exercise of authority is supremely important. As a practical matter, fathers should recognize that each child is a person,

40. Mary Stewart Van Leeuwen, *Gender and Grace: Love, Work and Parenting in a Changing World* (Downers Grove, Ill.: InterVarsity, 1990).

41. The Westminster Confession of Faith uses an odd expression with respect to civil magistrates. It calls them "nursing fathers." Though we may find the expression overly paternalistic when applied to the civil government, it nevertheless is in line with the biblical concept of fatherly nurture. Cf. Susanne Heine, "It is dangerous and contrary to basic feminist interests when a division of the male and female properties of God gives a boost to the usual stereotyping of roles." *Christianity and the Goddesses: Systematic Criticism of a Feminist Theology* (London: SCM, 1988), 28, cited in Anthony C. Thiselton, *New Horizons in Hermeneutics* (Grand Rapids: Zondervan, 1992), 458.

42. It is sometimes argued that *hoi pateres* (fathers) in Eph. 6:4 and Col. 3:21 is equivalent to *hoi goneis* (parents) as in Heb. 11:23, "By faith Moses' parents (*hoi pateres,* fathers) hid him for three months after he was born." But this seems forced inasmuch as *hoi goneis* in both contexts (Eph. 6:1 and Col. 3:20) is used when both parents are in view.

created in God's image, growing physically, intellectually, emotionally, and spiritually. In instruction and discipline the level of maturity in all these areas has to be taken into account.

Probably nothing in the Bible speaks more to the issue of overlapping parental roles than the mothering figure as expressive of God's relation to his people. The more predominant image of mother, however, is with reference to the church: "Jerusalem is the mother of us all" (Gal. 4:26; cf. Isa. 66:7–13 NASB). The figures serve to underscore the profound significance of the maternal vocation. The apostle Paul, for his part, highlights the dignity of the domestic sphere of labor by his encouragement to young Christian women to become household managers (*oikodespotein*, 1 Tim. 5:14) and homeworkers (*oikourgous*, "working at home," not *oikourous*, "staying at home," Titus 2:4–5).

The dignity of the vocation of mother—granting that it overlaps with the vocation of father—stands in need of cultural reaffirmation. The feminist movement, with all its gains for women by way of expanded equality of opportunity for pursuit of the cultural mandate, has also its downside in the denigration of the domestic sphere.[43] This is especially problematic as it impinges upon the high calling of "mothering," defined by Selma Fraiberg as "the nurturing of the human potential of every baby to love, to trust, and to bind himself to human partnerships in a lifetime of love."[44] Fraiberg cites the interdisciplinary consensus to the effect that "the human qualities of enduring love and commitment to love are forged during the first two years of life. The consequences of not addressing this concern are most serious: 'The absence of human bonds in infancy or the rupture of human bonds in early life can have permanent effects upon the later capacity for human attachments and for the regulation of aggression.'"[45]

The family provides the outstanding place to demonstrate grace in interpersonal relationships. To do so faithfully according to the Christian calling is to advertise its viability as a social institution.[46]

The Family and Public Policy

Sylvia Ann Hewlett writes perceptively on the movement in American society toward free-choice individualism and adult self-realization at the expense of children.

---

43. For documentation see Christina Hoff Sommers, "Philosophers Against the Family," in *Person to Person*, ed. George Graham and Hugh Lafollette (Philadelphia: Temple University Press, 1989); Ronald Fletcher, *The Abolitionists: The Family and Marriage Under Attack* (London: Routledge, 1988).

44. Selma Fraiberg, *Every Child's Birthright: In Defense of Mothering* (New York: Basic, 1977), xi, 4.

45. Ibid., 4, 61.

46. The flip side of parental responsibility, of course, is what used to be called filial piety. Not only the term but the very idea has fallen on hard times. See Christina Sommers, "Filial Morality," *The Journal of Philosophy* 83 (1986): 439–56.

Our legal system has given up on the idea that marriage should be a binding, lifelong commitment and that parents should take enduring responsibility for their children. Adults can now live with whomever they want for as long as they want; they can also abort or abandon babies and bear children in or out of wedlock. Indeed, individual Americans can pretty much do anything that tickles their fancy without fear that the state will step in and constrain their freedom "for the sake of the children."[47]

As a corrective, Hewlett proposes a ten-point action plan for children. But even though one of the basic principles behind the plan is that "government should strive to *empower families* rather than supplant them," nine out of the ten points call for more government action, such as number six, "Government should *provide substantial housing subsidies for families with children.*" Only the tenth point recognizes the "need to *complement government policy with a new level of personal commitment* to this nation's family of children."[48]

In other words, Hewlett sees clearly the problem of individualism, but not the danger of state power. Others observe the double threat: "The well-being of families [is] strained today by the twin forces of individualism and state power."[49] As Robert Nisbett and various colleagues argue, "Under the intent and rhetoric of ministering to the family, of reinforcing it in society, the state often winds up actually damaging the family as a repository of vital authorities and functions."[50] In contrast to some other Western democracies, the United States gives no constitutional recognition to the family, despite its crucial role as a "mediating structure" between the individual and the state.[51]

Will expansion of the welfare state strengthen the family? Among the doubters is Brigette Berger, who writes: "From a mediating structures perspective the central problem of the American family today is its loss of autonomy." Though still central in the lives of individuals, "the situation of the family has changed fundamentally with the expansion of the power of the state into the family's relations to its children."[52] There are two critical areas of concern:

47. Sylvia Ann Hewlett, *When the Bough Breaks: The Cost of Neglecting Our Children* (New York: Basic, 1991), 103.

48. Ibid., 239–58.

49. Pontifical Commission on the Family, "Charter of the Rights of the Family," 22 October 1983, published as a supplement to the *Catholic League Newsletter.* See also Pope John Paul II, *On the Family (Familaris Consortio),* 1981 (Washington, D.C.: U.S. Catholic Conference, 1982).

50. Robert Nisbett, Forward to *The American Family and the State,* ed. Joseph R. Peden and Fred R. Glahe (San Francisco: Pacific Research Institute for Public Policy), xix. Rousseau's statist attack on the family is remarked on here.

51. Mary Ann Glendon cites, for example, the West German Basic Law (1949), Article 6. *Rights Talk: The Impoverishment of Political Discourse* (New York: Free, 1991), 73.

52. Brigette Berger, "The Family as a Mediating Structure," in *Democracy and Mediating Structures: A Theological Inquiry,* ed. Michael Novak (Washington, D.C.: American Enterprise Institute, 1980), 158. See

parental responsibility for preschool child care and parental rights as well as responsibility in the whole area of education and nurture.

With respect to child care, Brigitte Berger and Sidney Callahan have developed the following guiding principles:

1. A national family policy should be based on the understanding that the family and not any other conceivable structure is the most viable locale for child care.
2. Insofar as professional services and agencies have to be involved in the process of child care, they should be ancillary to the family and as fast as possible held accountable to parents.
3. A national family policy should respect the existing pluralism of family life-styles and child care.
4. Any national family policy has to free itself from the pejorative myths that have surrounded the black family.
5. The thesis about the primacy of the family should apply to the various categories of 'special children' as well.
6. A national family policy must not become an instrument for further weakening the family by emphasizing children's rights more than the rights of their parents.
7. In the context of the current discussion of income support and incomes redistribution, a national family policy should be guided by the general principle that reforms intended to diminish poverty defeat their own purpose if they weaken the family.[53]

The question to ask in connection with child care is rightly put by Hewlett (herself a married working mother of four): "When substitute mother care is considered for a child of any age, the questions which need to be asked are: (1) What are the needs of my child at *this* stage of development? (2) Who can serve as a mother substitute for my child, given these needs?"[54] Government policy at the very least should not penalize those who seek home care for their children, even at the sacrifice of two incomes.

In the field of education, the principled pluralists in the Reformed tradition have articulated the case of disestablishment of the present secular system in favor of parental choice.[55] Pluralism is presented in a twofold light: "*Structural*

---

also Jessica Gress-Wright, "Liberals, Conservatives and the Family," *Commentary*, April 1992, 43–46; Barbara Dafoe Whitehead and David Blankenhorn, "Man, Woman, and Public Policy," *First Things*, August/September 1991, 28–35; *Families First: Report of the National Commission on America's Urban Families*, January 1993, John Ashcroft, chairman, Annette Strauss, co-chair (Washington, D.C.: U.S. Government Printing Office, 1993).

53. Berger, "The Family as a Mediating Structure," 167–69.
54. Fraiberg, *Every Child's Birthright*, 81.
55. Cf. Rockne M. McCarthy, James W. Skillen, William A. Harper, *Disestablishment a Second Time: Genuine Pluralism for American Schools* (Grand Rapids: Eerdmans, 1982); Gordon J. Spykman, *Society, State, and Schools: A Case for Structural and Confessional Pluralism* (Grand Rapids: Eerd' mans, 1981).

pluralism means that God has created the world with various structures—civil government, marriage, the family, the church, schools, the marketplace—which order life and coordinate human interaction. *Confessional pluralism* refers to the right of the various religious groups that make up a society to develop their own patterns of involvement in public life through their own associations—schools, political parties, labor unions, churches, and so on—to promote their views."[56] American public education violates both structural and confessional or religious pluralism. The remedy is to empower families to exercise freedom of choice by tax credit or tax reduction as a matter of public justice.

56. Gordon J. Spykman, "The Principled Pluralist Position," in *God and Politics: Four Views on the Reformation of Civil Government*, ed. Gary Scott Smith (Phillipsburg, N.J.: Presbyterian and Reformed, 1989), 79–80.

9

Divorce and Remarriage

Divorce creates a classical case, in sociological parlance, of structural
ambiguity.

—Furstenberg and Cherlin, *Divided Families*

What therefore God hath joined together, let not man put asunder.

—Matthew 19:6 KJV

The Scope of the Problem

Although the divorce rate in the United States is declining, it is still
high by any standard. In 1991 there were 1,170,000 divorces, which figures out to be 4.6 per 1,000 population, down from a high of 5.2 in
1980.[1] This brings the rate back to where it was around 1970, the year
California introduced the first no-fault divorce law in the Western
world since pre-Christian times. (Automobile insurance legislation
pending at the same time unfortunately lent the dubious no-fault terminology to the structurally crucial issue of divorce.) Before 1970 fault-
based grounds (adultery, desertion, or cruelty) were required in all fifty
states for divorce. The new law, which since 1985 has prevailed in all
U.S. jurisdictions, allows either party to secure a divorce not only without charging fault but by simply withdrawing consent. The practical
effect has been that the United States, along with Sweden and Canada
(since 1986), "have altered the legal definition of marriage itself by making it a relationship terminable at will."[2] Lenore J. Weitzman offers
these observations on how the movement for reform effected, in her
phrase, "the divorce revolution."

1. *The World Almanac and Book of Facts: 1992,* 938.
2. Mary Ann Glendon, *Abortion and Divorce in Western Law* (Cambridge: Harvard University Press,
1987), 81.

The new reformers altered each of the major provisions of the traditional law—and, in the process, redefined the norms of legal marriage. No-fault laws abolished the need for grounds and the need to prove fault in order to obtain a divorce. They abandoned the gender-based assumptions of the traditional law in favor of standards for treating men and women 'equally' in alimony and property awards. They negated the traditional role that fault played in financial awards and instead decreed that awards should be based on the divorcing parties' current financial needs and resources. And finally, the new rules shifted the legal criteria for divorce—and thus for viable marriage—from fidelity to the traditional marriage contract to individual standards of personal satisfaction. They thereby redefined marriage as a time-limited, contingent arrangement rather than a life-long commitment.[3]

"Traditional legal marriage," Weitzman notes, "created a unity that transcended the parties' individual interests. . . . [It] assumed that the spouses were engaged in a joint enterprise, were responsible for each other, and would share the fruits of their united endeavors."[4] Commitment to marriage as a lifelong partnership was reinforced by the clear moral framework of traditional family law by which "men remained legally obligated to support wives and children, while women remained responsible first and foremost for the care and custody of the children."[5] Weitzman herself believes that the new laws rightly reflect "altered social realities, evolving social norms, and everyday legal practice." Her problem is that "because the present laws do not *adequately* or accurately reflect social reality, they are exacerbating some of the grossest inequities in our society."[6] Weitzman's solution is for couples to write their own marriage contract.[7] But the idea of a contract, besides being "inimical to our notion of marriage," has the effect of perpetuating what many social critics say is the root problem, namely, "the rise of personal fulfillment as the main criterion for evaluating marriages."[8] Who suffers most, of course, are the children. Nor is this simply a matter of private morality. As Mary Ann Glendon points out, "American divorce law in practice seems to be saying to parents, especially mothers, that it is not safe to devote oneself primarily or exclusively to raising children."[9] Sylvia Ann Hewlett agrees:

---

3. Lenore J. Weitzman, *The Divorce Revolution: The Unexpected Social and Economic Consequences for Women and Children in America* (New York: Free, 1985), 367–68.

4. Ibid., 4–5.

5. Ibid., 367.

6. Ibid., 366–67.

7. Lenore J. Weitzman, *The Marriage Contract: Spouses, Lovers, and the Law* (New York: Free, 1981).

8. Frank E. Furstenberg, Jr., and Andrew J. Cherlin, *Divided Families: What Happens to Children when Parents Part* (Cambridge: Harvard University Press, 1991), 26, 100.

9. Glendon, *Abortion and Divorce*, 111.

In moving toward no-fault divorce, we thought that we were relinquishing the responsibility of arbitrating private morality. In fact, our new policies, by giving a green light to much easier methods of ending marriage, produced a major shift in private values. . . . no-fault divorce tells a very powerful story: that no one is to blame when a marriage breaks up, and no one need take responsibility for the consequences. . . . the new legislation changed public attitudes toward divorce, and, in the end, both weakened the institution of marriage and undermined the life prospects of children.[10]

These and other voices are telling us that it is time to reopen the question of public policy and divorce.[11] The divorce revolution has not produced a relational utopia. The destructive dynamic of divorce inevitably renders co-parenting unworkable. And as the authors of the first of a new Harvard series on the family and public policy pointedly observe: "Through divorce and remarriage, individuals are related to more and more people, to each of whom they owe less and less."[12] These same authors recognize that any effort to strengthen marriage now must have grass-roots support to be successful. In their view, "It would probably take a social upheaval such as a prolonged economic downturn or a nation-wide religious revival to create a greatly renewed commitment to family ties."[13] Are Furstenberg and Cherlin also among the prophets?

In this situation of both personal tragedy and structural deformation the church is called to a ministry that reflects the threefold mediatorial office of Christ: to declare the revealed will of God concerning marriage; to restore sinners through the gospel of repentance and forgiveness of sins; and to nurture persons so that by God's grace they are disposed toward marital fidelity. In this work we are necessarily concerned primarily with the first of these offices.[14] As a first step we take a look at three broad ecclesiastical traditions on the issue of divorce and remarriage.

The Teaching of the Churches

The Roman Catholic Church

The Roman Catholic Church teaches that the marriage bond is indissoluble in the specific sense that a consummated sacramental marriage cannot be dissolved except by death. This means that a married couple who have had

10. Sylvia Ann Hewlett, *When the Bough Breaks: The Cost of Neglecting Our Children* (New York: Basic, 1991), 257.

11. Cf. the provocatively titled article by Barbara Dafoe Whitehead, "Dan Quayle Was Right," *The Atlantic Monthly*, April 1993, 47–84.

12. Furstenberg and Cherlin, *Divided Families*, 95.

13. Ibid., 105.

14. Andrew Corner, *Divorce and Remarriage: Biblical Principles and Pastoral Practice* (Grand Rapids: Eerdmans, 1993).

sexual intercourse in marriage after both have been baptized cannot be divorced; not even adultery provides sufficient cause for dissolution of the marriage bond. Even so, marital indissolubility is not absolute on the Roman Catholic view; the Roman church does not rule out all divorces, nor is divorce the only way to be released from the obligations of a broken marriage. There are two distinct approaches.

Divorce as a privilege of the faith. According to Roman Catholic doctrine, no marriage can be dissolved by merely human authority. The church, however, has authority under certain conditions to dissolve marriages between Christians and non-Christians on the grounds that it serves the higher interests of the faith. The privilege of divorce reserved for the faithful takes two forms.

Divorce according to the Pauline privilege (so named for its basis in 1 Cor. 7:15) was first established by Pope Clement III in the twelfth century. The 1983 Code of Canon Law defines the conditions on which it may be granted as follows: both spouses were unbaptized when the marriage was contracted; one spouse converts and is baptized; an "interpellation" is made to the unconverted spouse who will neither convert nor live in peace with the converted spouse. The couple may then be divorced, and the Christian is free to remarry in the faith.

The Petrine privilege differs from the Pauline in that it applies to cases where one of the spouses was baptized when the marriage was contracted. Divorce for the sake of the faith under such circumstances may be granted only by papal dispensation. New canons on the Petrine privilege were proposed for the 1983 revised code but were not adopted. Though theoretically still a means of obtaining a divorce, in practice it has been supplanted by greater use of the annulment procedure.

Annulment as an alternative to divorce. There are some eight million divorced Catholics in the United States. The church does not excommunicate divorced persons as such, but if they remarry they are ineligible to receive the sacraments unless the original marriage is either dissolved or annuled. "An annulment is a declaration by a Tribunal to the Church that a marriage never legally existed as a sacramental union according to canon law."[15] In 1968 there were 338 such annulments in the United States; by 1978 the number had risen to 27,670, and twice that number of petitions were filed in 1981.

The grounds on which a marriage may be annuled include impediments such as impotence, consanguinity, and affinity; documentary grounds such as defective form or previous bond; simulated consent; consent elicited through force or fear; and psychological grounds, especially "lack of due discretion" in

---

15. Joseph P. Zwack, *Annulment: Your Chance to Remarry within the Catholic Church* (New York: Harper, 1983), 1.

contracting the marriage and "lack of due competence" or inability to fulfill the marital obligations.[16]

As a Catholic writer observes, "If, by civil standards, a marriage has irretrievably broken down, it is quite likely that by current Church standards there was never a true sacramental union."[17]

One can appreciate the pastoral concern of the Roman church, but its resolution of the question is more verbal than real. The resort to solution-by-definition could be obviated by openness to exegetical reconsideration of the notion of indissolubility.

The Eastern Orthodox Church

Unlike the Roman Catholic Church, the Eastern Orthodox Church does not have a single code of canon law that is binding on all local churches. Such a unified code, it is held, would be foreign to the spirit of Orthodoxy, which emphasizes autonomy in ecclesiastical government and discipline. As a result, it is difficult to state the church's position precisely in detail. Nevertheless, the basic principles and main lines of approach are clear.

The Eastern church teaches the ideal indissolubility of marriage, both in this life and in the life to come: "The union between husband and wife is an end in itself; it is an eternal union between two unique and eternal personalities which cannot be broken."[18] Thus, "Christian marriage is not only an earthly sexual union, but an eternal bond which will continue when our bodies will be 'spiritual' and when Christ will be 'all in all.'"[19]

In light of this, the church discourages remarriage on the part of widows and widowers, though second and third marriages are allowed as a concession to earthly human needs and desires. It follows that marital indissolubility is not absolute; the marriage bond may be dissolved as a consequence of either physical or moral death. As one Orthodox writer puts it, "The gift of Christian marriage needs to be accepted, freely lived, but can eventually be rejected by man."[20]

Divorce for adultery. The Eastern church recognizes divorce for adultery as a divine dispensation. "According to the Gospel, adultery destroys the very reality, the mystical essence, of marriage." Divorce for adultery declares "the absence, the disappearance, the destruction of love, and therefore it simply declares that a marriage does not exist."[21] The analogy of death is often appealed to in Orthodox teaching about divorce.

---

16. "Canons on Marriage," *The Code of Canon Law in English Translation* (Grand Rapids: Eerdmans, 1983).

17. Zwack, *Annulment*, 7.

18. John Meyendorff, *Marriage: An Orthodox Perspective*, 3d rev. ed. (Crestwood, N.Y.: St. Vladimir's, 1984), 14.

19. Ibid., 15.

20. Ibid., 14.

21. Paul Evdokimov, *The Sacrament of Love: The Nuptial Mystery in the Light of the Orthodox Tradition*, trans. Anthony P. Gythiel and Victoria Steadman (Crestwood, N.Y.: St. Vladimir's, 1985), 189.

In the words of our Lord, in the case of conjugal infidelity the ideal of Christian marriage is entirely defeated. For this reason the bond of mutual trust, love, and faith, the mutual exercise of power over each other's body, is broken; consequently, the scope of marriage is destroyed. Such a case is considered by Orthodox theologians and moralists as equal to spiritual death. As physical death is the only natural cause that may dissolve the nuptial tie, so moral death creates the same result, the dissolution of the marital unity. The chasm created between spouses on account of moral and spiritual death is much wider than that caused by natural death.[22]

It should be noted that there are two courses that may ensue following adultery: repentance, forgiveness, reconciliation, and restoration; impenitence, moral death, dissolution, and divorce.

Divorce as an exercise of pastoral care. Strictly speaking, adultery is the only cause for divorce mentioned in the teaching of Christ. The church, however, may grant divorces for other causes on the principle of *oikonomia*—the church's loving care for its members. *Oikonomia* (direction, administration) stands in contrast to *akribeia* (exactness, precision). The boundaries are not prescribed; "the Church reserves the right to deal with each problem in a pastoral way."[23] With respect to divorce, the rationale is expressed as follows:

Having in mind what our Lord has stated as the only cause of divorce, the Church always tries to study carefully and evaluate conditions in the family life in order to safeguard the sacredness of marriage and protect the moral growth of the persons involved, at the same time giving them an opportunity to find themselves again as living cells in the Body of Christ.

The Church will never justify herself as the dispenser of the grace of God if in her zealous effort to fulfill the letter of the law she kills the spirit of love and mercy by denying her lapsed people opportunity to repent and re-establish themselves in the life of grace.

The truth is that there is no alternative, except choosing the lesser evil. And in the case of broken families the lesser evil is divorce, which the Church, following the example of Moses, grants, not easily and gladly, but hesitantly and sorrowfully, to those who because of "the hardness" of their hearts, feel unable to continue living their married life "in two bodies as in one."[24]

22. Athenagoras Kokkinakis, *Parents and Priests as Servants of Redemption: An Interpretation of the Doctrines of the Eastern Orthodox Church on the Sacraments of Matrimony and Priesthood* (New York: Morehouse, 1958), 47.

23. Gregor Larentzakis, "Marriage, Divorce and Remarriage in the Orthodox Church," *Theology Digest* 26 (1978): 232–34.

24. Kokkinakis, *Parents and Priests,* 49–50.

The Eastern church seriously considers the following conditions in granting divorce and permitting remarriage: adultery, fornication, and all other immoral actions committed by either of the spouses; treacherous actions and threats against the life by either of the spouses; abortion without the consent of the husband; impotence existing prior to marriage and continuing two years after; either of the spouses abandoning the other for more than two years; apostasy or heresy; incurable insanity lasting four years after the marriage, or leprosy.[25]

The Classic Protestant View

Evangelical Protestants are distinguished by adherence to the principle of *sola scriptura*. The holy Scriptures are the only infallible rule of faith and practice, and the church has no authority to bind the conscience by laws of its own making. The church may ministerially determine cases of conscience, but the "supreme judge" in all such controversies "can be no other but the Holy Spirit speaking in the Scripture."[26] The Protestant principle of authority entails the doctrine of the sufficiency of the Scriptures which states that "the whole counsel of God concerning all things necessary for his own glory, man's salvation, faith and life, is either expressly set down in Scripture, or by good and necessary consequence may be deduced from Scripture."[27] The classic Protestant position on divorce framed in the light of these principles is concisely stated in the Westminster Confession of Faith:

> Although the corruption of man be such as is apt to study arguments unduly to put asunder those whom God hath joined together in marriage, yet, nothing but adultery, or such willful desertion as can no way be remedied by the church, or civil magistrate, is cause sufficient of dissolving the bond of marriage.[28]

It is of some interest that none of the antecedent Reformed confessions in the British Isles—neither the Scots Confession (1560) nor the Thirty-Nine Articles of the Church of England (1563) nor the Irish Articles of Religion (1615)—included a statement on divorce. Indeed, the only Reformed confession to contain any reference to divorce prior to Westminster is the First Helvetic Confession (1536). Its teaching on marriage includes a pertinent word directed to the civil government:

> We contend that marriage has been instituted and prescribed by God for all men who are qualified and fit for it and who have not otherwise been called by God to

---

25. Ibid., 54.

26. Westminster Confession of Faith, 31.2, 1.10.

27. Ibid., 1.6.

28. Ibid., 4.6. See also 24.5, which expressly asserts the right of remarriage: "In the case of adultery after marriage, it is lawful for the innocent party to sue out a divorce: and, after the divorce, to marry another, as if the offending party were dead."

live a chaste life outside marriage. No order or state is so holy and honorable that marriage would be opposed to it and should be forbidden. Since such marriage should be conformed in the presence of the Church by a public exhortation and vow in keeping with its dignity, *the government should also respect it and see to it that a marriage is legally and decently entered into and given legal and honorable recognition, and is not lightly dissolved without serious and legitimate grounds.*[29]

Although the Westminster article on divorce is without confessional precedent in the Reformed churches, it is understandable given the historical circumstances of the Westminster Assembly. By the Solemn League and Covenant (1643) both Assembly and Parliament were sworn to preserve and extend "the reformed religion" and to "endeavor to bring the Churches of God in the three kingdoms [Scotland, England, and Ireland] to the nearest conjunction and uniformity in [that] religion" (1st vow). As its dual title indicates, the Solemn League and Covenant was a political instrument as well as a religious commitment. At its heart lay "the conviction that the unity of a society inheres in its religion and church."[30]

Given the concept of a religiously unified society and the intimate connection between church and state that obtains under such circumstances, it is not surprising to find the social institution of marriage among the articles of religion addressed by the Westminster Confession. The Assembly no doubt judged that the unity of both church and society would be well-served by a confessional exposition of the doctrine of marriage, including the biblical grounds for its dissolution, a controversial issue in seventeenth century Britain.[31] The Scottish Parliament already in 1573 had enacted legislation that allowed divorce for desertion.[32] With Anglo-Catholics, on the one hand, still arguing that marriage was indissoluble, and Milton, on the other, lobbying for divorce on grounds of incompatibility, the question could hardly be ignored, as it was bound to have an effect on the civil law.[33]

29. Art. 27 (emphasis added). The Second Helvetic Confession (1566), although silent on divorce, is unique in making this proposal: "Let lawful courts be established in the Church, and holy judges who may care for marriages, and may repress all unchastity and shamefulness, and before whom matrimonial disputes may be settled." Art. 29.

30. John H. Leith, *Assembly at Westminster: Reformed Theology in the Making* (Richmond: John Knox, 1973), 59.

31. Cf. James Turner Johnson, *A Society Ordained by God: English Puritan Marriage Doctrine in the First Half of the Seventeenth Century* (Nashville: Abingdon, 1970). A useful discussion, but unaccountably does not include the Westminster Confession.

32. *Marriage and Divorce: A Report of the Study Panel of the Free Church of Scotland* (Edinburgh: Free Church of Scotland, 1988), 28. "These two causes for the termination of marriage [adultery and desertion] . . . remained the only two grounds for divorce in Scotland until 1938 when cruelty, incurable insanity, sodomy and bestiality were added by Act of Parliament" (p. 28). More radical legislation was enacted in 1976 and 1977 (p. 5).

33. John Milton, *The Doctrine and Discipline of Divorce: Restor'd to the Good of Both Sexes from the Bondage of Canon Law and Other Mistakes . . . to the Parliament of England with the [Westminster] Assembly,*

The Westminster divines took up the question of marriage and divorce in 1646, the year the Confession was completed (apart from the prooftexts requested by Parliament). Following preliminary work in committee, and not a little debate on the floor concerning the "willful desertion" clause, the entire chapter "Of Marriage and Divorce" was adopted November 11, their work on drafting a pan-British confession done at last. As it turned out, Parliament did not take the "humble advice" of its assembled divines on this issue but omitted the section on divorce in its authorized edition of the Confession published in 1648. The Church of Scotland, on the other hand, included it when it adopted the Confession in 1647, and it has since fallen to the Presbyterian family of churches to wrestle confessionally with its meaning and application.[34]

Between the rigorous Anglican view and the relaxed view of Milton, the Westminster position on divorce might seem to be a golden mean, but it was adopted not as a compromise but because it was believed to be biblical. The English Puritans had long since reached a consensus on remarriage following divorce for adultery, exegetically derived from the exceptive clause in Matthew. William Perkins (1558–1602) had included desertion as grounds for divorce under some circumstances on the basis of Paul's instruction regarding mixed marriages in the seventh chapter of 1 Corinthians.[35] Of the Westminster divines who published works on marriage prior to the Assembly, the most important is William Gouge, who chaired the Assembly's committee on divorce. Gouge's position on grounds for divorce is succinctly stated in opposition to "the error of the papists": "Concerning *adultery*, we deny not, but that it giveth just cause of divorce: but withall we say (as we have good warrant from Christ's words) that it is the only cause of just divorce."[36] Remarriage is permissible following divorce for adultery, but in case of desertion, the innocent party is free only from the obligation of conjugal relations; remarriage is not permissible because the marriage is not wholly dissolved. Gouge is aware of other Reformed interpretations of the Pauline release (1 Cor. 7:15) but does not deal with them because the problem is remote.

2d ed. (London, 1644). The first edition was published in 1643; both editions, along with Milton's other divorce tracts, are included in vol. 2 of *Complete Prose Works of John Milton,* ed. Ernest Sirluck (New Haven: Yale University Press, 1959).

34. Most recently the sixteenth General Assembly (1988) of the Presbyterian Church in America appointed a study committee to reexamine the biblical teaching on divorce and remarriage and to ask whether the Westminster Confession of Faith is more lax or more strict than Scripture on this issue. Mid-century revisions of the Confession by two other American Presbyterian denominations are included as an appendix.

35. William Perkins, *Christian Oeconomie: Or, A Short Survey of the Right Manner of Erecting and Ordering a Family According to the Scriptures,* trans. Thomas Pickering, vol. 3 of *The Workes of That Famous and Worthy Minister of Christ, in the Universities of Cambridge* (Cambridge: Iohn Legatt, 1612–13).

36. William Gouge, *Of Domesticall Duties Eight Treatises,* 3d ed. (London: W. Bladen, 1634), 2.2.16. Gouge's *Domesticall Duties* first appeared in 1622; a second and third edition followed in 1626 and 1634.

In many reformed Churches beyond the seas desertion is accounted so far to dissolve the very bond of marriage, as liberty is given to the party forsaken to marry another; and it is also applied to other cases than that which is above mentioned . . . the matter being heard and adjudged by the magistrate, the marriage bond may be broken; and liberty given to the party forsaken to marry another. *But because our church hath no such customs, nor our law determined such cases, I leave them to the custom of other churches.*[37]

One could wish that Gouge had published a post-Assembly volume on "How My Mind Has Changed." Perhaps the Scottish commissioners pointed out that divorce for desertion had not only the approval of Reformed churches beyond the seas but also parliamentary authorization (for three-quarters of a century!) in one of the three island kingdoms now in solemn league and covenant.[38]

The Confession as finally adopted does not restrict desertion as just cause for divorce to mixed marriages, a point observed at some length by John Murray in his widely-circulated *Divorce*.[39] Murray concluded that "the proposition respecting willful desertion in the Confession is not sufficiently guarded and delimited so as to confine itself to the teaching of the apostle in this passage" (p. 77). But this appears to have been intentional. The Assembly after all was advising the parliament of a commonwealth in which professed Christian belief was the norm. Had the Assembly meant to affirm that desertion was a just cause for divorce only when an unbeliever deserted a believer, unambiguous language was readily available. The fact that 1 Corinthians 7:15 was later appended as a prooftext is not decisive for the narrow construction as it is cited to substantiate the principle rather than the one and only circumstance of its application.

Recently the classic Protestant position has come under attack by some evangelicals for being too lax not simply for regarding "malicious desertion" as grounds for divorce, but for permitting remarriage following divorce for adultery. William Heth and Gordon Wenham in particular are critical of the Westminster position, which they call "the Erasmian view" inasmuch as "the exegetical tradition started by Erasmus and amplified by Luther and other Reformers was confirmed by . . . this Confession of

---

37. *Domesticall Duties*, 2.2.3; emphasis added.

38. According to the study panel of the Free Church of Scotland cited earlier, "The procedure required by the Act was surprisingly elaborate: the civil authorities were to make every effort to apprehend the deserter and oblige him to return to his wife and home; if they failed, they were to declare him an outlaw. They were then to notify the ecclesiastical authorities who if also unsuccessful, were to excommunicate him. The marriage could be ended by divorce provided the deserted spouse had always shown willingness 'to adhere'—i.e. to have the deserter back and to continue the marriage." *Marriage and Divorce*, p. 39.

39. John Murray, *Divorce* (Philadelphia: OPC Committee on Christian Education, 1953), 76–77. Murray's treatment of divorce was originally published in the *Westminster Theological Journal* (1946–49), and was subsequently reprinted by Presbyterian and Reformed (1961).

Faith."[40] The Heth-Wenham thesis is that Erasmus departed from the uniform teaching of the early church that remarriage following divorce for any reason was adulterous. We will examine their exegesis in due course, but for now it is important to note that what Heth and Wenham call "the early church view" is more accurately "the final Augustinian view." As late as 413 Augustine wrote: "Nor is it clear from Scripture whether a man who has left his wife because of adultery, which he is certainly permitted to do, is himself an adulterer if he marries again. And if he should, I do not think that he would commit a grave sin."[41] Augustine's definitive position according to which such a man would be an adulterer appears six years later.[42]

It is thus by no means certain that Heth and Wenham adequately represent the teaching of the early church. According to Jesuit scholar Theodore Mackin in his massive *Divorce and Remarriage*, "Christian writers on the subject of adultery, divorce and remarriage, beginning in the middle of the second century and continuing at least until Augustine . . . never call the following persons adulterers: [1] A husband who remarries after dismissing an adulterous wife. [2] A husband who remarries after being abandoned by his wife. [3] A woman who marries a man in either of these two cases."[43] Moreover, the final Augustinian view was never adopted by the Eastern churches, all of which permitted divorce and remarriage. Mackin summarizes the discipline of the Byzantine church in the thirteenth century:

> Where a marriage is indissoluble this comes of its being a sacramental marriage of two Christians. But even this indissolubility yields to divine dispensation as this was expressed by Christ in the exceptive clause recorded in Matthew 5:32 and 19:9. . . . In the circumstances envisioned by the Matthean passages the Church was thought to be authorized to separate the spouses, to dissolve their marriage in the name of and by the authority of God. . . . *Porneia* in the exceptive clause was taken to designate adultery; dismissal was taken to designate the dissolution of the marriage.
>
> But the adultery warranting dismissal and dissolution was understood to be not the only cause, but to be only a sample and a point of departure for other and equivalent causes. It was taken as self-evident that other crimes are possible

---

40. William A. Heth and Gordon J. Wenham, *Jesus and Divorce: The Problem with the Evangelical Consensus* (Nashville: Nelson, 1984), 83. The Westminster position is also implicitly criticized by J. Carl Laney in *The Divorce Myth: A Biblical Examination of Divorce and Remarriage* (Minneapolis: Bethany, 1981).

41. Augustine, *On Faith and Works*, trans. Gregory J. Lombardo (New York: Newman, 1988), chap. 19.

42. Augustine, *De incompetentibus nuptiis* (Adulterous Marriages), cited in Augustine, *On Faith and Works*, 98 n. 198.

43. Theodore Mackin, *Divorce and Remarriage* (New York: Paulist, 1984), 172. See also Roderick Phillips, *Putting Asunder: A History of Divorce in Western Society* (Cambridge: Cambridge University Press, 1988), 20–24.

to spouses that injure their marriages with equal or greater severity. Abortion and attempted murder of the spouse were only two of these.[44]

As we have seen, the historic difference between the Roman Catholic and the Eastern Orthodox churches on the doctrine of divorce persists down to the present day. Thus, while Erasmus should be given his due for his exegetical contribution to the discussion, to label the view that permits remarriage following divorce for just cause "Erasmian" is misleading and pejorative.

The Marriage Covenant and Divorce

The key biblical texts to be correlated are those that deal directly with the issue of divorce and remarriage: the Mosaic regulation (Deut. 24:1–4), the prophetic protest (Mal. 2:13–16), the teaching of Jesus (Matt. 5:32; 19:9; Mark 10:11–12; Luke 16:18), and the teaching of Paul (1 Cor. 7:10–16). These make sense, however, within the wider biblical teaching on marriage as a covenant.[45] As we have seen, the covenantal perspective on marriage is so much a part of Old Testament religion and culture that God's covenant with Israel is often pictured in such terms. Sadly, however, the figure of the marriage covenant is exploited primarily in dealing with Israel's apostasy. The prophets, especially Hosea, Jeremiah, and Ezekiel, represent Israel's infidelity to the Sinaitic covenant as committing adultery (nāʾap) and fornication (zānâ).[46] Hosea 2:2 (2:4 in MT and LXX) is typical:

> Contend with your mother, contend,
> For she is not my wife, and I am not her husband;
> And let her put away her fornication (zānâ) from her face,
> And her adultery (nāʾap) from between her breasts.[47]

According to the word of the Lord through Hosea, the problem with Israel was that "like Adam, they have broken the covenant—they were unfaithful (bāgad) to me there" (6:7); "the people have broken my covenant and rebelled against my law" (8:1). The stipulations of the Decalogue form the basis of the indictment: "There is no faithfulness, no ḥesed, no knowledge of God in the land. There is only cursing, lying and murder, stealing and adultery" (4:1–2). As a result of serious and unrepented of transgression of the covenant, the relationship between God

---

44. Mackin, *Divorce and Remarriage*, 373.

45. Cf. David Atkinson, *To Have and to Hold: The Marriage Covenant and the Discipline of Divorce* (Grand Rapids: Eerdmans, 1979); Ray Sutton, *Second Chance: Biblical Principles of Divorce and Remarriage* (Fort Worth: Dominion, 1988).

46. *Zenût* (the noun for fornication) is used with reference to covenant infidelity already in Num. 14:33. See also Exod. 34:15–16.

47. *Nāʾap* and *zānâ* are also used in parallel constructions in Jer. 3:8, 9; 13:27; Hos. 4:13, 14.

and his people became radically altered. Thus, Hosea at the Lord's direction names a son *Lo-ammi,* "for you are not my people and I am not your God" (1:9). In the figure of Hosea 2:2, the "marriage" between God and his people was dissolved; restoration would take nothing less than new covenant (Jer. 31:31–32).[48]

The language of divorce for the altered relationship between God and his "wife" is explicit in Jeremiah: "I gave faithless Israel her certificate of divorce and sent her away because of all her adulteries (*nāʾap,* LXX *moichaō*). Yet I saw that her unfaithful sister Judah had no fear; she also went out and committed adultery (*zānâ,* LXX *porneuō*)" (Jer 3:8). As we will see, this divinely established precedent is highly relevant to the teaching of Jesus and Paul. But first, what about Moses?

The Mosaic Regulation

The existence of practice of divorce is acknowledged in a few Pentateuchal texts without comment on its morality (Num. 30:9; Lev. 22:13; 21:14). It is similar to polygamy in this regard. Moses does regulate the practice, however, in one well-worn passage in Deuteronomy.

> Suppose a man marries a woman and later decides that he doesn't want her, because he finds something about her that he doesn't like. So he writes out divorce papers, gives them to her, and sends her away from his home. Then suppose she marries another man, and he also decides that he doesn't want her, so he also writes out divorce papers, gives them to her, and sends her away from his home. Or suppose her second husband dies. In either case, her first husband is not to marry her again; he is to consider her defiled. If he married her again, it would be offensive to the Lord. You are not to commit such a terrible sin in the land that the Lord your God is giving you. [Deut. 24:1–4 TEV]

This version captures the thrust of the passage, which is not to specify grounds for divorce but to provide a clear status for a divorced woman (hence a written declaration in her possession) and to prevent her being treated as a tradable commodity (hence the prohibition of subsequent remarriage to the divorcing husband after an intervening marriage). The Hebrew expression ʿerwat dābār, here translated "something about her he doesn't like," could be translated "some shameful conduct," as the Good News Bible indicates in the margin. The only other Old Testament instance of ʿerwat dābār (literally, "nakedness of a thing") is Deuteronomy 23:14 with excrement as the referent

---

48. Walter Brueggemann helpfully notes a threefold distinction with respect to prophetic ministry in the Old Testament: "The words of the prophet, in the service of the covenant, depend upon the situation of the covenant in his day. (1) When the covenant has been broken but the patient concern of Yahweh is still seeking, he admonishes repentance, summoning Israel back to covenant. . . . (2) When the covenant is broken and the anger of Yahweh has been provoked, he offers evidence that the covenant has been broken (indictment) and declares the punishment to come (sentence). (3) When Yahweh continues his gracious concern for Israel in spite of broken covenant, the prophet announces grace (promise)." *Tradition for Crisis: A Study in Hosea* (Richmond: John Knox, 1968), 99.

of "the indecent (or repulsive) thing." The context determines its use in Deuteronomy 24. Whereas the reason the woman finds no favor in the eyes of the first husband because he has found some vague "unseemly thing" in her, the second husband is said to divorce her simply because he dislikes her. Ugly is in the eye of the beholder. The hard fact is, divorce for aversion was tolerated under the Mosaic civil law, though its moral wrongness could be inferred from the creation ordinance.

The Prophetic Protest

Although technically legal, such divorce practice did not escape protest in the Old Testament, being vigorously challenged in Malachi 2:13–16. The overall theme of the whole of chapter 2 is broken faith among the covenant community on the part of both priests (2:1–9) and the people (2:10–16). The verb *bāgad* (act or deal treacherously, faithlessly, deceitfully) occurs five times in the latter seven verses, beginning with the question, "Why do we profane the covenant of our fathers by breaking faith with one another?" (v. 10), and closing with the exhortation, "So guard yourself in your spirit, and do not break faith" (v. 16). Malachi protests against two specific instances of covenant infidelity: entering into marriages with unconverted pagan wives ("the daughter of a foreign god") and divorce ("the wife of your youth"). These, of course, may be parts of a coordinated event, but they are treated in the text as separate instances of "treason."

We are used to reading the key phrase of verse 16 thus: "For I hate divorce, says the Lord God of Israel." But the Hebrew (with the vowel points supplied by the Masoretes) actually says, "For *he* hates divorce, says the Lord God of Israel." But if *he* refers to God, the parallel clause does not make good sense: "and he spreads violence upon his garment, says the Lord Almighty." The New International Version is compelled to take considerable liberties with the text of the second clause in order to make it conform to the first: "'I hate divorce,' says the Lord God of Israel, 'and I hate a man's covering himself with violence as well as with his garment,' says the Lord Almighty." One wonders whether there might not be a better way of reading the text, a way that will be able to do justice to both clauses as parts of a coherent whole.

Already in the last century the German Old Testament scholar Ewald suggested a slight repointing of the Hebrew that would yield this translation: "For he who from hatred breaketh wedlock, saith Yahvé Israel's God,—he covereth with cruelty his garment, saith Yahvé of Hosts."[49] Beth Glazier-McDonald in her recent commentary on Malachi follows this suggestion and translates the crucial clauses thus: "'For one who divorces because of aversion,' says Yahweh, the God of Israel, 'thereby covers his garment with violence,' says

---

49. G. H. A. von Ewald, *Commentary on the Prophets of the Old Testament*, trans. J. F. Smith (London: Williams and Norgate, 1881), vol. 5, 81–82. See also Alvin van Hoonacker, *Les Douze Petits Prophètes: Traduits et Commentés* (Paris: Gabalda, 1908), 728–29.

Yahweh of Hosts."[50] This makes excellent sense in the context, and the translations of J. M. Powis Smith, the New English Bible, and the New Vulgate Edition reflect the same reading of the text.[51]

The Septuagint supports this reading of the consonantal text, though it is widely and mistakenly assumed to have the same rendering as the Targum and the Vulgate: "If you hate, divorce!" As Glazier-McDonald notes, "Such a command would be totally out of place here, coming as it does directly after an exhortation not to deal deceitfully with the wife of one's youth (2:15)." Correctly parsed, however, the Septuagint is not a subjunctive and an imperative, but a participle and a subjunctive. It does not say, "If you hate, divorce!" It says, "If hating you divorce," with apodosis still to come, as in the Hebrew.[52] For the sake of clarity, the text may be written thus:

> But if you divorce out of hatred,
>   Says the Lord God of Israel,
> Then ungodliness covers your thoughts
>   Says the Lord Almighty.

This rendering is congruent with Malachi's general style as Malachi often inserts "says the Lord" before completing the thought (1:10, 14; 3:10, 17). In one other verse he places it as here, between the protasis and the apodosis of a conditional sentence (2:2). Contextually it addresses precisely what the situation calls for. The verb for "hatred" is the same as in Deuteronomy 24, and there is external evidence for the practice of "hating" and "divorcing."[53] Malachi aims his protest directly at the practice falsely assumed to be morally permissible from the merely descriptive terms of a case. He appeals to God as witness to the broken marriage covenant, highlighting the interpersonal dimension by references to "the wife of your youth," the covenant "companion and partner" now treacherously abandoned for no good reason.

Malachi's expression for the consequences of a husband's betrayal of the marital trust by divorcing his wife because he dislikes her is "violence (ḥāmās)

---

50. Beth Glazier-MacDonald, *Malachi: The Divine Messenger* (Atlanta: Scholars, 1987), 82.

51. J. M. Powis Smith, *The Old Testament: An American Translation* (Chicago: University of Chicago Press, 1927): "'For one who hates and divorces,'/Says the Lord God of Israel,/'Covers his clothing with violence,'/Says the Lord of hosts." NEB: "If a man divorces or puts away his spouse, he overwhelms her with cruelty, says the Lord of Hosts the God of Israel." *Bibliorum Sacrorum: Nova Vulgata Editio* (Rome: Vatican Library, 1979): *Si quis odio dimittit, dicit Dominus, Deus Israel, operit iniquitas vestimentum eius, dicit Dominus exercituum.*

52. For the technical details see David Clyde Jones, "A Note on the LXX of Malachi 2:16," *Journal of Biblical Literature* 109 (1990): 683–85.

53. Cf. David Daube: "It should also be noted that from two papyri of the 5th cent. B.C. it looks as if at Elephantine at least a Jewish wife could legally terminate the [marriage] union by 'disliking and leaving' (*sene' unephaq*) her husband or by a public declaration of 'dislike' (*sene'*)." "Terms for Divorce," in *The New Testament and Rabbinic Judaism* (New York: Arno, 1973), 366.

covers his garment (*lĕbûš*)." The phrase is somewhat obscure, and the Septuagint ("ungodliness covers your thoughts") does not help us here. *Ḥāmāṣ* is used in the Old Testament specifically of physical violence, but also more generally of serious injury inflicted by wrongdoing.[54] *Lĕbûš* has been variously interpreted. Gesenius's lexicon calls attention to the Arabic word for garment (*libasun*) and its use in the Qur'an as a metaphor for spouse (Sura 2:183, "Wives are your garment and you are theirs"), but there is no parallel use in the Old Testament. A more likely explanation is that the prophet alludes to the betrothal pledge in which the man spread the "wing" (i.e., extremity) of his garment over the woman as a symbol of his protection and commitment (cf. Ruth 3:9; Ezek 16:8). *Lĕbûš* would then be a metonymy for the marriage relationship, which is radically abused through arbitrary divorce.

The latter view does makes sense in the context, especially in light of the repeated expression "the wife of your youth," which calls attention to the early stage of the marital relationship. The wrongdoing of divorce is something obvious and serious, and divine worship is no substitute for righteousness in human relationships. To paraphrase what the Lord said through the prophet Hosea, "I will have *fidelity*, not sacrifice."[55] Such divorce constitutes treachery (*bāgad*) against the marriage covenant.[56]

So far from weakening the Lord's protest against marital infidelity, the prophetic word against divorce is rendered more forceful by being more definite. Divorce for "hatred" is a radical breach of fidelity; it is "violence" against the companion to whom one has been joined in marriage. It therefore stands condemned by the God of justice, mercy, and troth.

The Teaching of Jesus

The fullest presentation of Jesus' teaching on divorce (Matt. 19:3–12; Mark 10:2–12) is given in response to a test question posed by the Pharisees, a question we know from the Jewish Mishnah (promulgated ca. A.D. 200) was answered differently by the contemporary rabbinical schools of Shammai and Hillel. The longer and more complex Matthean account warrants a number of separate observations.

---

54. E.g., Gen. 16:5, "Then Sarai said to Abram, 'You are responsible for the wrong (*ḥāmāṣ*) I am suffering [from Hagar].'"

55. Cf. Joyce G. Baldwin: "[Malachi] sees divorce to be like *covering one's garment with violence*, a figurative expression for all kinds of gross injustice which, like the blood of a murdered victim, leave their mark for all to see." *Haggai, Zechariah, Malachi: An Introduction and Commentary* (Downers Grove, Ill.: InterVarsity, 1972), 241.

56. The lexical meaning of *bāgad* is "act or deal treacherously, faithlessly, deceitfully, in the marriage relation, in matters of property or right, in covenants, in word and in general conduct" (Francis Brown, S. R. Driver, and C. A. Briggs, *Hebrew and English Lexicon of the Old Testament* [Oxford: Clarendon, 1977], 93). It is parallel to the (now rare) use of the English word treason for "betrayal of trust" or "breach of faith."

The dominant concern. The purpose of Jesus' teaching is to guard his disciples against divorce, to preserve marriages rather than to prevent remarriage. The dominant concern is faithfulness to the original ideal of marriage expressed in the creation ordinance. The climactic exhortation, "What God has joined together let not man separate," is addressed to the couple, particularly the husband, whose prerogative to end the marriage is falsely assumed. Divorce under Jewish and Roman law did not require the pronouncement of some third party (civil or religious) that the couple was no longer bound to each other. Divorce was a matter of repudiation of the marriage on the part of the husband (Jewish law) or of either husband or wife (Roman law). All that was required was evidence of intent, normally by written documentation, always a requirement under Jewish law. In the Roman empire couples dissolved their own marriages by withdrawing consent. In Judaism the husband dismissed the wife; he was the sole agent of the dissolution (though he could be compelled under certain circumstances to dismiss his wife at her insistence).

The practical point of the exhortation is that attitudes and actions that contribute to the breakdown of the relationship fall under the principle of keeping intact what God has joined together. Emotional disengagement is already a step in the wrong direction.

The Mosaic regulation. The relevant section of the tractate on divorce from the Mishnah (*Gittin* 9.10) is brief and may easily be cited in full.

> The School of Shammai say, A man may not divorce his wife unless he has found in her aught improper [*děbār ʿěrwâ*], as it is said, *because he hath found some unseemly thing* [*ʿerwat dābār*] *in her.* But the School of Hillel say, Even if she spoiled a dish for him, as it is said, *because he hath found some unseemly thing* [*ʿerwat dābār*] *in her.* R. Akiba says, Even if he found another more beautiful than she is, as it is said, *Then it cometh to pass if she find no favour in his eyes.*[57]

Both schools cite the same Old Testament text (Deut. 24:1), but with a different emphasis. Shammai places the emphasis on ʿerwat and reads, "*unseemly* in anything." Hillel places the emphasis on *dābār* and reads, "unseemly in *anything.*" Hillel's "ground" is subjective and open-ended; the husband decides what is unseemly. Shammai's "ground" is more objective, but the expression on which he bases his argument is too vague to support it. Understandably, given the sin of men, the Hillelian "exegesis" became the dominant view, which Rabbi Akiba (A.D. 90–135) simply extends to its logical conclusion with equal exegetical warrant.

Jesus, for his part, challenges the assumption common to all disputants, namely, that the passage in Deuteronomy was intended to provide grounds for divorce. His scriptural proof is the original will of God expressed in the

---

57. *Tractate Gittin,* ed. and trans. Philip Blackman (New York: Judaica, 1963), 444.

creation ordinance. Viewed in that light, it becomes evident that the Mosaic permission was enacted as an accommodation to the hardness of men's hearts—who might resort to something worse to rid themselves of an unwanted wife. As Lane observes, "When Jesus affirmed that Moses framed the provision concerning the letter of dismissal out of regard to the people's hardness of heart, he was using an established legal category of actions allowed out of consideration for wickedness or weakness."[58] The intent of the Mosaic "command" was not to approve arbitrary divorce but to limit the consequences of male-domineering sin. Stonehouse's conclusion is correct: "Although the use made of this passage in order to substantiate laxness was illegitimate, the fact remains that the Mosaic provision for the protection of the woman assumes that divorce was permissible. Christ condemns what Moses accepted as part of the *status quo*."[59] The civil provision must be read within the broader teaching of the Torah as a whole with its preeminent concerns for justice, mercy, and especially in this case *fidelity*.

The exception clause. Most of the controversy over Jesus' teaching on divorce surrounds the interpretation of the exception clause, which appears twice in Matthew, here in the divorce pericope and also in the Sermon on the Mount.

> Anyone who divorces his wife, except for marital unfaithfulness (*mē epi porneia*), and marries another woman commits adultery. [Matt. 19:9]
> Anyone who divorces his wife, except for marital unfaithfulness (*parektos logos porneias*), causes her to become an adulteress, and anyone who marries the divorced woman commits adultery. [Matt. 5:32]

The exception clause provokes two questions: What is the meaning of *porneia* in this context? How does the exception clause affect the issue of remarriage?

The lexical question. *Porneia* is the general term for all illicit or immoral sexual intercourse. The specific form may sometimes be indicated by the context. If payment of wages is involved, it is prostitution. If it involves close relatives, it is incest. If it involves persons of the same sex, it is homosexuality. If it involves an unmarried couple, it is unchastity. If it involves a married person outside of marriage, it is adultery.[60] The Septuagint uses *porneia* with reference to prostitution and adultery, but not premarital unchastity, homosex-

---

58. William L. Lane, *The Gospel According to Mark* (Grand Rapids: Eerdmans, 1974), 355. See further David Daube, "Concessions to Sinfulness in Jewish Law," *The Journal of Jewish Studies* 10 (1959): 1–13; David F. Wright, "Calvin's Pentateuchal Criticism: Equity, Hardness of Heart, and Divine Accommodation in the Mosaic Harmony Commentary," *Calvin Theological Journal* 21 (1986): 33–50.

59. Ned B. Stonehouse, *The Witness of Matthew and Mark to Christ* (Grand Rapids: Eerdmans, 1944), 204.

60. *Porneia* originally meant prostitution. "But the word had been picked up in Hellenistic Judaism, always pejoratively, to cover all extramarital sexual sins and aberrations, including homosexuality." Gordon D. Fee, *The First Epistle to the Corinthians,* New International Commentary on the New Testament (Grand Rapids: Eerdmans, 1987), 200.

uality, or incest. What is crucial for the right interpretation of the exceptive clause in Matthew is the observation made earlier that Israel's covenantal infidelity, leading to her "divorce" by the Lord, is alternately described in the Old Testament as fornication and adultery (*porneia* and *moicheia* in the LXX; see, e.g., Hos. 2:2; 4:13–14; 6:7; 8:1; Jer. 3:6–9; 13:27; Ezek. 16:15, 32, 59; 23:43–45). This usage continues in the intertestamental period, as in Ecclesiasticus 23:22–23:

> The woman who deserts her husband
> and provides him with an heir by another man:
> First, she has disobeyed the Law of the Most High;
> Secondly, she has been false to her husband; and
> Thirdly, she has gone whoring in adultery
> (*en porneia emoicheuthē*).[61]

There are those who argue that *porneia* more plausibly refers to incest in the exceptive clause in Matthew, and consequently that adultery is not grounds for divorce. In an influential article published some sixty years ago W. K. Lowther Clarke made the case by appealing to the apostolic decree or "compromise" in Acts 15:29. The argument in a nutshell is "Since the first three articles of the compromise are concerned with practices which were abhorrent to the Jews but seemed innocent enough to the Gentiles, the fourth must be of a similar nature. The passage in 1 Corinthians gives us the clue. *Porneia* here means *marriage within the prohibited Levitical degrees.*"[62]

By taking the exceptive clause to refer to marriage within the prohibited Levitical degrees, Matthew may be brought into harmony with Mark and Luke. Clarke concludes, "There is no divorce, but causes of nullity may be recognized."[63] The argument, however plausibly it may seem to satisfy considerations of harmonization, is nevertheless flawed at the outset when Clarke asserts that "*porneia* cannot have meant infidelity within the realm of marriage, for in Matt. xv. 19 it is distinguished from *moicheia.*"[64] The point has been reasserted more recently in an influential article by Joseph A. Fitzmyer: "Elsewhere in Matthew [*porneia*] occurs only in 15:19, where it is . . . lined up side-by-side with *moicheia*, 'adultery,' and obviously distinct from it."[65]

---

61. For additional examples see F. Lövestam, "Divorce and Remarriage in the New Testament," *Jewish Law Annual* 4 (1981): 9–27.

62. W. K. Lowther Clarke, "The 'Excepting Clause' in St. Matthew," *New Testament Problems: Essays—Reviews—Interpretations* (London: SPCK, 1929), 60.

63. Ibid.

64. Ibid., 59.

65. Joseph A. Fitzmyer, "The Matthean Divorce Texts and Some New Palestinian Evidence," *Theological Studies* 37 (1976): 208. Fitzmyer dismisses an earlier critique of the idea that Matthew keeps *porneia* and *moicheia* distinct as "sciolist" (209 n. 49), but scholarly put-downs are no substitute for argument.

But is it so obvious? Matthew 15:19 says, "For out of the heart come evil thoughts, murder, adultery, fornication, theft, false testimony, slander." Both *moicheia* (adultery) and *porneia* (fornication) are listed as violations of the seventh commandment, but this does not mean that the specific (*moicheia*) is distinguished from the general (*porneia*) to the point of exclusion. In a similar use of the Decalogue Paul lists patricide, matricide, and murder (1 Tim. 1:9). Are the former not murder because they are lined up side by side with it? Is it not rather the case that they are specified as particularly heinous forms of murder? Again, Paul names liars and perjurers in the same list (1 Tim. 1:10). As with patricide and matricide, perjury is specified as a particular form of lying, not distinguished from it. The same reasoning applies to Matthew 15:19.

There is thus no reason why *porneia* may not refer to adultery in the exceptive clause. Of course it is lexically *possible* that it might refer to incest.[66] As with the actual use of any word, the intended meaning has to be determined from the context. Given the situation that the question specifically concerns divorce (not annulment), and given the well-known divine precedent of Israel's divorce for fornication and adultery, it makes excellent sense to take the clause to refer to exceptional circumstances under which divorce is just.

Another common argument against the understanding that the exceptive clause justifies divorce for adultery is that "Jesus, then, would be siding with the conservative school of Shammai which allowed divorce only in the case of adultery," and, if so, then "Jesus' teaching did not rise above that of Shammai and the Pharisees, contrary to His usual pattern . . . [as] Christ customarily rebuked the superficiality of the Pharisees with His own more stringent interpretation of the Law."[67] There are two issues here: what Shammai actually taught and whether the comparative "stringency" of Jesus is a viable hermeneutical principle.

To take the latter first, Jesus' interpretation of the law is not invariably more stringent than that of the Pharisees. Indeed, sometimes the opposite is the case. Responding to the Pharisees' stringent interpretation of the fourth commandment, Jesus twice reproves them for failure to incorporate into their hermeneutic the principle of Hosea 6:6: "I desire mercy, not sacrifice" (Matt. 9:13; 12:7). Jesus said, "Unless your *righteousness* surpasses that of the Pharisees and the teachers of the law, you will certainly not enter the kingdom of heaven" (Matt. 5:20). But this is not to say that our standards must in every instance be more stringent than theirs. Standards are not righteous for being rigorous.

---

66. 1 Cor. 5:1 is the only biblical instance of *porneia* where incest is *required* by the context, though a case can be made for such in the letter of the apostolic council to the Gentile believers (Acts 15:20, 28). Although *porneia* is not used with reference to incestuous marriage in the LXX, an instance of the Hebrew equivalent *zĕnût* has been found in the Dead Sea Scrolls. Cf. Fitzmyer, 218–21.

67. Laney, *The Divorce Myth*, 67–68. Again: "Had Jesus permitted divorce for adultery or other illicit sexual behavior, His teaching would not have risen above that of Shammai, and would not have provoked such a response" (76–77).

As for the teaching of Shammai, the only source is an ambiguous phrase in the Mishnah (*Gittin* 9.10) quoted in full above. Robert H. Gundry argues that *logos porneia* in the exceptive clause (Matt. 5:32) represents the *ʿerwat dābār* of Deuteronomy 24:1. (The LXX has *aschēmon pragma*, shameful thing or disgraceful conduct). According to Gundry, Matthew, like Shammai, "reverses the order of words to . . . get the meaning of unchastity, immorality."[68] But reversing the phrase—if that is what Matthew does—only shifts the emphasis from *thing* to *nakedness*; it does not in itself turn it into the equivalent of *porneia* as a synonym for adultery. It overreaches the evidence to confidently conclude, as many do, that "the more rigorous school of Shammai held that [*ʿerwat dābār*] meant adultery, and that divorce was not permitted for any lesser offence."[69]

The syntactical question. Heth and Wenham along with Gundry apply the criterion of stringency not to divorce, which they agree is permitted in the case of adultery, but to remarriage, which they argue is never permitted during the lifetime of the other spouse, not even when the divorce was for adultery. As Gundry puts it, "Matthew's exceptive clause allows formalization—according to Jewish requirement—of the break between husband and wife that has already occurred through the wife's immorality. But Matthew does not let the husband remarry."[70]

It is this absolute prohibition of remarriage following divorce that is supposed to distinguish Jesus from even the most exacting of the rabbinical schools and alone accounts for the disciples' astonished reaction, "If this is the situation between a husband and wife, it is better not to marry" (Matt. 19:10). Gundry takes verses 11–12 as a reaffirmation of no remarriage following divorce for adultery: "After they have had to divorce their wives for immorality . . . [Jesus' true disciples] out of obedience to Christ's law concerning divorce do not remarry, but live as eunuchs, lest their righteousness fail to surpass that of the scribes and Pharisees and entrance into the kingdom be denied them (cf. vs. 12 with 5:20)."[71]

Gundry, however, focuses on the disciples' reaction without discussing the prior question of the syntax of the exceptive clause. The syntactical question is whether the exceptive clause refers to divorce and remarriage or only to

---

68. Robert H. Gundry, *Matthew: A Commentary on His Literary and Theological Art* (Grand Rapids: Eerdmans, 1982), 90. A separate problem is Gundry's view that the exceptive clause "comes from Matthew, not from Jesus, as an editorial insertion to conform Jesus' words to God's Word in the OT" (90). If so, Matthew was a poor editor since Matthew's Jesus, if we must call him that, goes on to say that the provision of Deut. 24:1 was not God's word from the beginning but was given on account of the hardness of men's hearts.

69. Francis Wright Beare, *The Gospel According to Matthew: Translation, Introduction, and Commentary* (San Francisco: Harper, 1981), 387.

70. Gundry, Matthew, 377.

71. Ibid., 382.

divorce. In other words, does Jesus make the single assertion that divorce and remarriage is adultery, except when the divorce was for *porneia*; or does he make the double assertion that divorce is adultery, except when for *porneia*, and divorce and remarriage, with no exception, is adultery.

As the title of one of Wenham's articles indicates, this is an old crux revisited.[72] The syntactical question has been dealt with by Murray, who observed that "in this sentence as it stands no thought is complete without the principal verb, *moichatai*. The ruling thought of the passage is that of committing adultery (*moichatai*) by remarriage.

> The very exceptive clause, therefore, must have direct bearing upon the action denoted by the verb that governs. But in order to have direct bearing upon the governing verb (*moichatai*) it must also have direct bearing upon that which must occur before the action denoted by the principal verb can take effect, namely, the marrying of another. This direct bearing which the exceptive clause must have on the remarriage and on the committing of adultery is simply another way of saying that, as far as the syntax of the sentence is concerned, the exceptive clause must apply to the committing of adultery in the event of remarriage as well as to the wrong of putting away.[73]

More recently Phillip H. Wiebe has examined the crux from the point of view of the logic of statements containing an exceptive clause. Such statements, Wiebe points out, make two assertions. He illustrates the point with this example: "Whoever exceeds the speed limit, except as authorized by law, and hits another vehicle, is liable to criminal prosecution."[74]

This statement means not only that ordinary drivers who speed and crash may be prosecuted, but also that drivers of emergency vehicles cannot be prosecuted if they hit another vehicle while speeding in the line of duty. The propositions implied by the presence of the exceptive clause are two:

> (1) Whoever exceeds the speed limit, but is not authorized by law to do so, and hits another vehicle, is liable to criminal prosecution.

and

> (2) Whoever exceeds the speed limit, but is authorized by law to do so, and hits another vehicle, is not liable to criminal prosecution.[75]

72. G. J. Wenham, "Matthew and Divorce: An Old Crux Revisited," *Journal for the Study of the New Testament* 22 (1984): 95–107.

73. Murray, *Divorce*, 40. Murray presents six arguments against the opposing view.

74. Phillip H. Wiebe, "Jesus' Divorce Exception," *Journal of the Evangelical Theological Society* 32 (1989): 328.

75. Ibid., 329.

When the divorce statement with the exceptive clause in Matthew is subjected to logical analysis it is evident that it also implies two propositions.

(1) If a man divorces his wife, and the ground for the divorce is not his wife's unchastity, and the man marries another, then he commits adultery.

and

(2) If a man divorces his wife, and the ground for the divorce is his wife's unchastity, and the man marries another, then he does not commit adultery.[76]

The exceptive clause thus permits remarriage as well as divorce where there is sufficient cause for dissolving the marriage bond. This coheres with the meaning of divorce in first-century Palestine, which was never thought of as a permanent separation of partners who remained married. According to the Mishnah (*Gittin* 9.3), "The essential formula in the bill of divorce is 'Lo, thou art free to marry any man.'" Where divorce is justified there is freedom to remarry.

Mark and Luke mention no exception (Mark 10:11–12; Luke 16:18). But such a radical breach as adultery—in fact, a capital offense, though not enforced—was not in question as grounds for divorce (cf. Mishnah, *Sotah* 1.1, 5). The principle enunciated by Murray in connection with Romans 7:2–3 is applicable also here: "The contingency of perverse and wanton violation of marital sanctity need not be taken into consideration when appeal is made to the law that governs marriage."[77]

The disciples' startled reaction ("If this is the situation between a husband and wife, it is better not to marry") is not unique—they're still very much learners (cf. Matt. 16:22–23; 20:20–21, 24), and it is entirely intelligible apart from the question of remarriage. As Martin Franzmann puts it, "The disciples were startled to hear Jesus bind man to woman so absolutely, with no concession to sentiment, or desire, or utility; the woman claims man's love and loyalty, not because she pleases him, or comforts him, or gives him children, but simply because God has put her there at man's side."[78] The disciples' "better off single" is just the kind of chauvinistic attitude you would expect when they were confronted with Jesus' radical challenge to their self-serving assumptions about the "right" to divorce.

---

76. Ibid., 327–28.
77. Murray, *Divorce*, 92.
78. Martin H. Franzmann, *Follow Me: Discipleship According to Saint Matthew* (St. Louis: Concordia, 1961), 174.

The Teaching of Paul

The apostle Paul speaks to the question of divorce in 1 Corinthians 7:10–16, addressing first the Christian couple by recalling the teaching of Jesus in the Gospels, then applying the principles of Jesus' teaching to the situation where only one of the marriage partners has entered the new covenant through faith in Christ.

> To the married I give this command (not I, but the Lord): A wife must not separate from her husband. But if she does, she must remain unmarried or else be reconciled to her husband. And a husband must not divorce his wife. [vv. 10–11]

> To the rest I say this (I, not the Lord): If any brother has a wife who is not a believer and she is willing to live with him, he must not divorce her. And if a woman has a husband who is not a believer and he is willing to live with her, she must not divorce him. . . . But if the unbeliever leaves, let him do so. A believing man or woman is not bound in such circumstances; God has called us to live in peace. [vv. 12–13, 15]

In verses 10–11 the apostle, appealing to the express teaching of the Lord ("not I, but the Lord"), instructs the wife not to separate from (*chōrizō*) her husband and the husband not to send away (*aphiēmi*) his wife. Both verbs refer to divorce performed by actual separation.[79] Contemporary English should translate "divorce" in *both* instances to avoid confusion with the modern idea of legal separation (from bed and board, as the expression concretely puts it). This is confirmed by the use of "unmarried" (*agamos*) for the status of the separated partner.

Like Mark and Luke, Paul cites Jesus without the exception clause. Calvin's comment at this point affirms the hermeneutical principle: "When teachers intend to deal with something briefly, they teach in a general way, and exceptions are dealt with in detailed, as well as more inclusive and yet precise discussion."[80] Paul's "but if she does" is frankly realistic about the fallenness of human nature and the likelihood of marital breakdown even among Christians. The divorced partners remain in the church's fellowship and subject to its nurture and discipline. It would be wrong to regard "remain unmarried" and "be reconciled" as two equally valid alternatives for the Christian spouse.

---

79. Raphael Taubenschlag, *The Law of Greco-Roman Egypt in the Light of the Papyri, 332 B.C.–640 A.D.* (New York: Herald Square Press, 1944), 91. Cf. Moulton-Milligan: The verb *chōrizō* (separate oneself from, depart) "has almost become a technical term in connection with divorce." *The Vocabulary of the Greek Testament Illustrated from the Papyri and Other Non-literary Sources* (1930; reprint, Grand Rapids: Eerdmans, 1974), 696a.

80. John Calvin, *The First Epistle of Paul the Apostle to the Corinthians,* trans. John W. Fraser (Grand Rapids: Eerdmans, 1960), 145.

In light of what Paul has just said concerning conjugal duty (vv. 2–5) it is hardly likely that he would suggest divorce without remarriage as a permanent solution for marital difficulties. Whether the deserted husband is also under obligation to remain unmarried indefinitely to keep open the possibility of reconciliation is a question Paul does not answer but leaves to be worked out by further discernment of the principles that apply. Although the Scriptures are certainly sufficient, it is unrealistic to expect explicit answers to every conceivable contingency.

In verse 15 when an unbeliever "deserts" a believer, Paul's advice is, "Let him (or her) depart," that is, let divorce take its course. Instead of an exhortation to remain unmarried we find instead that the believer is not bound (*ou dedoulōtai*) to the marriage. Does this imply freedom to remarry? Or only nonobligation to marital duties? The context determines. The verb *chōrizō* we know was in common use for divorce by which all marital duties come to an end. The difference of tone between verses 12 and 15 may be accounted for by Paul's hope for reconciliation in the case of a marriage where both partners are Christians, and his realistic appraisal of the situation in which an unbeliever divorces a believer. The marriage bond, as in the case of adultery, has been dissolved, not by the religious incompatibility of the couple but by the irremediable infidelity on the part of the unbelieving spouse.[81]

Divorces that have occurred in preconversion "hardness of heart" would not be inconsistent to overlook so far as the marital status of the person is concerned. Because of unregenerate hardness, such divorces amount to willful, irremediable desertion on the part of one or both partners, and so the marriages are dissolved. But is this principle applicable when a professed Christian divorces a Christian spouse? If the desertion is willful and can in no way be remedied, including through the ministry and the discipline of the church, the answer is cautiously affirmative, especially with respect to the one against whose will to maintain the marriage the definitive actions that led to its dissolution were taken. At the same time, the action of the offending party may be a censurable offence.

Scripture does not forbid remarriage in such cases of irremediable desertion. Where there is genuine conversion, evidenced by sincere and heartfelt repentance and faith in Christ, the church, after providing pastoral counseling and instruction in the biblical teaching about marriage, may approve remarriage in the Lord.

---

81. The freedom to remarry is possibly confirmed by 1 Cor. 7:27–28. Are you bound (*deō*)? Are you loosed? = Are you unmarried? or Are you divorced? *Lysis,* while it only occurs here in the NT (in the LXX it is used only of solving hard sayings), is common in papyri for "discharge" of bonds or debts.

The Analogy of Faith

This leads to the question of the intent of the exception clause. Does it state the one and only exception? If so, does *porneia* have an exclusively sexual reference?

John Stott answers yes on both counts: "Porneia means physical sexual immorality; the reason why Jesus made it the sole permissible ground for divorce must be that it violates the 'one flesh' principle which is foundational to marriage as divinely ordained and biblically defined."[82] Similarly, John Murray: "Fornication is unequivocally stated to be the only legitimate ground for which a man may put away his wife."[83] However, both Stott and Murray concede that Paul permits a believer divorced by an unbeliever to remarry.[84] Both are careful to limit the Pauline privilege to the precise conditions of the apostolic text.[85] But no matter how narrowly conceived, "desertion" (1 Cor. 7:15) constitutes "cause sufficient of dissolving the bond of marriage." Either *porneia* is not the one and only ground for divorce, or it does not have an exclusively sexual reference in the exceptive clause.

The only satisfying approach to this question is by way of the analogy of faith, which seeks the theological rationale that unites the two exceptive passages. Why is adultery (which is at least included in the term *porneia*) cause sufficient for dissolving the bond of marriage? Because it is a radical breach of marital fidelity, violating the commitment of exclusive conjugal love. Why does the departure of the unbeliever in a mixed marriage leave the believer free to remarry? Because it is a radical breach of marital fidelity, violating the commitment of lifelong companionship. The exceptional circumstance common to both instances is *willful and radical violation of the marriage covenant.*

Now the crucial assertion of Jesus in the discussion of divorce in the Gospels is his conclusion drawn from the creation ordinance: "Therefore what God has joined together, let not man put asunder" (Matt. 19:6; Mark 10:9). It is important to recall that this is addressed in the first instance to the marriage partners themselves and not to a third party. Neither Jewish law nor Roman law required a decree of divorce by an ecclesiastical or a civil authority. Divorce was effected by a simple act of renunciation on the part of the husband (Jewish law) or of either husband or wife or both (Roman law).[86] As we have seen, the burden of Jesus' teaching is directed toward preventing divorce

---

82. John R. W. Stott, "Marriage and Divorce," in *Involvement: Social and Sexual Relationships in the Modern World* (Old Tappan, N.J.: Revell, 1984), 170.

83. Murray, *Divorce,* 20.

84. Stott, "Marriage and Divorce," 174–76; Murray, *Divorce,* 69–78.

85. For Stott this means that the permission is not applicable to preconversion marriages; the believer may not take the initiative; and the believer's freedom is due "only to the specific unwillingness of an unconverted person on religious grounds to continue living with his or her now converted partner." Ibid., 176.

86. Cf. *The Oxford Classical Dictionary,* ed. N. G. L. Hammond and H. H. Scullard, 2d ed. (Oxford: Clarendon, 1970), 649–50.

by fostering commitment to the one-flesh relationship established by the marriage covenant. The crucial words are spoken not to the divorced but to the married as Jesus calls husbands and wives to preserve their marriages and to guard against their willful destruction. In short, he calls for covenant fidelity.

The exceptive clause illustrates the tragic possibility of marriages being destroyed through marital infidelity. It would be perverse to take this as an invitation "to study arguments unduly to put asunder those whom God hath joined together in marriage."[87] As Ridderbos aptly says, "The point of Jesus' qualification . . . is that divorce is only permitted in cases where one of the two partners, by radically betraying the marital bond, has already irreparably broken the marriage *in fact*."[88] Nevertheless, such betrayals and such breaches do occur in a fallen world, and the exceptive clause is realistic about the ravages of sin upon the marriage relation.

So while it is true that divorce is always an abnormality arising out of human sinfulness, it is also true that it is divinely sanctioned in circumstances of grave infidelity. Though *porneia* in the exceptive clause in Matthew may refer in the first instance to the specifically sexual sin of adultery, its pervasive use in the Old Testament for Israel's covenant breaking creates the possibility that it is used here as a synecdoche, that is, as a part (adultery) for the whole (gross violation of the marriage covenant). As Bullinger put it: "With [whoredom or adultery] no doubt [Christ] hath not excepted like and greater occasions but understood and comprehended them therein. For the holy Apostle also did leave infidelity as an occasion of divorce."[89] Though it is unwise to attempt to draw up an exhaustive list of such sins, it is clear that some violations of the marriage covenant are the moral equal of adultery: a husband who forces his wife to have an abortion; a wife who has an abortion without the knowledge of her husband; a husband who habitually beats his wife or children. All these actions strike at the heart of the marriage relationship. The inveterate abuser in particular falls within the standard legal definition of desertion, which "may be done by leaving or physically departing from the other spouse, or constructively, by one spouse so treating the other that he or she is driven to, and held justifiably to, leave the deserting spouse."[90] As such, it surely provides cause sufficient for dissolution of the marriage bond for, as the apostle says, "God has called us to live in peace."

---

87. Westminster Confession of Faith, 24.6.

88. H. N. Ridderbos, *Matthew*, trans. Ray Togtman (Grand Rapids: Zondervan, 1987), 109. Similarly, William Hendriksen: "The exception . . . permits divorce only then when one of the contracting parties . . . by means of marital unfaithfulness ('fornication') rises in rebellion against the very essence of the marriage bond." *New Testament Commentary: Exposition of the Gospel According to Matthew* (Grand Rapids: Baker, 1973), 305.

89. Heinrich Bullinger, *The Christen State of Matrimonye*, trans. Miles Coverdale (Antwerp: M. Crom, 1541), final chapter, fifth principle. See also *The Decades of Henry Bullinger*, ed. Thomas Harding, trans. H. I., 4 vols. (Cambridge: Cambridge University Press, 1852) 1:403, 2:228, 4:511.

90. David M. Walker, *The Oxford Companion to Law* (Oxford: Clarendon, 1980), 353.

Summary of Biblical Principles

1. Marriage is more than a bilateral contract in which only the will of the two parties is involved, and certainly more than a romantic liaison based on erotic attraction. Marriage is a covenant witnessed by God whereby he joins the couple in a relationship he intends to be a permanent, sexually exclusive union.

2. Divorce is not a solution for marital disappointment or difficulty. Christians should be encouraged to believe that resources are available for making their marriages "work"; to face up to responsibilities and failures, seeking God's grace and forgiveness; and to believe that to endure hardship and suffering is preferable to disobeying a clear command of Christ.

3. The covenantal commitment of a man and a woman to each other to be joined in a lifelong companionship of common life and conjugal love provides the context for trust and patience when disappointments and difficulties arise.

4. Nevertheless, it must be recognized that some marriages are destroyed by radical breaches of covenant troth. Such are the ravages of sin upon the marital relation, the bond of which is moral, not metaphysical. The wrong in such cases is the destruction of the relationship so that the covenant cannot be fulfilled, of which divorce is the public and legal attestation.

5. God hates covenant infidelity in all its hideous marital forms: adultery, incest, arbitrary divorce, malicious desertion, marital violence. All these are destructive behaviors that strike at the very heart of the unique one-flesh union of husband and wife. The adulterer, the deserter, and the inveterate abuser are alike guilty of gross betrayal of their marriage companion. By their actions they willfully repudiate the one-flesh relationship of the marriage covenant and so provide just cause for the dissolution of the marriage bond.

6. Whether a given case of marital violation is both radical and irremediable can be judged only in the particular circumstances. The premium that the Bible places on commitment to lifelong marital union and on seeking reconciliation even in circumstances of extreme provocation means that there is always a strong presumption against divorce. The Westminster Confession wisely counsels that the persons concerned be "not left to their own wills, and discretion, in their own case" (24.6). With this the focus shifts to the practical question of how the church may become available to persons with troubled or broken marriages to help and to heal.[91]

91. Cf. Bob Burns, *Through the Whirlwind: A Proven Path to Recovery from the Devastation of Divorce* (Nashville: Nelson, 1989). Burns is a minister in the Presbyterian Church in America and founder of Fresh Start Seminars, Inc., a support group for persons who are going through divorce.

Appendix

Presbyterian Church in the U.S.A., 1953

Because the corruption of man is apt unduly to put asunder those whom God hath joined together in marriage, and because the Church is concerned with the establishment of marriage in the Lord as Scripture sets it forth, and with the present penitence as well as with the past innocence or guilt of those whose marriage has been broken; therefore as a breach of that holy relation may occasion divorce, so remarriage after a divorce granted on grounds explicitly stated in Scripture or implicit in the gospel of Christ may be sanctioned in keeping with his redemptive gospel, when sufficient penitence for sin and failure is evident, and a firm purpose of and endeavor after Christ marriage is manifest. (24.2)[1]

Presbyterian Church in the U.S., 1959

It is the Divine Intention that persons entering the marriage covenant become inseparably united, thus allowing for no dissolution save that caused by the death of either husband or wife. However, the weaknesses of one or both partners may lead to gross and persistent denial of the marriage vows so that marriage dies at the heart and the union becomes intolerable; yet only in cases of extreme, unrepented-of, and irremediable unfaithfulness (physical or spiritual) should separation or divorce be considered. Such separation or divorce is accepted as permissible only because of the failure of one, or both, of the partners, and does not lessen in any way the Divine Intention for indissoluble union. (24.5)

The remarriage of divorced persons may be sanctioned by the Church, in keeping with the redemptive Gospel of Christ, when sufficient penitence for sin and failure is evident, and a firm purpose of and endeavor after Christian marriage is manifested. (24.6)

Divorced persons should give prayerful thought to discover if God's vocation for them is to remain unmarried, since one failure in this realm raises serious question as to the rightness and wisdom of undertaking another union. (24.7)[2]

---

1. The Constitution of the United Presbyterian Church in the United States of America, part 1, Book of Confessions (Philadelphia: Office of the General Assembly, 1967), 6.124.

2. *Minutes of the Ninety-Ninth General Assembly of the Presbyterian Church in the United States* (Atlanta: Office of General Assembly, 1959), 69. Twelve commissioners protested the revision (p. 72).

Index of Subjects

Index of Scripture